*The Daniel Boone Wagon Train*

*--a journey through 'the Sixties'*

**Other titles by Randell Jones**

*Trailing Daniel Boone*
2012, Daniel Boone Footsteps, publisher
2012 Kentucky History Award, Kentucky Historcial Society
Willie Parker Peace History Book Award, 2012
North Carolina Society of Historians

*Before They Were Heroes at King's Mountain*
2011, Daniel Boone Footsteps, publisher
Willie Parker Peace History Book Award, 2011

*A Guide to the Overmountain Victory National Historic Trail*
2011, Daniel Boone Footsteps, publisher
Willie Parker Peace History Book Award, 2011

*In the Footsteps of Daniel Boone*, 2005, John F. Blair, Publisher
Willie Parker Peace History Book Award, 2006

*On the Trail of Daniel Boone*, companion DVD,
2005, Daniel Boone Footsteps, publisher
Paul Green Multimedia Award, 2006

*In the Footsteps of Davy Crockett*, 2006, John F. Blair, Publisher

*Scoundrels, Rogues, and Heroes of the Old North State*
by Dr. H.G. Jones, co-editors: Randell Jones and Caitlin Jones
2004, The History Press

All titles available through Daniel Boone Footsteps
*www.danielboonefootsteps.com*
1959 N. Peace Haven Rd., #105
Winston-Salem, NC 27106
DBooneFootsteps@gmail.com

**www.danielboonefootsteps.com**

THE DANIEL BOONE WAGON TRAIN

# The Daniel Boone Wagon Train

## – a journey through 'the Sixties'

by Randell Jones

**Daniel Boone Footsteps**
Winston-Salem, North Carolina

Copyright 2013 Randell Jones
All Rights Reserved

Daniel Boone Footsteps
*www.danielboonefootsteps.com*
*DBooneFootsteps@gmail.com*

THE DANIEL BOONE WAGON TRAIN

*For my grandchildren,*
*who have way more history to learn than I did*

THE DANIEL BOONE WAGON TRAIN

"Knowledge of our past,
of our struggles and sacrifices
that were required to bring us to where we are today,
can give us strength
for the challenges of the future."

U.S. Secretary of Commerce Luther H. Hodges,
former governor of North Carolina,
Carolina Charter Tercentenary Celebration
Boone, NC,
1963

THE DANIEL BOONE WAGON TRAIN

# Preface

Daniel Boone is America's pioneer hero. The truth and the myths of his life have captured the imagination of generations of Americans since his remarkable 86 years ended peacefully in 1820, now almost two centuries ago. Stories of his adventures have been told and retold across those years and more than a few authors have written about his life. My own book, *In the Footsteps of Daniel Boone*, led me into researching the biography of a man whose life I have continued to admire since my days in Scouting, leading up to my Eagle Award earned in 1965.

During that research of his life, I came across accounts of others who had sought to commemorate Daniel Boone and his heroics. I learned about J. Hampton Rich, a North Carolinian from Winston-Salem, and his placing of over 380 plaques between 1913 and 1938 for the Boone Trail Highway Memorial Association. (See *Rich Man: Daniel Boone*, by Everett G. Marshall.) I learned about the Daughters of the American Revolution and their work from 1912 to 1915 to mark Daniel Boone's Trail from North Carolina to Kentucky. They were the first group to undertake that effort and their work salvaged for us today a history of that frontier landscape, a history that would have otherwise disappeared with modernization. The Daughter who originated the idea for marking Daniel Boone's Trail and who saw it through to completion was Mrs. Lindsay (Lucy) Patterson, a North Carolinian from Winston-

Salem. I wrote about that DAR effort in *Trailing Daniel Boone*, a book recognized in 2012 with awards from the Kentucky Historical Society and the North Carolina Society of Historians. The Daughters of the American Revolution are celebrating the centennial anniversary of their historic accomplishment during 2013 to 2015.

During that research, I also came across information referring to a curious event held in North Carolina during the 1960s, something called the "Daniel Boone Wagon Train." In time, I knew I would have to write that story, too. It was just too rich with stories of its own colorful characters; and, it had happened during my lifetime. I felt as if I could reach back and touch it. Besides, I am a North Carolinian and I live in Winston-Salem.

I am, also, a child of "the Sixties." That was my time, my season for coming of age. The music, the movies, the cars, the television shows—it was a time to remember. It was a time recalled by some as simpler, slower, more peaceful than today; but, such thinking is an illusion suffered by every generation, I suspect. Our childhoods, at least those of many middle-class Baby Boomers, were generally carefree because we were not paying much attention to the things that troubled our parents. The Sixties were deeply troubled and troubling times. History certainly bears that out. They were a time of social revolution and turmoil, of personal and collective loss, a time when the status quo could not remain still and unchanged, or at least, remain unchallenged. They were also a time of great achievement.

As I learned, the Daniel Boone Wagon Train was an annual event conducted from 1963 to 1973, and as such it overlaid a decade of significant change in America. Those times ran from "I have a dream" to "I'm not a crook." In considering writing this book, I thought it might be interesting to look at the two stories simultaneously, sharing in some detail the lives of North Carolinians in the northwestern part of the state coming together for fellowship and mutual appreciation of their American heritage while also reviewing a chronology of events—social, political, economic, scientific, technological—which unfolded during the same time frame. The product of that effort is *The Daniel Boone Wagon Train—a journey through "the Sixties."*

As you read this book, if you are of a certain age, you may find yourself recognizing people—some notables, of course, but others as well. If not by face and name, you may certainly know them by character, habit, propensity, and personality. Human nature does not change that much and perhaps we have all known people just like some of those met in the stories of the wagon train. As well, you may find yourself surprised to be reminded of the events that unfolded during those years: the space race, assassinations, Beatlemania, civil rights demonstrations, race riots, the Viet Nam War, anti-war demonstrations, the Summer of Love, the moon landing, Woodstock, Apollo 13, Watergate, and more. These were wondrous years, filled with amusement and delight, fear and anger, inspiration and pride. They were the Sixties.

To make this walk down memory lane perhaps a little more tangible for some, the Appendix includes a listing of the music, movies, and television shows that were the soundtrack of the lives lived during the time of the Daniel Boone Wagon Train, 1963 to 1973.

Ready? Wagons, Ho!

RJ
Winston-Salem
2013

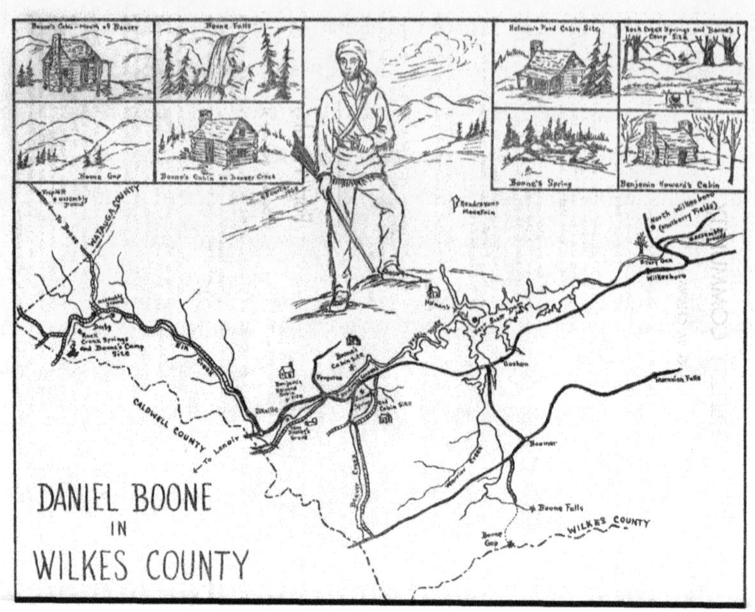


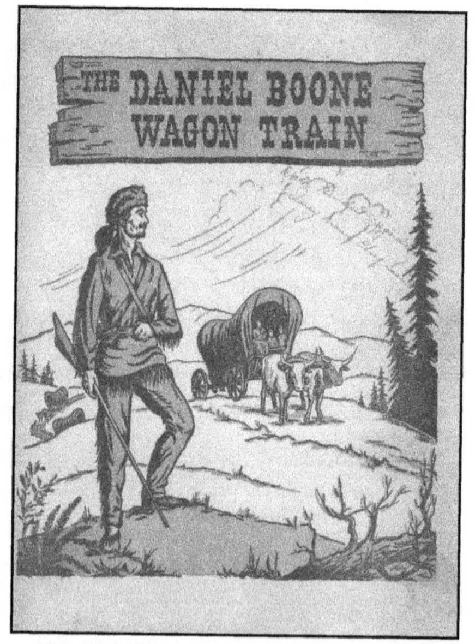


Map and cover from 1964 souvenir booklet
illustrations by Edith Ferguson Carter

# Foreword

The tiny Wilkes County community of Ferguson—earlier known as Yellow Hill and Kendall—must have presented a strange picture when on a June day in 1963 an estimated 5,000 people descended upon it, many of them by horse, mule, ox, wagon, and one stagecoach. Nobody was happier than Tom Ferguson, whose book *Home on the Yadkin* had stimulated interest in the history of the area and whose farm provided much of the space needed to accommodate the motley gathering.

It was the beginning of the Daniel Boone Wagon Train, a three-day "living history" trek to help commemorate the 300th anniversary of King Charles II's charter granting to eight Lords Proprietors the vast area of Carolina named for him. Of course, Daniel Boone lived a century later than the event being commemorated, but the legend of his crossing the Blue Ridge was familiar to every school child, and the adventure deserved to be celebrated, even if it did not qualify as one of the Carolina Charter Tercentenary Commission's "scholarly" activities.

Boone's story has been told by scores of authors, among them North Carolinians like Francis L. Hawks, Archibald Henderson, Robert B. Downs, James W. Wall, and Robert Morgan, but of all biographers, no one has traced the backwoodsman more closely than Randell Jones.

See, for example, his *In the Footsteps of Daniel Boone* (2005) and *Trailing Daniel Boone* (2012). In the present book, Jones describes how one serious celebration of Boone led to a decade of annual imitations, each accompanied by its own genuine and sometimes hilarious opportunities and problems. In the end, it is not clear whether history or myth was the winner in the series.

After Ferguson, an even more remarkable scene occurred when the wagoners and their fellow travelers stopped for the night at tiny Darby, still in Wilkes County. There, too, several thousand visitors joined the wagoners in devouring so many barbequed chickens that egg sales dropped off the next year. Surprisingly, in view of the later fame of Doc Watson and his wife Rosa Lee, the young couple from Deep Gap could win no higher than second place in a campfire musical competition.

As the road became increasingly rough, sometimes almost impassable, both humans and animals strained uphill to reach the crossing in the mountains called Cook's Gap (near present-day Milepost 285 of the Blue Ridge Parkway), the site of the next night's camp. There, appropriate obeisance was paid to a commemorative marker placed for Boone many years earlier by the Daughters of the American Revolution; a speech was made by Dr. Christopher Crittenden, writer of the original legislation creating the Carolina Charter Tercentenary Commission; and the train was "attacked" by mock-Indians before being saved by a Daniel Boone impersonator. The historicity of the night, however, was spoiled by a bunch of locals more interested in mayhem than history. Even so, the wagon train's parade was appreciatively received the next day by "the biggest crowd ever seen" in the Watauga County seat named for Daniel Boone. Thus, despite vicissitudes along the way, the wagon train experiment was successful in the eyes of its sponsors, and Tercentenary Day featured state and national figures during the opening of the Daniel Boone Native Gardens and the new season of Kermit Hunter's outdoor drama, *Horn in the West.* In Raleigh, stodgy General John Phillips, executive secretary of the Carolina Charter Tercentenary Commission, proudly published in *Tercentenary News* a photograph showing the twenty-four-wagon train curving through the mountains, thus authenticating its contribution to the anniversary observances.

The wagon train in 1963 having been considered a success, some sponsors in Wilkes and Watauga counties proposed an annual repetition, moving its starting point eastward to the two Wilkesboros. Wider interest and support assured success in 1964, and even the rescue squads of North Wilkesboro and Boone provided assistance to the estimated five hundred participants and seventy-five wagons of all kinds. Again the chicken populations at Ferguson and Darby were drastically reduced (1,800 plates were said to have been sold at Ferguson alone), and the program of music and dance was more successful. Rain and broken wagon parts, however, were the chief spoilers on the climb up the mountain. Boone's namesake town again welcomed the parade despite the weather.

Similar events continued annually for a decade, but after1965 the purpose of the emphasis of the wagon trains became less historical than adventuresome. Without further sanction from state historical forces, successive trains—one of them claiming to have sold $3,000 worth of ham at Triplett alone—placed more emphasis on outdoor experience, fun, food, and, ultimately, tourism. Commercialism became an engine fueling them. Nevertheless, Randell Jones follows each of the annual projects to the last whimper in 1973. Throughout his commentary, the author points out inconsistencies between history, imagination, and outright commercialism. For example, Daniel Boone's early trips westward were on horseback, not on wagons for which there were then no roads; buckskin and calico were not worn until the nineteenth century; and Daniel Boone is not known to have ever worn a coonskin cap. After the 1965 trek, Jones writes, "Again, what passed for 'historically correct' was given a wide berth, prompting one young girl to show up dressed as a pilgrim of the 1620s Plymouth Plantation." He tempers his criticism, however, by adding that although participants on the wagon trains "were unwittingly inappropriate to the period in their dress and reenactment, they were at least sincere. A new telling of Daniel Boone's life [TV's *The Adventures of Daniel Boone*] was about to trump their effort to educate; and, this new effort was not in the least bit concerned with sharing the story with any sense of authenticity or accuracy."

In an appendix summarizing a few unrelated activities contemporaneous with the respective wagon trains, Jones reminds the reader how even recent history can be forgotten or misinterpreted—perhaps his way of softening his judgment of those who wittingly or unwittingly distort history. For example, a program titled *Wagon Train* remained one of the most viewed national television programs during the early years of the Daniel Boone Wagon Trains in western North Carolina.

This small book reminds us again of the enduring interest in Daniel Boone, both in life and in myth.

H. G. JONES

January 2013

*Note: Dr. H.G. Jones is curator emeritus of the North Carolina Collection at UNC-Chapel Hill and is former director of the NC Division of Archives and History. Dr. Jones and the author are not related. -- RJ*

# Contents

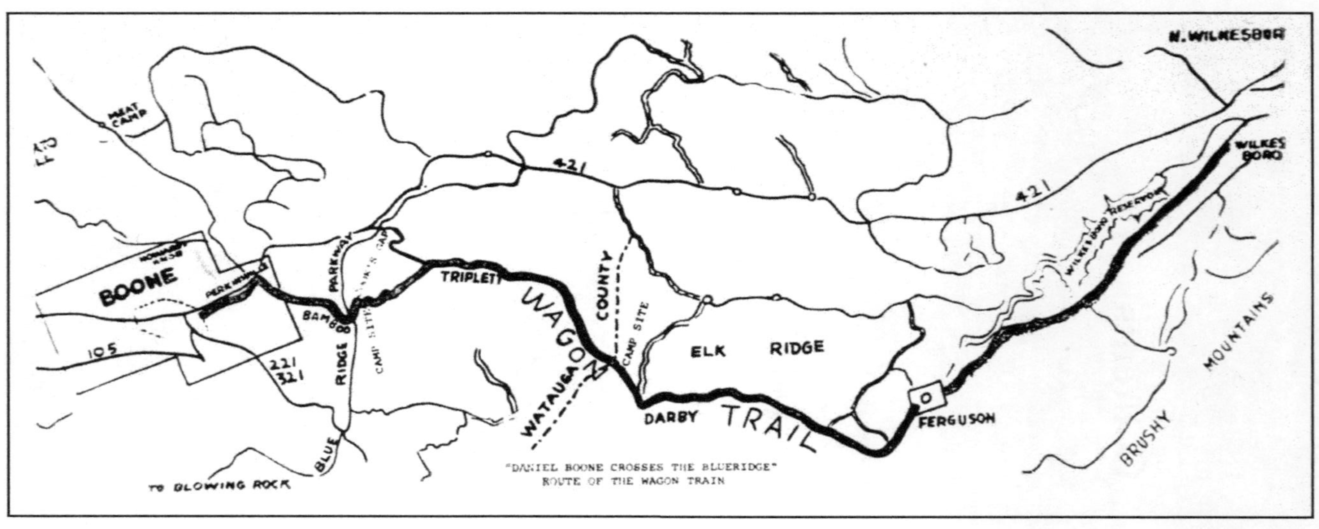


# Route of the Daniel Boone Wagon Train

1963-1973

Map by Edith Ferguson Carter, 1964

# Wagons, Ho!

"Wagons, Ho-o-o-o-o!"

People might have expected that call to start the Daniel Boone Wagon Train in 1963, the very first one, but no records seem to suggest it. The closest we know for sure was "Mount up and move out," the signal enthusiastically given by Wagon Master DeWitt Barnett on June 27, the first day of the three-day trek.

The television show *Wagon Train* had been a popular staple of the western genre that filled the primetime airwaves at the time.[1] The

**The Daniel Boone Wagon Train approaches Triplett.**
from microfilm, photo by George Flowers, courtesy of *Winston-Salem Journal*

show's opening, with Wagon Master Major Seth Adams, played originally by veteran actor Ward Bond, calling out "Wagons, Ho!," was a clear signal that the television audience should prepare itself to be immersed in another adventure on the American frontier.[2] But, even if that TV show did not inform the language of the Daniel Boone Wagon Train's trail bosses in 1963, it most certainly seemed to inform the thinking of the wagon train participants. Unfortunately, they were about 100 years out of sync with the theme of the Daniel Boone reenactment event; but, that did not dampen their spirits or their enthusiasm for joining in. They would have plenty of foul weather, a challenging trail, some ornery livestock, and some rowdy interlopers to do that.

From 1963 into the early '70s, the Daniel Boone Wagon Train was an annual celebration in Northwest North Carolina that garnered the attention and participation of enthusiastic pioneer "wannabes" from across the Southeast and even farther away. After the first year, it became a longer, four-day sojourn across an historic landscape, one deep into the heritage of the region. Daniel Boone had trod this ground two centuries before, in 1773 notably, and these folks were proud to connect with his legacy. They did so with more enthusiasm than authenticity, but the story of that 20th century celebration, which began 50 years ago, has become its own history, an event and cultural phenomenon worth remembering in itself.

The Daniel Boone Wagon Train began as a way of joining in the celebration of North Carolina's 300th birthday, the Carolina Charter Tercentenary. The first Daniel Boone Wagon Train was so successful it was repeated annually for nearly a dozen years. The citizens of Wilkes, Watauga, and surrounding counties can take a great measure of pride in how they organized and conducted such a bold effort to celebrate their heritage and to recognize America's pioneer hero,

Daniel Boone. Thousands of people and families from the Southeast and beyond can today recall with fondness the fun and entertaining experiences they had by joining in a half-century ago the celebrations which were part of the Daniel Boone Wagon Train.

**The Times They Are a-Changin'**

While the Daniel Boone Wagon Train was an honorable and sincere effort to celebrate the history and heritage of the Blue Ridge Mountain region, it is interesting to recall the social, economic, scientific, and political events that were occurring during the times surrounding the reenactments. The world and America were changing in the 1960s in dramatic ways, just as America had always changed. In Daniel Boone's time, he had to adjust his thinking and actions to the altering circumstances in which he found himself. The residents of Great Britain's American colonies were becoming an independence-minded people, eager to be citizens of a self-governing nation; and, in 1773 when Daniel Boone was moving west, crossing the Blue Ridge Mountains, he was seeking the opportunities that would come with that freedom. He relinquished the relative safety of the somewhat settled, socially established, status-quo world that he knew.

Daniel Boone was venturing into a new world he would help create. During the 1960s, so was America.

# THE DANIEL BOONE WAGON TRAIN

# 4

# Daniel Boone Wagon Train, 1963

The Daniel Boone Wagon Train was put together in 1963 with a great deal of enthusiasm; but, on the day before the event, the planners were still uncertain about the number of participants. Even one of the event's principal organizers, Chief Scout Ivey Moore, was unsure how many people would show up. Moore, a long-time resident of North Wilkesboro, was a fourth great nephew of Daniel Boone. He dressed the part for his role as chief scout, decked out in buckskin. He even grew a beard for the occasion although beards were not really customary in Boone's day. During the event, Moore carried with him a family rifle from the Revolutionary War era. "Ivey was quite a character," said Edith Ferguson Carter, owner of Whippoorwill Academy and Village in Wilkes County. Her family hosted the first night's camp. "Through the years, he would ride on horseback around the camp and up and down the train of wagons, making sure that everyone knew that he was 'Daniel Boone.' He was one of the real champions of this event."[1]

**Chief Scout Ivey Moore**

photo by Larry Penley, from 1964 DBWT Souvenir Booklet

For the first year, the plans

were for wagons to gather near Ferguson on Wednesday afternoon, June 26 and then leave out on Thursday morning at 7:00 a.m. for a historic and historical trek to Boone, North Carolina. The plans included stops at Darby and Cook's Gap for overnight camps and then arrival in Boone in time to be part of a parade on Saturday morning. The whole route was some 35 miles. Some would have thought it an exciting thing to do; others would have called it crazy. Not knowing exactly what to expect, organizers guessed at participation somewhere from 100 to 200 people.[2]

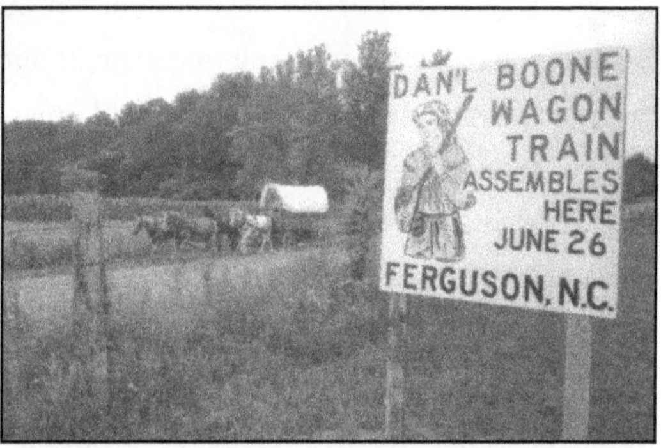


**The wagon trainers gathered at Tom Ferguson's farm for the 1963 wagon train.**
photo by Frank Jones for *Winston-Salem Journal*, Courtesy of Forsyth County Public Library Photograph Collection, Winston-Salem, NC

"The first two years we had the wagon train, it stopped on our farm," Edith Carter recalled. "The participants camped down along Beaver Creek near where it flows into the Yadkin River. Across from the mouth of the creek is the little knoll where Daniel Boone built his third cabin in the Upper Yadkin River valley. Where the wagons circled up on our farm was a beautiful setting for the campers. My family has owned this land since the 1760s when Thomas Ferguson and his two brothers came into the area having left Scotland some time before. My Ferguson ancestors were here when the Boones were here."

Not everyone who planned to go on the wagon train arrived by Wednesday evening that first year, but those who did had a grand time.

The campers circled the wagons, pitched their canvas tents, and brought out the fiddles. By the light of their campfires, they entertained themselves as their ancestors would have done with singing and square dancing. That evening frolic got the wagon trainers in the right mood to tackle what lay ahead. Ivey Moore called it a "whoop and hooraw."

The concept of a wagon train left a lot open for people to imagine. The ones who came on Wednesday and Thursday arrived with a range of vehicles. Some were in wagons, some on horseback, and one fellow drove a stagecoach he had built himself. The wagons were not old enough to have been around when Boone was, but they were old enough to be tested by the rigors of the trip. Some were Nissen wagons, built in Winston-Salem at the rate of 50 per day at the Nissen Wagon Works on Waughtown Street. Others were built by Spach Bros. Wagon Works, in business since 1854 also in Winston-Salem. Both brands were notably reliable and durable; they were legendary among

**Wagon trainers brought their old farm wagons pulled by horses, mules, and oxen.**

from 1964 DBWT Souvenir Booklet

farmers of the region. Some of the wagons which were brought were over 100 years old and had been restored and were well maintained. [3] Some were drawn by horses, some by mules, some by steers, and one by oxen.[4] As was discovered along the route, those were more than enough ornery and stubborn animals to have to tend with. The event was deemed a wagon train, and it was imagined that a few folks would ride along with each family's wagon. Riding clubs joined in, however, and many participants were on horseback and not attached to any wagon party. These outsiders lent a decidedly anachronistic "western" theme to the reenactment of an 18th century event.

The most common term used in accounts and by participants to describe the era these wagon trainers were reliving was "old-fashioned." Indeed, most seemed to be reflecting the clothing and manner of people who lived well after Daniel Boone. Again, that was probably caused by an overreliance on the TV shows *Wagon Train*, *Gunsmoke*, *Bonanza*, and *Rawhide* and a host of movies that showed wagons and people moving west in the post-Civil War era. The problem was this was supposed to be the Daniel Boone Wagon Train; and, American life in the 1770s was a good bit different than in the 1870s, the time frame that seemed to influence the participants most of all.

**No Wagons**

For the record, Daniel Boone was indeed a wagoner. His family had moved south in 1750 from the Oley Valley of southeast Pennsylvania down the Shenandoah Valley along the Great Philadelphia Wagon Road. They moved in Conestoga wagons, the "U-haul" freighters of their day. After settling in the Forks of the Yadkin (today's Davie and Yadkin counties) with his parents, Daniel drove the produce in a wagon from his family's farm to trade in Salisbury. Also, during the French and Indian War, Boone drove a supply wagon in the back of

**This Conestoga wagon, shown here on display at Fort Dobbs SHS, was a long-haul freighter of its day. A team of four horses would pull this loaded wagon. The drover would ride one horse. In the 18th century, people walked beside the wagon.**

Maj. Gen. Edward Braddock's entourage, marching to recapture Fort Duquesne in the summer of 1755. Daniel Boone was more than a little familiar with wagons. (See *In the Footsteps of Daniel Boone*, 2005). The wagons of Boone's era, however, were just for hauling goods. None included a seat on which the teamster sat. Instead, the teamster, or drover or wagoner, saddled up and rode the lead horse, the left front in a four-horse team. Or the drover walked along leading the horses who were pulling the wagon. Although young children may have ridden at times in the wagon, the teamsters did not. Most, if not all of the wagoners in the Daniel Boone Wagon Train, however, controlled his or her team from a seat inside the wagon.

Moreover, the route westward from North Carolina toward Kentucky in 1773 was a different kind of path from the route the Boones had taken into that Carolina colony from Pennsylvania in 1752. In 1773, no wagon roads ran into the Blue Ridge Mountains and certainly none ran through them. Daniel Boone and his family traveled on foot and horseback with packhorses carrying what supplies they intended to take into Kentucky. Indeed, no one passed through the Cumberland Gap in a wagon until after 1795 when the Commonwealth of Kentucky, after the American Revolution, widened and rerouted the packhorse trail Boone had laid out in 1775. Boone's 1775 route was called Boone's Trace. The Wilderness Road, built in 1795, followed another route except for a few miles where they overlapped. As it was, Boone's 1775 route into Kentucky followed along the water courses where eastern bison, searching for salt licks and eating river cane, had rambled along over centuries and worn a sizeable path. That path was adequate for packhorses to pass along. When wagon roads were built later, they tended to stay near the ridge lines, away from the water courses where wagons could get mired more easily. Such preferences for the "high road" gave us the modern term "highway."[5]

In frontier North Carolina, Daniel Boone had more than one route he followed into the hunting lands atop the Blue Ridge plateau and beyond. But in 1963, the route that seemed the most accommodating to a modern wagon train was the route along Elk Creek from Ferguson to Boone by way of Darby and Triplett and through Cook's Gap. The Daughters of the American Revolution had commemorated this route in 1913 with the placing of bronze markers. (See *Trailing Daniel Boone.*) These 20th century paths were public roads, but even in 1963 not all were paved—and that was fortunate. Still, the roads and landscape at midcentury presented enough of a challenge to make the reenactment of Boone's crossing of the Blue Ridge Mountains a worthwhile undertaking for the committed wagon trainers who joined in the celebration.[6]

### A Fashion Risk

Besides conflating the means of transportation across several eras into one, the participants in the Daniel Boone Wagon Train also dressed more in the manner they imagined the Boones might have than from any documented research.[7] On the Daniel Boone Wagon Train, women wore bonnets and dresses from the 1800s and men wore a good bit of "western" gear. Again, anything deemed "old fashioned" seemed old enough to some of the participants. Mention was made in accounts of the Wagon Train of women in calico dresses, but such printed cloth was not economically feasible until 1783 and that was in England. It would be the middle-to-late 19th century before calico would have been prevalent in America. Many women Wagon Train participants wore bonnets with broad visors like those used to shield the sun when crossing the open prairie, again an historic venture of the late 19th century. A gathered bonnet to keep one's hair out of the way would have been more prevalent in the East and certainly something Rebecca Bryan Boone and her daughters would have worn.

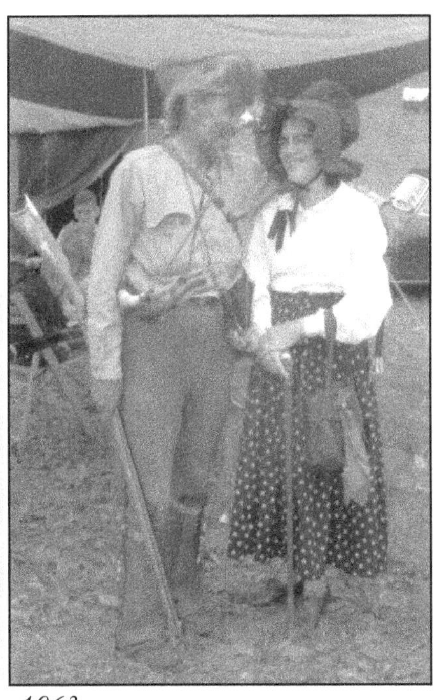

**Sun bonnets, long dresses of printed cloth, buckskin, and coonskin caps were popular attire for the wagon train participants, but these were not worn generally in the 1700s.**
photo by Frank Jones for *Winston-Salem Journal*, Courtesy of Forsyth County Public Library Photograph Collection, Winston-Salem, NC

*1963*

The Chief Scout Ivey Moore wore some buckskin; but, surprising to many, buckskin was not worn until the early 1800s and then more in the west by mountain men. In the late 1700s, Daniel Boone and his fellow pioneers wore wool and linen clothing and goods made from a coarse linsey-woolsey, a durable cloth made from weaving together a linen warp and a woolen weft. Of course, leather leggings were worn to turn a briar and a thorn, but not leather britches. Again, facial hair was not popular in the 1700s; beards were rare. And, notably, despite the one thing that everybody just "knew" was absolutely true, Daniel Boone never wore a coonskin cap. His children were on record declaring that Boone thought such a fur cap was highly impractical. Boone wore instead a broad-brimmed, beaver-skin hat. The 1999 statue of Daniel Boone on the Appalachian State University campus portrays Daniel Boone in camp attired in the clothing he would have worn. He is outfitted with the accoutrements of a long hunter of his day. Few, if any, of the wagon trainers in 1963 came close to emulating the real Daniel Boone. But in the early years of the Daniel Boone Wagon Train, they were earnest and sincere, and that counted for a lot.

**The Gathering**

The wagon trainers were to assemble at the farm of Tom Ferguson at 7:00 a.m. on Thursday, June 27. They were welcome to arrive the night before and many did. As the families and participants for the wagon train arrived, they got to know one another and word spread around the camp about one group or another. Some people had come from not so far away in Watauga, Caldwell, and Wilkes counties, but others joined in from King and Hickory and Winston-Salem. One brave soul, a woman from North Wilkesboro, organized 24 children from the YMCA day camp there. Another family brought most of what was their own "day camp." Spencer Miller, of the Wildcat community near Deep Gap, and his wife, Doris, brought some of their 18 children to

**The Spencer Miller Family included their 18 children in 1963.**
photo by Larry Penley, Daniel Boone Wagon Train, Inc.

Ferguson. The older ones stayed at home to do the chores, but were planning to join up with the whole family at the campsite at Darby at the end of the first day. Miller was celebrating his 50$^{th}$ birthday on the wagon train; his oldest child was 28 years and his youngest was 21 months. Mrs. Miller looked tired.[8]

"There was one family," Edith Carter recalled, "that brought a whole wagonload of children. They were real characters. They must have had 10 or more children, all their own; and, they were all dressed up, you know. That was a real sight for everybody, to see a whole family come all dressed up with their wagon and all their children. There was another family that came and they had such a large family that everybody got worried that they didn't have enough to eat. So people started bringing food and going to find this family in their wagon to make sure they had plenty of food. My husband [the late Hill Carter] went to the grocery store and to the garden and got piles of food to take to that family. Everybody on the train was watching out for each other."

Clyde Greene, the chairman of the Wagon Train Committee (See next chapter), listed the following men and equipment for the Daniel Boone Wagon Train:

> "Vance Harman, Sugar Grove, two-horse wagon; Monroe Hampton, Boone, one-horse wagon; Mrs. Blair Gwyn, North Wilkesboro, two-mule wagon; Foy Norman, East Bend, two-horse wagon; Howard Hendrix, Hayes, two-horse wagon; Floyd Hodges, Vilas, two-horse wagon; D.N. Vestal, East Bend, two-horse wagon; J.E. Smith, King, two-steer wagon; Mrs. Worth Tomlinson, North Wilkesboro, two-horse wagon; Spencer Miller, Wildcat, two-steer wagon; Roll Shirley, Wildcat, two-steer wagon; Thomas Winkler, Patterson, two-horse wagon; Allie Greene, Patterson, two-horse wagon; Clyde Watson, Hickory, one mule wagon; Rufus Estes, Lenoir, two-mule wagon. Men and packhorses include Joe J. Welborn, Deep Gap; Bruce Simmons, Hickory; and, G.D. Barnett, wagon master. Chief Scout Ivey Moore would be assisted by Willard Watson, Wildcat, and ten other men."[9]

**Day One**

The wagon train pulled out from the Tom Ferguson farm at 8:30 a.m. on Thursday, June 27. The field and the wagon trainers were a bit soggy. It had rained on Wednesday night; it had rained a lot. But the spirits of the participants were high. As the wagon train rolled out, they numbered "158 people, 24 wagons, a stagecoach, 88 horses and ponies, 14 mules, 6 oxen, and 2 dogs." They were followed by a host of cars and "a Coca Cola stand on wheels."[10] They were led and followed part of the way by the North Carolina Highway Patrol, at least until they got off NC Hwy 268 and onto Elk Creek Road.

**The wagon train began from the Ferguson farm with everyone in high spirits.**

from 1964 DBWT Souvenir Booklet

"The wagon train had rain, hot weather, steep mountain roads, and altogether too much inexperience with the rigors of outdoor life," the *Wilkes Journal-Patriot* later proffered.[11] Although the "steep mountain roads" were still a day away, the rest of these calamities struck on the first day. Indeed, Mother Nature and the gremlins soon began to play tricks on the wagon trainers. "One minute the '63 model Boones would be hot and dusty; next minute they'd be soaked, shivering, and muddy," wrote Roy Thompson, staff reporter for the *Winston-Salem Journal* and a wagon train participant. He also witnessed some mishaps, but only heard about others. "Something happened and an axle broke ...," he wrote about one incident early in the day. That was Mrs. Worth Tomlinson's wagon that broke down shortly after departure; but, she just got another wagon and kept on going.[12] Another wagoner, O.L. Abernethy of Hickory, had a spindle nut work off his wheel and then the wheel fall off. "I'm too old for this sort of thing," Mrs. Abernethy declared. Others were not as discouraged. Jack Hines of Lincolnton declared that if his four horses got tired, he would get a wrecker to pull them all. Ernest Smith of King nearly did the same, bringing his flatbed along to haul his weary oxen and Nissen wagon farther down the road. It seems the oxen's unshod hooves had gotten tender walking along the pavement of NC Hwy 268.

"A horse is reported to have thrown a rider," Thompson added, and then he noted the passion these participants had for the experience. "The rumor was that the injury was only a broken wrist. It would take at least a broken back to get these people off the train." Even Abernethy defied disappointment. Asked if his broken wagon was going to make him quit, he declared with true pioneer spirit and determination, "I'm going on if the world never turns another crank."[13]

The broken arm belonged to Warren Gillette, age 9, from Charlotte. He fell from his horse. He was part of the group of two dozen children with the YMCA Day Camp, headed by Mrs. J.H. Winkler of North Wilkesboro. He was a true trooper, too. After getting the cast put on his arm, he returned to ride on to Boone. [14]

The train moved along all day covering 12 miles in six-and-a-half hours while making frequent stops to rest the livestock and the wagon trainers. The sun, which had then come out, and the heat were taking their toll; but, Helen Bumgarner of Roaring River was there to help. She brought along a collection of coonskin caps and passed them out to the neediest among the wagoners—the baldheaded men. "We may have been hot when the sun was out," wrote Thompson, "but … we were stylish as the dickens."[15]

Heavy rains began in the afternoon and soaked the wagon trainers on the road to Darby, but they arrived there about 4:00 p.m. They pitched their camp in the mud during the continuing rain, which stopped

**The line of wagons approached Darby at the end of the first day.**
from 1964 DBWT Souvenir Booklet

about 6:30. The participants were rewarded with a delightful campsite, a spacious meadow, along Elk Creek. There was a swimming hole there at Dugger Creek. They unhitched the horses and mules and steers and oxen and led them into the water to cool off. The wagoners joined in getting cooled off too.[16] The wagoners were greeted by a barbeque chicken dinner, prepared by the local community to raise money for their respective missions. The Ferguson Ruritan Club, the P.T.A., and the Home Demonstration Club and Grange were all busy cooking.[17] Joining them in the effort were churches from Beaver Creek, Darby, and Elkville along with Sharon Walker Baptist.[18] They fed the wagoners and hordes of visitors who drove in to see the encampment along Elk Creek.

Not everyone depended on someone else cooking his meal. The Spencer Miller family "found itself short of food at supper time," the *Wilkes Journal-Patriot* reported. "The problem was solved in true pioneer way when Miller went out and got two young groundhogs and a son pulled some fish from Elk Creek."[19]

**Food for the table, the old-fashioned way.**
from 1964 DBWT Souvenir Booklet

In her article printed in the *Watauga Democrat*, Nancy Alexander, a columnist for the *Lenoir News-Topic*, captured some of the characters and the spirit of folks who had joined in the wagon train on that first day:

"In one of the wagons which formed a circle in the wide green meadow surrounded by high green mountains was Rufus Estes, who lives near Union Grove Baptist Church in Caldwell County. A friendly, slender man, wearing a vivid shirt, he dismounted, unhitched his horses and led them to an oat-filled trough.

"'I've had my covered wagon about 20 years. I keep it in dry storage at my father's, Frank Estes, barn at Mulberry, just to use for outings such as this. Mr. I.T. Barnette of Boone, who is my saw mill boss, has been driving my wagon. I've been sawmilling for him for 18 years and working at night as night watchman at American Efird Mills at Whitnel. First time in all these years I've got to boss him,' he laughed.

"Barnette spoke, 'I've enjoyed this trip. Last night we sat up most of the night drinking coffee around the camp fire and talking with friends. Seems this day and time people don't visit like they use to. I've seen friends from Wilkes and other places I hadn't seen in years.'

"Estes added, 'I've got a kick out the whole trip, rain and all; some Girl Scouts were camped near us. I got up about four o'clock this morning to feed my horses and some of 'em [were] way over on the hill and were so confused they wouldn't come back 'til I went over to lead 'em. I've got seven children. My wife and all of us work. Two of my boys, Lloyd and Harold, are riding two of my three ponies. I can remember my ponies' ages, but not my boys. On my wagon here are relics I've collected, a very old saddle with wooden stirrups, an old Spanish American War sabre, and a muzzle-loading rifle.'

"He rubbed his beard of several days' growth. 'I'm not going to shave until the trip's over, but I'm going to jump in that river and take a bath in a little while. Back here just behind my wagon is a stagecoach I'd love to own. I offered the man $300 for it. He told me he'd recently refused $3,500 for it. Here's the owner, Claude Minton.'

"Minton, who is from North Wilkesboro, explained he owns not only the stagecoach, but an old hearse, a three-seated carriage, a buggy, and a covered wagon. The wagon, too, was in the train. He pulled out pictures of his stagecoach parading down Constitution Avenue in Washington, [D.C.] where he takes it each year for the Cherry Blossom Festival. It's been in numerous wagon trains in Tennessee, 'where they really have them, with 120 wagons or more.' There was a picture of A.W. Drinkwater and Thad Eure riding in the vehicle in the Pirate

**Claude Minton brought a home-made stagecoach to the wagon train.**
from 1964 DBWT Souvenir Booklet

Jamboree at Manteo two years ago. Drinkwater, who died this past year, was the man who telegraphed the first news of the Wright Brothers' first flight. [Thad Eure (1899-1993) was North Carolina's longest serving Secretary of State, 1936 to 1989.]

"Camp fires were lit. Spencer Miller of Watauga's Wildcat community, a man who has 18 children, was busy stirring the evening's stew in a big black pot. Fragments of age-old ballads floated over the meadow, children raced hither and yon, women hurried about in long calico dresses and bonnets performing wifely tasks.... The day was ending."[20]

The day was ending, yes, but not the fun. A talent show began at dark and included performances by 11 groups who had auditioned for the Ferguson Ruritan Club. Ralph Smith of the WBTV Crackerjacks served as master of ceremonies.[21] The groups performed old-time music and dances deemed by the organizers to be in keeping with the times of Daniel Boone. The spectacle, the music, and the food attracted quite a crowd, estimated at 3,000. They arrived in more than 1,000 automobiles that converged on Darby. "The road was lined with cars for over three miles, and every side road was filled," the *Journal-Patriot* reported.[22]

The talent performances were judged and prizes were given. A ballad-singing quartet from North Wilkesboro called the Migrants took first place and the $50 prize. Relegated to second place, in what today must seem an egregious breach of good sense on the part of the judges, were Doc and Rosa Lee Watson performing on guitar and autoharp. They won $15.[23] (Doc Watson and Rosa Lee Watson each passed away in 2012 during the writing of this book. One wonders if they performed in 1963 his moving song, "Your Long Journey.")

The first day of the excursion had been long and difficult, but the experience was rewarding for more than just the wagon trainers. "Despite the rain and mud and accompanying discomforts," the *Wilkes Journal-Patriot* concluded, "the thousands on hand at Darby apparently enjoyed their visit; and, the wagon train camp was filled constantly by people visiting the various campfires and inspecting wagons, horses, and oxen. For many of the younger people, it was their first visit to a wagon camp, while older people told of seeing wagon trains some 50 or 60 years ago in the area before the days of motor transportation."[24]

"It was quite a spectacle," recalled Edith Carter. "People brought their children out to see such a sight. They wanted them to see something from the old times, something like what their grandparents and great-grandparents might have done. The whole experience was educational and quite memorable. A lot of our neighbors would go on the wagon train and they would dress up. To a lot of them it was just a

**Thousands converged from all around Northwest North Carolina to see the wagon train, shown here at Darby.**
from newsprint, courtesy of *Wilkes-Patriot Journal*

nice family vacation, a good experience for them to take their children on."[25]

Edith Carter's father, Tom Ferguson, wrote his column, "News from Ferguson," for the July 4 edition of the *Wilkes Journal-Patriot*, praising the event organizers and giving approval of the unique effort. "More people from far and wide poured into the village of Ferguson on Wednesday and Wednesday night, June 26, than ever in its history," he wrote. "It was estimated that there were five thousand people gathered at the assembly grounds and an equal number at Darby; and most of them partook of the excellent chicken barbeque prepared at Ferguson and Darby."[26]

**Day Two**

Again at 8:30 a.m. the wagon train pulled out for the second day of the three day excursion. They had 14 miles to make that day from Darby to Cook's Gap. As far as Triplett the road was not too bad, but the weather was hot. When the wagoners reached Triplett, they were treated to soft drinks by Stewart Simmons who owned a general store there. "The drinks are on the house," he offered. The thirsty wagon trainers were most appreciative.

The road beyond Triplett was a real challenge, for everyone including the horses, mules, steers, and oxen. It was unpaved, which was better for the animals, but it was all uphill—steep uphill. It was also narrow and the road had to be closed from both ends to other traffic. No room was available for passing.

"Two yokes of oxen gave up and hitched rides on trucks," wrote Thompson. "One wagon was left along the trail. It broke an axle within a few miles of the Promised Land, and there was nothing to do but move on and leave it." One horseman arrived at Cook's Gap, the crest of the Blue Ridge, but let his horse drink too much water too quickly; the animal suffered greatly. "Chief scout Ivey Moore, who has walked all the way from Ferguson, has blisters all over his feet," wrote

**The wagon train climbed toward Cook's Gap on a dirt road.**
from microfilm, photo by Miriam Rabb, NC Tourism Bureau, courtesy of *Watauga Democrat*

Thompson. "Wagon master DeWitt Barnett, who has ridden a horse all the way from Ferguson, declined comment on blisters, but when he arrived there he had a pillow between him and his saddle."[27]

Tom Ferguson offered his view of the second day's effort in his column: "It was amazing to see with what perfect harmony the long train of about 30 wagons and an equal number of horseback riders wended their way up the rather crooked, steep and gravel highway to the summit of the Blue Ridge at Bamboo with scarcely a mishap." Acknowledging its purpose and also its oddity, he added, "If [Daniel Boone] could have returned to witness this great event in his honor, he would perhaps have been more frightened at it than we would at a band of roving Indians."[28]

The wagoners may have been doing this for fun, but they were not really wheeling along at a vacationer's pace. They had places to be and things to do when they got there. There was a schedule to keep. The Wagon Train was a major feature of events to unfold at Cook's Gap on the evening of the second day, Friday night. The occasion had been selected for the dedication of a marker where Daniel Boone's Trail crossed the Blue Ridge Parkway. The Daughters of the American Revolution had placed a marker at Cook's Gap in 1914. It was a bronze tablet they had placed to commemorate America's pioneer hero. (Five other identical DAR markers were placed elsewhere in Watauga County in the fall of 1913. The Cook's Gap marker was placed in the spring of 1914. See *Trailing Daniel Boone,* 2012.) The 1914 marker at Cook's Gap had disappeared during the ensuing 50 years, and the powers that be wanted to replace it. They decided to move one of the other DAR markers, the one from the site of Three Forks Baptist Church on the New River, and to place it on the Blue Ridge Parkway. The church had since moved a quarter mile or so north to face US Hwy 421; and, although the graveyard was still there at the original site, that DAR marker for Daniel Boone's Trail certainly did not get the attention it would if it were placed on the Blue Ridge Parkway near Cook's Gap.

The ceremony was set as part of a "Big Pow Wow Campfire" planned for 7:00 p.m. with the wagons arriving at 5:30. Dr. Christopher Crittenden, the Director of the Department of Archives and History, was the scheduled, featured speaker for the dedication. That department was, after all, one of the three standing members of the Carolina Charter Tercentenary Commission. (See next chapter.) The unveiling would be followed by hymn singing, square dancing and "old time games."[29] The wagoners would be treated to a feast of buffalo meat, too. Clyde Greene and his scouts had found a good supply of it from the Buffalo Ranch of Concord. Spencer Miller would cook a buffalo stew in a "huge iron pot of the 1773 vintage."[30]

After leaving Ferguson early on Thursday morning, the wagon train

**The wagon trainers made camp at Cook's Gap and prepared for a "big pow-wow."**

from 1964 DBWT Souvenir Booklet

had maneuvered its way through the Elk Creek valley during two pretty rough days full of heat, rain, blisters, sore feet, sore muscles, and a host of unexpected surprises. Especially in the face of so many doubts that they could make it at all, they were delighted to be at the top of the Blue Ridge and waiting for an easy six mile trek into Boone in the morning.

The wagoners were exhausted but pleased to reach Cook's Gap and Bamboo at the crest of the Blue Ridge Mountains. The next day would be an easy route into Boone where they would parade through downtown and that night go see the season-opening performance of *Horn in the West.* But some of these performers could not wait to see the wagoners, so they came out from town—to attack them. Cast members from *Horn in the West* dressed as Indians rode out to Bamboo to lay in ambush of the wagon train. "The Indians are reliably reported to have come to the campsite in station wagons ..." Thompson wrote. Rumors of the attack had gotten out and tourists began arriving, milling around, looking at their watches and asking, "When are the Indians going to attack?" Meanwhile the cast members, being the publicity hounds their art demands them to be, were coming out of their hiding places to have their pictures taken by tourists. Just when the whole ambush was about to be ruined, Glenn Causey, who played Daniel Boone in the outdoor drama, "Horn in the

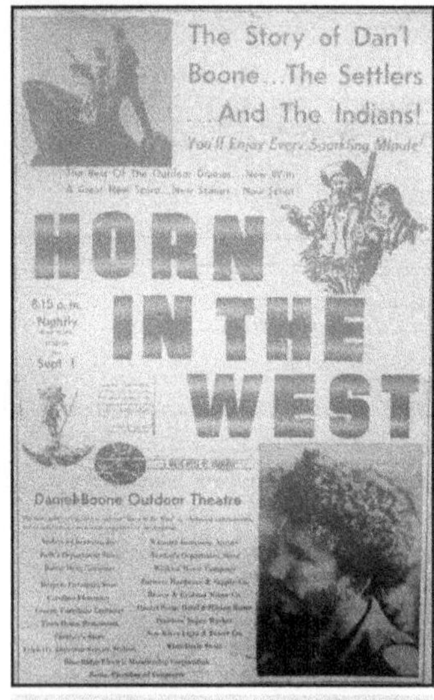


**The wagoners would attend opening night of the 12th season of *Horn in the West.***

from microfilm,
courtesy of *Watauga Democrat*

**"Indian" cast members from *Horn in the West* staged an attack on the wagon train. Glenn Causey, in coonskin cap, portrayed Daniel Boone in the outdoor drama. Ivey Moore is at left.**
from 1964 DBWT Souvenir Booklet

West," broke from his heroic, protector character by chasing the Indians back into hiding so they could attack the wagon train. But eventually, the "Indians" did attack with a great deal of whooping, much to everyone's delight.

But it was not the "redskins" who almost ruined the Daniel Boone Wagon Train. It was the rednecks.

By Friday night, word of the wagon train had spread broadly throughout the community and indeed throughout Northwest North Carolina. Everybody wanted to go see it and nearly everybody did. "Thousands of people swarmed into the camp," Thompson wrote. "A few of them brought booze." Alcohol and drinking had been prohibited during the wagon train. Most of the participants had abided by that rule diligently. Not so, the visitors.

"The wagon train people turned in early," Thompson continued, "but a few of the outsiders stayed on to keep the party going. It grew louder and louder." Then a few shots were fired. "Some of the horses, terrified by the gunfire, stampeded. At least two of the horses crashed into a barbed wire fence. One was cut badly. Another horse charged into the big circle formed by the wagon train as 'protection against Indians.' People were sleeping there in tents. Some were on the ground in sleeping bags. Luckily the horse was caught before anyone was trampled.

"Doc Hines of Lincolnton tried to explain the danger involved in stampeding horses and asked them [the revelers] to move the party somewhere else. A few minutes later one of Hines' horses galloped off. Someone had cut him loose. Later on, a car slid at high speed into the big, muddy circle made by the wagons. The driver put the car into a power slide, and he made at least two 360-degree spins among the campers."

With affordable cell phones yet 40 years into the future, there was no way to call the Watauga sheriff's deputies. "It was a long and sleepless night," wrote Thompson, "but most people on the train thought they were lucky to lose nothing more than sleep."[31]

**On Parade**

The remainder of the night passed without additional trouble and the wagon trainers were glad to see the morning. They had only six miles to cover that morning before becoming a parade through downtown Boone. They had put up with the rain, the heat, the steep climb, and stupid drunks. But before they could get into Boone, they faced one more challenge—a snarl of traffic. More tourists had flooded into Boone that morning for the parade and the Tercentenary celebration. Many of them drove out just to see the wagon train roll into town.

The wagon trainers made a spectacular crossing at the ford of the New River. The night's rain had made the water a little deeper, and the beasts and wagons coming across the stream was a sight to see. The wagon trainers then walked into town with, perhaps, a little less spring in their steps than they had at Thursday morning's departure, but with a lot more pride beaming from their faces for what they had accomplished. "They've been hot and dusty this week," wrote Thompson, "and they've been thirsty while soaked to the skin. … They've been plagued by bugs and frightened by rumors of rattlesnakes and copperheads. But they kept coming and they finally made it."

**The wagons forded New River at the historic crossing before reaching Boone.**
photo by Frank Jones, courtesy of *Winston-Salem Journal*

The Daniel Boone Wagon Train paraded through Boone "in front of the biggest crowd ever seen here," the *Watauga Democrat* reported. "People smiled and pointed as [the wagon trainers] marched through Boone in their old-fashioned clothes," Thompson wrote, "but it was good to know that there are still people who can do this sort of thing."[32]

Reporter Dale Gaddy described in the *Watauga Democrat* the parade through town:

> "Time, 11:45 – People were gathering in clusters along the parade route, talking in excited tones. The sun shined bright-

**Their smiles were broad and their pride shone brightly as the wagon trainers neared the end of their trek. Ivey Moore, on foot, is followed by Wagon Master Dewitt Barnett.**

from 1964 DBWT Souvenir Booklet

ly, a brisk wind fought carefully combed hair, and powder puff clouds dotted the crystal sky above.

"It was a beautiful day—a perfect day for a parade. And everyone and his cousin was in town to see the Wagon Train. Dan'l Boone himself couldn't have brought more people to the town which bears his surname. They formed a blanket of many-colored clothes on the Daniel Boone Hotel lawn. They stood thick as molasses along the narrow sidewalks. They sat in second story windows and waved to persons below. And the usual number made their way between Northwestern and the theater, "socializing." It was a sociable day. And the parade was beginning.

"Time, 12:30 – A siren whined in the distance. Chief Thomas

led the procession in. 'Right on time,' one Floridian said with amazement. One by one the covered wagons rolled by. Drivers and passengers waved to the throngs which lined the streets. Periodically a rumble of applause passed through the crowd as an especially authentic wagon passed by, or as familiar faces were seen. People liked the wagons and the hearty mountaineers who had made the two-day trek over the mountainous wilderness as Boone, the pioneer, had done nearly 200 years before. The smell of animal droppings brought back nostalgic memories of the times when Boone, the town, was just a village with dirt streets and horse-drawn carriages. The town has grown; yet, her people are no less friendly, no less homey, than the original wagoners.

"A chubby little lady, who looked like Mrs. Santa Claus, drew quick breaths in the heat of the afternoon sun. Fanning her round face with a newspaper, she never once relaxed her smil-

**The wagon trainers parade down King Street in Boone before, reportedly, the largest crowd ever to assemble there.**

from microfilm, photo by George Flowers, courtesy of *Winston-Salem Journal*

ing expression. Three dogs—probably strays—scampered down the street, barking madly. A small colored girl, her hair in pig-tails, gazed intently at the proceedings. Newsmen from TV stations, radio stations, and newspapers far and near wrote, snapped pictures, and danced in front of the lines of people, trying to get into "just the right position" for that next shot.

"Floats came bearing bathing beauties. Antique cars—some 30 in all—passed down the narrow streets of Boone. The high school band marched proudly in their smart uniforms. A television cowboy from Charlotte rode high in the air on his stagecoach. And a farm tractor of bygone decades blew its shrill whistle, much to the glee of the young boys in the crowd.

"Time, 1:24 – The parade had passed. And the clusters of people broke into singles or pairs, and the mountain folks found their way back to their homes. It had been a good parade. And Dan'l Boone would have been proud of the pageantry."[33]

The Daniel Boone Wagon Train clearly took center stage that day in events that commemorated the state's 300th birthday anniversary. Ten thousand people, by one estimate, lined the streets of the parade route. About 1,000 of those in town for the celebration joined in ceremonies at Conrad Stadium on the campus of Appalachian State Teachers College when former Governor and then-U.S. Commerce Secretary Luther Hodges spoke to celebrate the occasion. Secretary Hodges, of course, had organized the Carolina Charter Tercentenary when he was North Carolina's governor. (See next chapter.) He was delighted to be speaking at this gathering, which had turned out to be one of the top events in the state to celebrate the anniversary. "It is these local observances, such as your celebration here," he said, "which make this 300th anniversary meaningful. It is at the community level that we get our keenest understanding of how we stand on the shoulders of the past and bear on our shoulders the responsibility for the future."[34]

Alluding to what he saw as corruption in local governments (in general, not specifically in Boone) at the time, he called attention to the story told in *Horn in the West* when colonial residents in the Piedmont rose up against unfair treatment during the Regulator movement to "throw the rascals out," as he said. He concluded his remarks with a nod to the importance of history in preparing citizens for a future which seemed destined to continue in a Cold War with the Soviet Union:

"Today we are part of a great democratic nation in a world in

**(l to r) Dr. Frank Porter Graham, Congressman Charles R. Jonas, Secretary of Commerce Luther H. Hodges, and Mrs. May Gordon Latham Kellenberger (rebuilt Tryon Palace in New Bern during 1950s) attended the celebration in Boone as members of the National Commission on the Charter Tercentenary.**

from microfilm, photo by Hugh Morton, courtesy of *Watauga Democrat*

> which freedom and self-government face their greatest challenge. Our country, and the future of freedom, requires that we be strong in our faith in ourselves, in our beliefs, and in our sense of destiny. Knowledge of our past, of our struggles and sacrifices that were required to bring us to where we are today, can give us strength for the challenges of the future."[35]

Also speaking at events that day at the Daniel Boone Hotel was Dr. Frank Porter Graham, United Nations special representative and former U.S. Senator from North Carolina.

**Wagons and Taxis**

Old wagons and horses might have been a good draw to bring people into the mountains of North Carolina, but word of mouth has always been the best means of promotion. That was what Miss Honey Lucas, representing Gov. Terry Sanford, and the State Department of Conservation and Development had in mind when they invited 100 New York cabbies to come take a three-day tour of North Carolina, to learn about "Variety Vacationland." That was the official phrase used to promote tourism in the state.

Miss Lucas personally selected the New York taxi drivers based on their charm and talkativeness and invited them to North Carolina. Herman Wilcox arranged for their bus to be "attacked" by Indians from "Horn in the West" and to ride in the Daniel Boone Wagon Train parade. From there, they were to drive to Hickory and then fly to Raleigh for a tour of the capital, by taxi, and a meeting with Governor Terry Sanford.[36] The governor did not attend the "Daniel Boone Crosses the Blue Ridge" events in Watauga County to which he had extended invitations to numerous governors and dignitaries, most of whom also did not attend.

**Daniel Boone Native Garden**

After the parade and the speeches at the stadium, the Daniel Boone Native Gardens were dedicated as part of the Tercentenary celebration, although the gardens had been planned well beforehand. (See next chapter.) Mrs. Roscoe D. McMillian, of Red Spring, was the president of the state garden club. She presided at the dedication. U.S. Secretary of Commerce Luther H. Hodges and British Minister Dennis A. Greenhill attended.[37]

The concept for the gardens came from Mrs. B.W. Stallings of Boone. They were designed by Asheville landscape architect Dean Ogden. The gardens were sponsored by the state's garden clubs, by the Southern Appalachian Historical Association, and by Appalachian State Teachers College. During the dedication ceremony, wrought iron gates for the garden's entrance, fashioned by Daniel Boone IV of Burnsville, were presented. The gardens would include a marble figure of St. Francis in a prayer nook, a rock garden known as the Rockery, a stream, a natural spring, a rustic arbor, a wishing well, a path through the woods, and a 75-year-old "black heart" cherry tree.[38]

**The Daniel Boone Native Gardens were dedicated in 1963.**
from 1964 DBWT Souvenir Booklet

Those attending the opening performance of *Horn in the West* for the 1963 season were greeted by Dennis A. Greenhill, British minister to the United States. One can only assume that he winced a little at the end of Kermit Hunter's play, when the backcountry Americans, ancestors perhaps of some of those who had endured the rigors of the wagon train reenactment that week, gave a bruising black eye at the 1780 Battle of Kings Mountain to the British effort to subdue the rebels of the recently declared independent states in the South.

### A Success

The *Watauga Democrat* was glowing in its praise of the community's role in the state's birthday celebration:

> **"It Was A Big Day**
>
> "As the years multiply, Boone people will be apt to date everything back to the part the community played in the observance of North Carolina's Tercentenary celebration.
>
> "It was one of Boone's biggest days …. There's no way of knowing how many people lined the path of the gay parade, but the town was jam packed with the gay throngs, who saw one of the most spectacular parades in the city's history. One world traveler tells the *Democrat* that he had never viewed such a varied and compelling sort of exhibition in all his experiences.
>
> "There were the oxen and the wagons, and the horse drawn vehicles which included a stage coach, and many lumbering and sheeted vehicles, the like of which moved back the western frontiers. And there were old automobiles and new, and bands, and all sorts of things to delight all ages, and bring a pleasant nostalgia to those whose hair is sprinkled with the snows of many winters.

"Windows of the stores in the town drew great interest with their displays of old pictures, old clothing, and implements used in the days before the machines came … . It was an event of which all Wataugans are proud."[39]

The *Tercentenary News*, July 1963 issue, printed a photograph of the wagon train approaching Cook's Gap and gave a resounding report of the successful effort in Watauga County to celebrate North Carolina's 300th anniversary with a commemoration of "Daniel Boone's Crossing of the Blue Ridge Mountains." The caption for the photograph mentioned the formal address by Secretary Luther Hodges and the outdoor drama, *Horn in the West*, but the Daniel Boone Wagon Train had clearly become the center of attention.[40] (See next chapter.)

**Historic Premonition**

During the celebration, of course, no mention was made that during

**The Daniel Boone Wagon Train approaching Cook's Gap.**

Wide use of this photo has obscured its origins. Photo probably by Larry Finley. This image courtesy of *Wilkes Journal-Patriot*

this crossing of the Blue Ridge in 1773, Daniel and Rebecca suffered a great personal tragedy—the murder of their oldest child, James Boone, on October 10. Just a fortnight after leaving the Yadkin River valley, James, age 15, and Henry Russell, also 15, of Castle's Wood, Virginia, were among the small party of migrating settlers attacked in camp along Wallen's Creek and near the Warrior's Path. They had passed over Kane's Gap and were proceeding west through the Wallin's Creek portion of the Powell River valley in today's Lee County, Virginia, trying to catch up with Daniel Boone's larger party.

Neither did the reenactors in late June 1963 know that only five weeks after the 190$^{th}$ anniversary of the murder of James Boone, America would suffer the assassination of its youngest President, John F. Kennedy. They did know, however, that the world was shifting around them. In the same month of the first Daniel Boone Wagon Train, demonstrations at college campuses were calling for an end to racial segregation. Change was in the air. At the time of Boone's departure from North Carolina, America was on the cusp of the Revolution. In 1963, another revolution in America was starting as well.

And the world turned:

> On July 1, 1963, Zip Codes were introduced by the U.S. Post Office Department. 
>
> In August, James Meredith became the first black person to graduate from the University of Mississippi; and, the Rev. Dr. Martin Luther King, Jr. led the March on Washington for Jobs and Freedom with 250,000 demonstrators. Dr. King delivered his stirring "I have a dream" speech from the steps of the Lincoln Memorial.

On September 15, the racially-motivated bombing of the 16th Street Baptist Church in Birmingham killed four young girls. Push-button telephones were first made available to customers. And, on November 22, the nation was stopped cold in its tracks, and the times changed irrevocably: President John Fitzgerald Kennedy was assassinated in Dallas, Texas, while riding in a motorcade.

In the last week of the year, Beatlemania, part of the British music invasion, began with the release of two songs in the United States.

In January, 1964, the Surgeon General first announced officially that smoking tobacco might cause lung cancer. The 1964 Winter Olympics were held in Innsbruck, Austria. In February, 1960 Rome Olympics gold medalist boxer Cassius Clay, who later changed his name to Muhammad Ali, defeated Sonny Liston to become World Heavyweight Champion. In March on Good Friday, Alaska was rocked by a devastating earthquake, killing over 120 people and causing $500 million in damages. The Supreme Court ruled that under the First Amendment, speech that criticized public figures could not be censored. Malcolm X left the Nation of Islam to start a black nationalist party.

In April, General Douglas McArthur passed away at age 84. *Gemini 1* was launched as an unmanned test of the two-astronaut system. Sidney Poitier received the Academy Award for Best Actor (*Lilies of the Field*), the first black person to receive

that award. Ford Motor Company introduced the Mustang, which became its most successful launch since the Model A. The New York World's Fair opened, running April to October in 1964 and 1965.

In May, President Lyndon B. Johnson intended to tour Appalachia to kick off his "War on Poverty," ending up for reasons unknown in Rocky Mount, North Carolina, where he made the announcement. Twelve men in New York burned their draft cards following protests by several hundred students in New York, San Francisco, Boston, and Madison, Wisconsin, to protest U.S. involvement in Vietnam.

In June, 1964, the Catholic Church condemned the oral contraceptive pill. After a 75-day filibuster, the U.S. Senate passed the Civil Rights Act of 1964; and, three civil rights workers on a voter registration campaign disappeared in Mississippi.

Meanwhile:
On television, America was introduced to instant replay in football and Ed Sullivan hosted The Beatles in a show that set new audience records. *The Pink Panther* and *Tom Jones* entertained movie-goers, and "Blue Velvet," "Sugar Shack," and "Ring of Fire" were popular songs before Beatlemania overran the pop charts.

For more about television, movies, and music of the following 12 months, see Appendix, Popular Culture: July 1963-June 1964.

# The Carolina Charter Tercentenary

Happy Birthday, North Carolina!

Three centuries is a long time, and when the 300$^{th}$ anniversary of any notable event finally rolls around, especially one in American history, it is an occasion most certainly worth celebrating, perhaps with great fanfare and passion. Such was the situation in the early 1960s when the state's authorities took note to celebrate the 300$^{th}$ anniversary of North Carolina's beginnings.

**Carolus**

North Carolina may have been enticed into holding its 300$^{th}$ anniversary celebration by the success of Virginia's recent 350$^{th}$ anniversary celebration in 1957 for the settling of Jamestown in 1607. That grand celebration lasted eight months and welcomed then-Vice President Richard Nixon and Queen Elizabeth II to its gathering. Her Majesty was then only five years into her reign that since has stretched across and into seven decades to reach her Diamond Jubilee in 2012. (Only Queen Victoria has reigned longer, so far.) The focus on Jamestown garnered for the Commonwealth of Virginia some impressive tourism credentials and prompted them to create the Colonial Parkway connecting the tourist destinations of Jamestown, Yorktown, and Williamsburg. They built Jamestown Festival Park (now Jamestown Settlement) as an interpretive and educational center. The event was hugely successful for economic development and for developing heritage prestige. North Carolina must have felt it could do the same.[1] The planners of North Carolina's celebration had also looked at what was done in Maryland and in Connecticut in the 1930s to celebrate their founding, but the recent success of Virginia's celebration probably loomed largest in its influence.

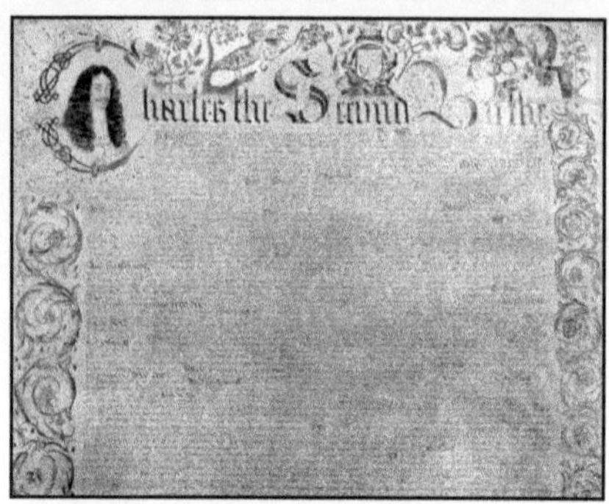

**King Charles II issued the Carolina Charter in 1663.**
NC Division of Archives & History

North Carolina's story, however, was not the same as those of other early colonies. North Carolina had no Jamestown or Plymouth Rock moment on which to focus. And even though attempted English settlement in North Carolina preceded all others absolutely, and Jamestown by 20 years, another event's anniversary was chosen to celebrate as the origin of North Carolina. In 1660, King Charles II was restored to the throne of England, Ireland, and Scotland after the death of Oliver Cromwell, a man who had ruled as a virtual dictator after he beheaded King Charles I in 1649. In appreciation for their help in Charles II regaining the throne, the restored monarch granted a charter to eight Lords Proprietors for land in the Americas. He did so in March 1663. Given that *carolus* is the Latin name for Charles, this chartering of Carolina was indeed the birth of the Tar Heel State. That land, the Province of Carolina, made up what is today North Carolina, South Carolina, and Tennessee.

### Carolina Charter Tercentenary Commission

To celebrate the 300th anniversary of the historic occasion, the North

Carolina General Assembly created a Carolina Charter Tercentenary Commission in 1959 to organize commemorative events across the state. The Honorable Francis E. Winslow from Rocky Mount was appointed as chairman of the commission in fall 1959. Governor Luther Hodges (1954-1961), who is remembered notably today in the state for his championing the creation of Research Triangle Park, appointed 22 of the 25 members of the commission. The other three were standing, ex-officio members—the Superintendent of Public Instruction, Director of Archives and History, and Director of Conservation and Development. Gov. Hodges got the celebration started and he would participate in the later events; however, at the time of the tercentenary observances, Terry Sanford, later U.S. Senator, actually served as North Carolina's governor (1961-1965).

**Gov. Terry Sanford and the First Lady celebrated the state's 300th birthday all year beginning at an opening ball on Jan. 4, 1963.**
NC Division of Archives & History

In the early planning, the commission realized that not much of the state had actual history that reached back into the 1600s, so they broadened the era to be commemorated by the observance to the first century of Carolina, 1663 to 1763. The end date was a convenient break as well, as it marked the end of the Colonial era. That stopping point also gave some impetus to the celebration of the country's bicentennial which was to follow 13 years later in 1976.

That first century of Carolina settlement gave most North Carolina communities some opportunity to celebrate something. The French and Indian War had ended by then and settlement had moved westward across most of the colony. Although Daniel Boone and his family did not live along the Upper Yadkin River at the foot of the Blue Ridge Mountains until 1766, Boone had hunted on the Blue Ridge plateau since at least 1760 and had lived in the "forks of the Yadkin" just a little farther east in Rowan County (today's Davie County) since 1752. Daniel Boone was America's pioneer hero and North Carolina had a strong claim on at least 21 years of his remarkable legacy, from 1752 to 1773. And besides, it was from North Carolina that Daniel Boone first ventured forth into Kentucky:

> "I sold my farm at Yadkin, and what goods we could not carry with us, and on the 25th of September, 1773, we bade farewell to our friends, and proceeded on our Journey to Kentucky, in company with five more families ..."[2] (*The Adventures of Col. Daniel Boon*, by John Filson)

All that remained was for someone to suggest a way for "Daniel Boone" to join in the state's grand birthday celebration.

Celebrating a statewide event such as the Carolina Charter Tercentenary is not an easy task to organize. Many people had different ideas on what could be done and ought to be done. One of the top ambitions of the tercentenary commission, was to help promote the State's construction of a new repository for the state's archives and historical items. Another was to update and complete the compilation of the colonial records. Commission Chairman Winslow was championing the tercentenary celebration for its educational value and encouraging activities that would enhance a greater understanding and appreciation of Carolina's history during that first century. Along with the focus on a repository and the colonial records a series of historical pamphlets was published, a mobile museum was created, essay contests were held around the state, and a documentary film, *The Road to Carolina*, was produced. In addition, individual schools and colleges across the state performed pageants, and musical and dramatic programs, each imparting some educational aspect of the Carolina Charter.[3]

**Southern Appalachian Historical Association**

The educational focus by the commission was important and warranted, of course, but as that other iconic frontiersman, Congressman David Crockett, remarked during his political campaigns in Tennessee of the 1820s and 1830s, "People don't want to be informed; they want to be entertained." That sentiment set the stage for when the folks in Watauga County got wind of the celebration opportunity.

Brig. Gen. John D.F. Phillips, U.S. Army (ret.), served as executive secretary of the Carolina Charter Tercentenary Commission. In the spring of 1962, he wrote a letter to Dr. Daniel J. Whitener, dean of Appalachian State Teachers College, inviting him to a meeting in Asheville about planning celebration events for the western part of the state. Watauga County had no representative for a Committee of Commemorative Events, but Dr. Whitener already served on the Committee for Programs in Schools, Colleges, and Universities, so he went. After the meeting, Dr. Whitener was enthused about the potential and immediately contacted Herman W. Wilcox, executive vice-president of the Southern Appalachian Historical Association (SAHA) and also chairman of Boone's Chamber of Commerce. (Wilcox was a fireball of ideas and community engagement. He had served as chairman of the chamber for 22 of the years since he first served in that role in 1939. In 1951, he was the board director who suggested and championed that SAHA sponsor and produce *Horn in the West,* the outdoor drama. Wilcox, a baldheaded man, was known affectionately throughout the community as "Curly."[4]) Internal meetings were held and in a few months, Wilcox was writing to Phillips suggesting a series of events surrounding the opening of the 12th season of Kermit Hunter's *Horn in the West.* This outdoor drama had been successful since its debut in 1952, attracting large crowds for nightly shows during each summer season.

**Herman Wilcox (r) greets visiting British Minister Dennis Greenhill.**
photo by Larry Penley, courtesy of *Tarheel Wheels,* June 1964

Clyde R. Greene, president of SAHA, suggested having a small celebration at Cooks Gap to unveil a Daniel Boone marker on the Blue Ridge Parkway and then coming to Boone for a larger celebration at either the new football stadium at the college or the outdoor theater. He suggested trying to get some oxen and covered wagons for the celebration. Ideas began to percolate within the group. Some caught on right away and grew with the enthusiasm and imagination of the planners. Throughout all the planning and execution, Herman Wilcox served as the chairman of Watauga County Carolina Charter Tercentenary observance.

**Clyde Greene prepares for the wagon train he organized.**
from newsprint, courtesy of *Watauga Democrat*

**Making It Happen**

During that fall of 1962, as the world held its breath during the Cuban Missile Crisis, more ideas for the celebration in Watauga County developed and some were rather grand. In November a special committee reported its suggestions for inviting notables including President John F. Kennedy, Gov. Terry Sanford, former N.C. Gov. Luther Hodges, the Chief of the Cherokee Nation, and the governors of all the states which grew out of the land included in the Carolina Charter. The collective committee also suggested having "a wagon train leaving from Bamboo" as well as "a square dance with hillbilly music." Other suggestions included a golf tournament, a bicycle race, and a fox hunt. Someone suggested including the dedication of the Daniel Boone Native Gardens, a living tribute to the pioneer hero. Others proposed adding a specially written historical prologue to the opening weekend's performances of *Horn in the West.* It could be crafted by the drama's author, Dr. Kermit Hunter, then a professor at Hollins College (later University) in Roanoke, Virginia, from information provided by Dr. William S. Powell, all to commemorate the 300th anniversary of the Carolina Charter.

**A special prologue was added to *Horn in the West* to celebrate the Tercentenary.**
from 1964 DBWT Souvenir Booklet

During the winter, all these ideas were mulled over, modified, and considered. The event took shape as "Daniel Boone Crosses the Blue Ridge, A Watauga County Carolina Charter Tercentenary Celebration" with Herman W. Wilcox serving as overall chairman. He organized a host of committees, such as Golf Tournament, Parade, Publicity, Invitation of Distinguished Guests, and Wagon Train, each with its own responsibilities for the specific events.[5]

In early April 1963, a press release from chairman Herman Wilcox announced the plans for the late June celebration. It included the language to be used in the invitations issued by Gov. Sanford to all the dignitaries:

> "I wish to extend to you a most cordial invitation to attend in Boone, North Carolina, June 29, 1963, a celebration honoring our state's 300th Anniversary. The celebration which will be known as 'Daniel Boone Crosses the Blue Ridge' is a part of the Carolina Charter Tercentenary. It will commemorate the opening of the first prong of the renowned Wilderness Road to the West and will coincide with the opening of 'Horn in the West,' one of America's fine outdoor dramas, beginning its twelfth successful season. The Celebration is expected to attract national attention, and governors of all states of the original Carolina Charter and states into which Daniel Boone pioneered are being invited. I sincerely hope that you will join us in this outstanding event."

**Ivey Moore appeared with Sue Teele on WSPV-TV to promote the wagon train.**
courtesy of *Wilkes Journal-Patriot*

By that time, word had begun to circulate in the region about plans for some sort of wagon train experience. In the same month, the Wagon Train Committee met in Boone at the Daniel Boone Hotel to make the final plans. Clyde Green was committee chair. At the meeting, Ivey Moore was selected to be the chief scout. Moore's selection put him in a promotional frame of mind. He eagerly sought out opportunity at every turn to promote the wagon train event, appearing on TV and visiting the regional newspapers. Moore was already known as a bit of a publicity hound, but he was then set upon the stage that would give him perhaps his greatest notoriety, at least in North Carolina.

### Westward Movement

"As nearly as possible, the Wagon Train will duplicate Daniel Boone's Trek in 1773," the *Journal-Patriot* reported a week after the meeting. "Such equipment as Kentucky rifles, broad axes, old cooking utensils and clothing will be typical of Boone's party. … The last night's camp will be pitched in Cook's Gap where a picnic dinner will be spread around the open fire, and where there will be old time music and singing." Wagon Master DeWitt Barnett expected to have "eight covered wagons, six scouts, and a number of packhorses." [6] He would discover soon enough there was more interest than that.

News of the upcoming celebration was reported in the May 1963 issue of *Tercentenary News*, the official newsletter of the Carolina Charter Tercentenary Commission. The Wagon Train was indeed a central attraction:

> **"Boone Wagon Train Forming for 3-Day Trek, June 27-29, Honoring Tercentenary**
>
> The beginning of the Westward Movement will be relived June 27-29 as men, wagons, and oxen pit their strength against the hardships of the wilderness trail in an effort to duplicate Daniel Boone's Crossing of the Blue Ridge in the big Carolina Tercentenary celebration in Boone.
>
> "The wagon train, which will consist of ten wagons, six scouts, and five pack horses, will follow Boone's route from Ferguson into Boone. First night's camp, when the wagons

> will be drawn into a circle and camp fire built, will be between Darby and Triplett and the second night at Cook's Gap.
>
> "At Cook's Gap the wagon train will have open house with string music singing, square dancing, and roasted buffalo meat. G.D. Barnett of Boone is wagon master.
>
> "The wagon train will be one of the top attractions during the ceremonies of the Carolina Charter Tercentenary celebration in the William J. Conrad Stadium at Appalachian State Teachers College on June 29 at 2 p.m.
>
> "A large number of state, national, and international dignitaries will be present for the colorful celebration which honors the State's 300th anniversary."[7]

During April, local plans were made for the parade through Boone as part of the Saturday celebration. Bob Breitenstein was chairman of the Parade Committee and the minutes from the meeting revealed the arrangements for the route and types of floats to be included. "Items in the parade will be typical of the early history of this region. Some of the features of the parade will include the following: 'Horn in the West' Cast, an old steam engine from Pioneer Village, a number of antique cars, National Guard, the Wagon Train, bands, and many other special features." After organizing the wagons in the parking lot of *Horn in the West*, they planned to parade through Boone along King Street, Water Street, and Rivers Street, and over to the new stadium.[8]

As the date for the event got closer, more details about the wagon train developed. It was becoming one of the significant elements of the entire celebration in Watauga County, but not the only element.

The *Tercentenary News*, June issue, reported that the Honorable Luther H. Hodges would be the keynote speaker at the Boone celebration. He then served as Secretary of Commerce in the Kennedy administration. The dedication of the Daniel Boone Native Gardens, adjacent to the Daniel Boone Theater, was indeed added to the festivities. This botanical garden project had been under way for two years, but this event served well as the occasion to dedicate it. And, an invitation to the British Embassy had resulted in the attendance of Her Majesty's minister Dennis A. Greenhill and his wife. Watauga County's celebration, "Daniel Boone Crosses the Blue Ridge," was becoming quite an enterprise and undertaking. And among all the celebrations that had been planned around the state, it sounded as if it would provide the best opportunity for people to be—quite honestly—truly entertained.

## A Time of Change

In early October 1957, Great Britain's Queen Elizabeth II visited Jamestown, Virginia, to celebrate the 350th anniversary of a world-changing event, the establishment of the first permanent English settlement in the New World in 1607. As she did so, the world's first man-made satellite, the Soviet-launched *Sputnik*, circled the earth to the great alarm of Americans. Three months later, as America raced to catch up, a U.S. Vanguard rocket exploded on the launch pad at Cape Canaveral. (By contrast—and to some a commentary on America's technological prowess—that year Wham-O did, however, successfully launch the Frisbee.) America was awakened from its false sense of technological superiority as a nuclear power, even after having dedicated the nation's first nuclear power reactor in April at Fort Belvoir, Virginia. The nation took on the challenges of a changing world, championing for its youth education in math, science, and technology. This was knowledge that would soon enable America once again to showcase its innovative spirit.

In the month before *Sputnik*, in September 1957, integration of public schools as decreed by the Supreme Court in *Brown v. Board of Education (Topeka, KS), 1954* had been contested in Little Rock, Arkansas, by Gov. Orval Faubus. President Dwight Eisenhower sent in federal troops to assure the enrollment of nine black students into Central High School.

Earlier that year, in the spring of '57, President Eisenhower and South Vietnam's President Ngo Dinh Diem had affirmed their commitment

to prevent the spread of communism in the world. Senator John F. Kennedy had received the Pulitzer Prize for his biographical, *Profiles in Courage.* Elvis Presley, already an international sensation, appeared in the movie *Jailhouse Rock;* in December, he received his draft notice for the U.S. Army.

The next years, from 1958 to 1963, saw more changes—some slow and steady, some surprising and urgent.

In Moscow during spring '58, a 23-year old pianist, Van Cliburn from Kilgore, Texas, won the first International Tchaikovsky Competition. That summer, the National Aeronautics and Space Administration (NASA) was formed. On January 1, 1959, Alaska became the 49th state, and in August Hawaii became the 50th. On July 3, Vice President Richard Nixon toured the

Cumberland Gap National Historical Park the day before its official dedication. In February 1960, four freshmen students from Agricultural and Technical College of North Carolina staged a sit-in at the Woolworth's lunch counter in Greensboro, North Carolina, sparking a series of sit-ins across the country to protest "whites only" serving practices. In May, international tensions rose as Russia announced it had shot down an American U2 spy plane, seizing the pilot. That summer, citing the increasing hostility of Fidel Castrol, the U.S. cut its imports of Cuban sugar by 95%.

In fall 1960, the first televised presidential debates produced an advantage for the young and energetic Democratic nominee, Senator John F. Kennedy, over the experienced but haggard-looking Republican nominee, Vice President Richard Nixon. Kennedy was elected by a margin of only 113,000 popular votes out of 68 million cast. In his farewell address, President Eisenhower warned of the threat to the country of a growing "military-industrial complex." In his 1961 inaugural address, President Kennedy optimistically declared, "Ask not what your country can do for you, but what you can do for your country." He created the Peace Corps, as he also directed the CIA to train anti-Castro Cuban exiles for what became the failed invasion of Cuba at the Bay of Pigs in mid-April. On May 5, 1961, astronaut Alan Shepard in the Mercury capsule *Freedom 7* became the first American in space (on a sub-orbital trajectory), following the first human in space, Soviet cosmonaut Yuri Gagarin's orbit of the earth on April 12. President Kennedy then challenged America to land a man on the moon and return him safely by the end of the decade.

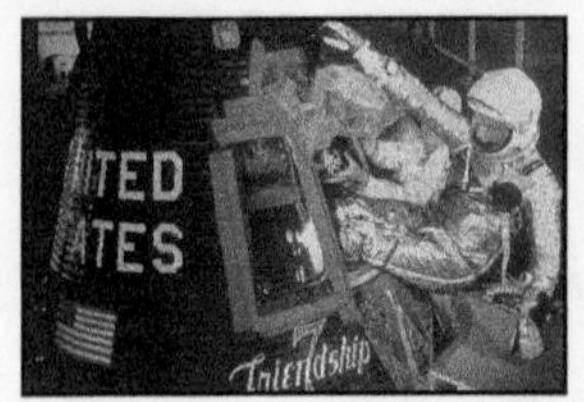


In January 1962, the Soviets released captured U2 pilot Gary Powers; and, Astronaut John Glenn orbited the earth three times on February 20. Astronauts Scott Carpenter and Wally Schirra followed with orbiting flights of their own that year. In May, Kennedy sent naval and land forces to support anti-Communist Laotian troops. In July, *Telstar*, the world's first communications satellite, an American success, was put into orbit and transmitted the first trans-Atlantic television signals. On August 5, actress Marilyn Monroe died at 36 of a drug overdose.

That fall 1962, James Meredith enrolled as the first black student at the University of Mississippi, amidst great protest and opposition. And publication of Rachel Carson's *Silent Spring* began the modern environmental movement.

In October, the world held its breath as America and the U.S.S.R. stood "eyeball to eyeball" over America's discovery that the Soviets had installed ballistic missiles in Cuba. The U.S. Navy quarantined Cuba with a blockade. Soviet Premier Nikita Khrushchev "blinked" and removed the missiles. Nuclear war was narrowly averted.

After a three-and-a-half month journey, in mid-December the American space probe *Mariner II* completed the first interplanetary exploration, passing by Venus.

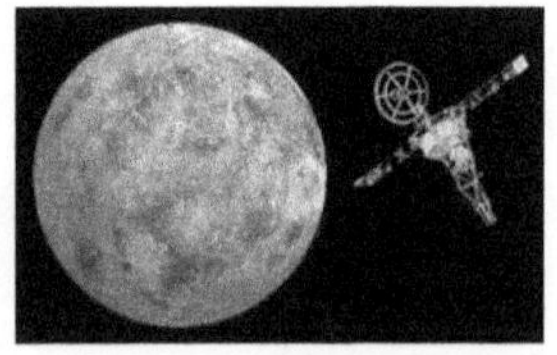

As 1963 began, the cost of first class postage rose 25%, increasing to

5 cents. In the wake of the Cuban Missile Crisis, the cost of not staying in touch was deemed too dear. The U.S. and the Soviets, immersed in a Cold War, established a telephone "hot line" to help avoid an accidental, world-ending nuclear conflagration.

In his January 1963 inaugural address, Alabama Gov. George C. Wallace declared, "Segregation now, segregation tomorrow, segregation forever." After "promises to keep And miles to go before I sleep," poet Robert Frost passed away at age 88.

In February, President Kennedy made it illegal for Americans to travel to Cuba or to engage in financial transactions with that country. Betty Friedan published *The Feminine Mystic*, reigniting the Women's Movement. In March, superstar singer Patsy Cline was killed in a plane crash; and the Beatles released their first album, *Please, Please Me.* Alcatraz Prison was closed.

Winston Churchill became an honorary U.S. citizen; and the Rev. Dr. Martin Luther King, Jr. was arrested in Birmingham, Alabama, and thousands protested across the city. In May, peaceful demonstrators in Birmingham were harassed by Commissioner of Public Safety Bull Connor and attacked with fire hoses and vicious police dogs. In June, Gov. George Wallace stood in the doorway of the University of Alabama to prevent the enrollment of black students; and, civil rights activist Medgar Evers was killed in Mississippi by a member of the White Citizens' Council. The U.S. Supreme Court declared that reading the Bible in public schools was

unconstitutional. As atheists and believers went 'round and 'round about that decision, astronaut Gordon Cooper circled the earth, 22 times on one flight.

Convinced that outside agitators were sparking unrest on college campuses regarding racial integration, the North Carolina General Assembly, controlled by conservatives, hurriedly wrote and passed without debate on June 26 the Speaker Ban Law preventing "known communists" and others as specified from speaking on UNC campuses. (This law set in motion events that would play out over the next five years at UNC-Chapel Hill and engage staunch conservative radio commentator (later US Senator) Jesse Helms, who frequently opposed what he saw as the liberalism of the Chapel Hill campus.)

On that same day, the eve of the first Daniel Boone Wagon Train, President John F. Kennedy was greeted in Germany by two million cheering West Berliners. He charmed them with his greeting, 'Ich bin ein Berliner.'' ("I am a Berliner.") He was there to support West Berlin 22 months after the building of the Berlin Wall by Soviet authorities. Kennedy continued his trip, visiting Great Britain and Italy and missing his chance to help North Carolina celebrate its 300th anniversary.

And the world turned.

# Daniel Boone Wagon Train, 1964

The success of the 1963 Daniel Boone Wagon Train encouraged a repeat excursion, one the organizers hoped would become an annual event. They began talking about it during the first wagon train before they even reached the top of the Blue Ridge. The 1964 event would be bigger, longer, and better, they imagined, and they were blessed with a cooperative calendar such that the next Wagon Train parade in Boone would fall on Saturday, July 4. The whole thing had captured such attention that they created a souvenir program with photographs from the 1963 event. They sold ad space to pay for the printing and included a wealth of information about the pioneer history of the area. Dr. Daniel J. Whitener had the first word in the program, but sadly it was among his last. He passed away on March 23, 1964, as plans were well under way for a second celebration. He was 67, and then serving as dean of Appalachian State Teachers College (ASTC).

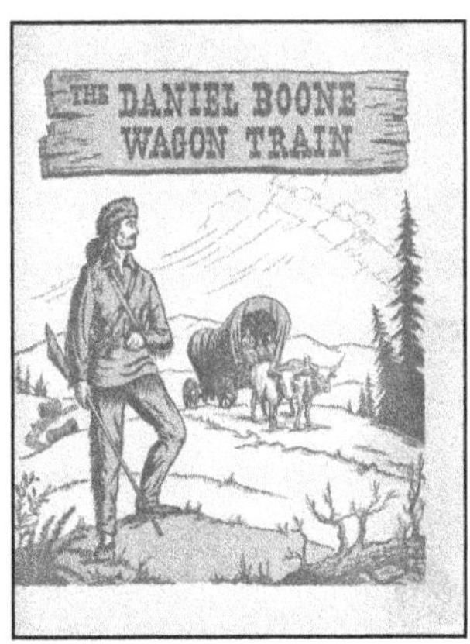


**A souvenir booklet was created for the 1964 wagon train; cover art by Edith Ferguson Carter.**
author's collection

Dr. Whitener's preface to the souvenir program championed the purpose of celebrating this particular bit of history related to the westward movement and called that telling of history a responsibility:

**Dean D.J. Whitener**
from 1964 DBWT
Souvenir Booklet

> "For long, history books have said that the first crossing of the Appalachian mountains and the settlement of the land of Tennessee and Kentucky just before the American Revolution were decisive events in our history. Much emphasis has been given to what these pioneers did in the new lands, but too little emphasis has been given to who they were and how they crossed the mountains.
>
> "These Boone-led English, Scotch-Irish, and German pioneers, largely from North Carolina, laid the foundations for westward expansion, culminating three quarters of a century later in the expansion of the United States to the Pacific Ocean under President James K. Polk, also a native of North Carolina. Surely a people who did so much to create our present Union of fifty states have a duty to tell their history!"[1]

The organizers took to heart Dr. Whitener's interest in promoting historical education and had organized an essay contest during the 1963-64 school year. Over 800 essays came in from elementary and secondary students extolling the virtues Daniel Boone as empire builder and recounting his role as hunter and (incorrectly) Indian fighter. Dr. Cratis Williams, director of graduate studies at ASTC, reviewed all the essays.[2] Further tribute was paid to Dr. Whitener with the establishment of a memorial fund for purchasing books for the school's library.

In addition, the N.C. Department of Archives and History presented 28 volumes of rare books to the college library "in grateful memory of Dr. Whitener." The presentation was made by Director Dr. Chris Crittenden and State Archivist Dr. H.G. Jones.[3] Dr. Whitener would be missed.

**Dr. Cratis Williams (l) and Herman Wilcox review essays.**
from microfilm, courtesy of *Watauga Democrat*

Many of the same people who were involved in the 1963 version of the Wagon Train reprised their roles or took on new responsibilities, but did so primarily for the Watauga County portion of the trek. Wilkes County had formed a cooperating set of committees to handle their portion of the expanded celebration. Excitement for the event, it seemed, had grown in the wake of its first success. But, that first year's experience had taught the planners some valuable lessons, too. Not surprising, Wilkes County had introduced a new committee, the Police Protection Committee, with Col. Roy Forehand and Sheriff Fred Myers taking the lead. The memory of the intoxicated rowdies at Cook's Gap the year before weighed heavily on the organizers. Let it not be said that these folks did not learn from history.

### "The Farmer's Cursed Wife"

The participants were eager for the experience, but such a large crowd needed some rules to assure that everyone had a good time. All the wagon trainers were asked to take a pledge swearing off profanity (if that is an acceptable oxymoron) and promising not to drink alcohol or allow others in their camp or travelling party to drink alcohol. Jesse

Poindexter, reporter for the *Winston-Salem Journal/Sentinel*, pointed out the irony of such a rule in Wilkes County "where many a man's corn field is measured in gallons instead of bushels."[4] Wagon Master Barnett also shared with the *Watauga Democrat* that the original Boone expedition carried some spirits in its wagon. "We know that and we want our re-enacting of Boone's crossing the Blue Ridge as authentic as possible. But, when it comes to hard drink, we're compromising. Many of us are Baptists, and like Charlie Elledge [who played Rev. Sims] in the 'Horn in the West' show, we leave that 'bust head' stuff to the Methodists and Episcopalians."[5] So, the pledges were taken and good intentions prevailed.

As if to test their mettle against these two specific prohibitions for alcohol and profanity, the organizers of the 1964 Wagon Train added a day to the actual trek and made the route a little longer, starting in the heart of Wilkes County. No Doubt, cussing and drinking would surely have helped. The wagon trainers would parade through North Wilkesboro on Monday, June 29, and then retire to Memorial Park for "Games, Horseshoes, Climbing pole, Catching pig, Shooting, Sack Races and Hog Calling." After a night of music and square dancing, they would on Tuesday morning parade through Wilkesboro on their way to Ferguson where the wagon train had begun the year before, at the farm of Tom Ferguson. A night of entertainment was planned. The second day's trek would end at Darby where they had camped the year before, with more games and dancing, music, singing, and prizes. The third day out would end at Triplett, not Cook's Gap. They would wagon train into Boone on July 3 in time to go see *Horn in the West* that Friday evening. On Saturday, July 4, the wagon trainers would parade through Boone in an Independence Day celebration.

The importance of the commemorative event did not escape the notice of the newspapers, a news medium which in the 1960s provided a community with a collective sense of itself. On June 24, Dwight Nichols, Editor of the *Wilkes Journal-Patriot* offered his thoughts on the upcoming event:

> "One weakness of this hectic and fast civilization in which we live is that it gives excuse to forget the people who founded and expanded our country and who gave us the greatest heritage known to any people.... If the wagon train shall serve to call attention to the courage, foresight and stamina of our forefathers, it will be well worth while."[6]

The 1964 Wagon Train started in North Wilkesboro with a weekend celebration and parade called "Pioneer Days." Many of the wagoners arrived on Saturday, June 27. Although they would have liked to open the event to all comers, the planners were constrained by the land available at each campsite. So, they limited the event to the first 75 wagons to register, but there was a catch. Those who wanted to participate had to bring authentic covered wagons in keeping with the theme of the event. Chief Scout Ivey Moore was in charge of registration.

The planners also anticipated the crowds of visitors who would flock to the camps to see this spectacle, so they made plans to keep people entertained. They held a talent contest before Pioneer Days began to select the groups who would perform each night at the camps in Ferguson, Darby, and Triplett and even during the gathering at North Wilkesboro. They insisted on ballads of the frontier and expected to hear "Barbara Allen," "Black Jack Davey," "Dandoo," and "The Farmer's Cursed Wife." "How Firm a Foundation" would be sung, of course, during planned daily devotionals, and folk songs "Green Gravel" and "Weevily Wheat" would add to the authenticity of the

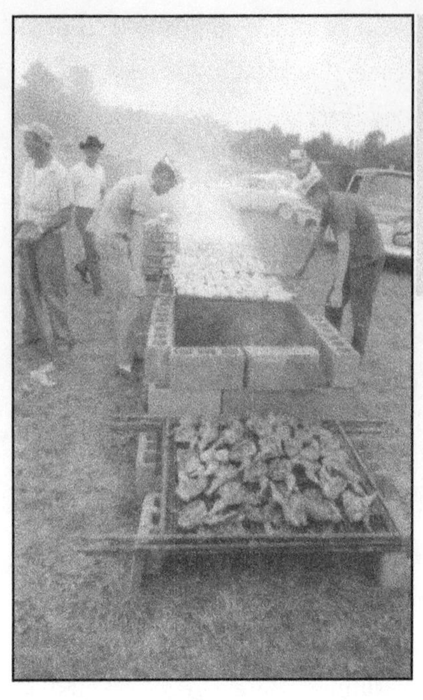

**Barbecuing chicken for all the people coming to see the wagon train was a major fundraiser for the communities.**
photo by Frank Jones for *Winston-Salem Journal*, Courtesy of Forsyth County Public Library Photograph Collection, Winston-Salem, NC

celebration.[7] With the Rev. G.W. Chapman of Beaver Creek Advent Christian Church as the chair of the entertainment committee, a family-friendly program of music was assured.[8]

They made arrangements with communities at those sites to prepare meals for sale to the hordes of people who would come to the nightly events. Even before the departure, the North Wilkesboro Optimist Club and the Boy Scouts prepared to barbecue 2,000 chickens on Saturday and Saturday night, continuing until the wagoners pulled out on Tuesday morning.[9] At Ferguson, the Ruritan Club had ordered another 500 chickens to feed their lot. The Daniel Boone Wagon Train was shaping up to be a rolling, rollicking party of music, food, and fun.

## A Mile Long

The wagons assembled at Memorial Park on Saturday in North Wilkesboro for their first camp. The park lay along the Yadkin River northeast of the NC Hwy 18/268 bridge. They had a community singing on Sunday, "but high temperatures and a broiling sun prevented any large number of spectators from assembling for the event."[10]

They paraded through town on Monday morning, June 29, going along Fifth Street, Main Street, Tenth Street, D Street and Forester Avenue before returning to the park for games and contests.[11] The parade jammed traffic for blocks, wrote Jesse Poindexter for the *Winston-Salem Journal*, "as the animals plodded along pulling the wagons loaded with people and water casks."[12] It included about 45 wagons and a host of horseback riders, but not everyone who would actually start the trek on Tuesday.[13]

That Monday night the participants and visitors held a square dance jubilee in the parking lot at Lowes Midtown Plaza. Singing groups and string bands competed, each again advised to prepare old songs in keeping with the times and theme of Daniel Boone.[14] "A crowd estimated conservatively at 5,000 people converged on Midtown Plaza," reported the *Journal-Patriot*, "jumping into the square dance area until microphone and record player cords were broken. Police tried to hold the crowd back. Everyone wanted to see, and continued to push in. All streets leading into the plaza area and Memorial Park were hopelessly snarled in traffic. When drivers could go no further, they parked the car and everyone walked in."[15] But the wagon trainers knew they were

**Square dancing was a big part of the celebrations and fun at all the campsites.**

from newsprint, courtesy of *Wilkes Journal-Patriot*

there for more than just fun and that they had a hard few days ahead of them of walking, riding, and driving teams of obstinate animals. Eventually the wagon trainers settled in for the night, even as the visiting revelers continued to party late.

Morning came too early for some, but not all. "Seems that just about everybody brought country ham," wrote Poindexter, "and it is a mouth-watering diversion to walk among the camp sites and smell the ham frying and the coffee."[16] That may have been a delight for some of the participants and perhaps seemed peculiar to others. People were there from New York, California, Maryland, Virginia, Tennessee, and South Carolina among others. But a lot of folks were from nearby and they were treating these out-of-staters to some real North Carolina hospitality.

The Wagon Train was much bigger in 1964 than it had been the year

**On the road to Ferguson, the 1964 wagon train stopped to rest along NC Hwy 268 at a pull off beside W. Kerr Scott Reservoir.**
photo by Howard Walker, from newsprint, courtesy of *Winston-Salem Journal*

before. Ivey Moore guessed it was three times as large. He expected between 500 and 600 people in the wagon train. "There will be perhaps 200 riders, and we have a lot more young people and children this year." If it got any larger, they were thinking, they would have to divide it into two trains. This one was already a mile long.[17]

**The Passing Spectacle**

The 1964 Daniel Boone Wagon Train departed North Wilkesboro at 8 o'clock on Tuesday morning, June 30, headed for Ferguson, 14 miles away. Walking in front were two local public figures, T.E. Story of Wilkes County and Herman Wilcox of Watauga County, co-chairs of the event. In a long career of community service, Story had served as a legislator in the state's General Assembly and his honesty was appreciated. Asked from the crowd if he was walking all the way to Boone, he simply said abruptly, "Nope," and kept on walking.[18]

The wagon train crossed the Yadkin River, which separated the two towns, and then followed Main Street through Wilkesboro, passing by the Tory Oak, a noted landmark from the Revolutionary War era.[19] They trailed along NC Hwy 268 adjacent to W. Kerr Scott Reservoir, which had been completed in September 1962 in response to flooding concerns; the devastating floods of 1916 and 1940 were hard to forget. The wagons were escorted by the State Highway Patrol and the Wilkes County Sheriff's Department, who directed traffic around the wagons. The North Wilkesboro Rescue Squad and then the Boone Rescue Squad accompanied the group during the event.[20]

Some of the people who had participated the year before returned for the '64 event. Some brought their friends. Six wagons formed up from East Bend with Foy Norman and his wife being the lead wagon, judged by Chief Scout Ivey Moore as the "best rig." As a group, the

**Foy Norman of East Bend was judged "best rig."**
from 1964 DBWT Souvenir Booklet

six wagons led the procession. Along the route, people came out of their houses and stopped work to stand, watch, and wave at the passing spectacle.

But problems did arise among the 75 wagons and their parties. Otis Wilcox of Boone fell and broke his leg before they even left town. With his new cast and some pain, he rejoined the wagon train declaring that it would hurt just as much anywhere and he might as well be with his outfitted wagon. And not far out of town, Cleo Edwards of Sparta had to stop and shod his oxen as the pavement was too rough on the shoeless beasts. The wagon train moved on, helped in some manner by Sheriff Fred Myers and his five deputies who were dressed for the times, they thought, "wearing western style boots in black, light colored-trousers, black shirts with pearl buttons and western hats." The *Journal-Patriot* continued, "They have laid aside their small, light revolvers for the long-barrel western models as were used by Wyatt Earp."[21] Apparently the idea of a "frontier era" had conflated about two centuries of history into one historical concept for many of the participants.

**An Inviting Place**

The campsite in Ferguson hosted shooting contests all day with contestants firing 19th century percussion cap rifles and period-correct flintlock rifles. And then the Ferguson Ruritans fed the whole crew—visitors and wagon trainers—with barbecued chicken dinners. "A long barbecue pit was fired up before noon and the aroma was present and pleasant thru the afternoon and far into the night," wrote the *Journal-Patriol*. "Community residents who watched the barbecue fires and dished out chick-n-que and accessories hour after hour counted the plates and came up with a figure of approximately 1,800 when the last ones ate near midnight."[22] "The entertainment events were well carried out at Ferguson. The singing and the string band groups performed on a flat bed truck in view of thousands of people with a PA system which could be heard to the far reaches of Tom Ferguson's big hay field where the wagon train camped."[23] Ballad singing, more string bands, and more square dancing filled up the night and kept the participants up later than they should have been. The road to Darby awaited them.

**Bill Miller tuned up his banjo for the evening frolic.**

from microfilm, courtesy of *Wikes Journal-Patriot*

On Wednesday, July 1, the wagon train processed from Ferguson to Darby. It was a long trip, but not as challenging as what was to come. The campgrounds at Darby were described as "a site locked away in the cool, quiet Elk Valley."[24] It was an inviting place and thousands of visitors thronged to the campsite to mingle with the wagon

**Cool waters welcomed weary wagoners and visitors alike.**
from newsprint, courtesy of *Lenoir News-Topic*

trainers. "A pall of dust from the unpaved road hung over the Elk Creek valley almost like a heavy fog and caused at least two [car] drivers to run off the road."[25] The campers took a dip in the swimming hole at Dugger Creek. The community was generally welcoming, offering food for sale including barbecued chicken, chicken salad sandwiches, hot dogs, and hamburgers;[26] but, restroom facilities were scarce. At the local recreation center, the bathrooms were locked. The only other inconvenience came when the talent contest lost electrical power for about an hour, plunging the campsite into the period-correct darkness of Boone's era, an aspect of the trek which had not been planned.[27]

**History in the Making**

Winston-Salem reporter Jesse Poindexter featured an exchange between two visitors from the local community. His story appeared on page 1 below the fold on Friday, July 3, 1964. He wrote:

"A few Negroes have lived in this fertile valley for genera-

> tions. They have worked amicably with and for their white neighbors. Two of the older inhabitants, both from Ferguson, sat together and talked about the old ways. They were Mrs. R.C. Woods and Mrs. Ninnie L. Hendrix, Negro. Mrs. Woods was in a wheel chair because of a broken hip. She is 75. Mrs. Hendrix, 76, was wearing her best dress. They chatted like Magpies at the Darby camp. 'I've lived here all my days,' said Mrs. Hendrix. 'My mother was a midwife. She was Sallie Hatton. She used to walk for miles to help out. She usually got one dollar.' Mrs. Woods, who had relatives from Ohio, remembers 'Aunt Sallie' Hatton very well. 'She delivered dozens of children,' recalled Mrs. Woods. 'She was a fine woman.'"[28]

As these two women of different races sat in the mountains of North Carolina on July 2, 1964, and reminisced about events from their long lives, history of another sort was being made in Washington, D.C. Only hours after Congress completed its work that afternoon on landmark legislation, President Lyndon Johnson signed the Civil Rights Act of 1964. But, reaction in the southern states was severe and predictable. The headline article above the fold in the same July 3rd issue of the *Winston-Salem Journal* noted "All 11 North Carolina representatives voted against the Civil Rights Bill Thursday." An adjacent article from the Associated Press titled "Reaction To Act Varies" noted: "Lester Maddox, operator of a segregated restaurant in Atlanta said he would go to jail before he would serve Negro customers." (In 1966, Lester Maddox was elected governor of Georgia.)

**New River**

The climb on Friday from Darby to Triplett was made more difficult by rain. It was a steady, pervasive drenching of the stalwart re-enactors. "The feed grain was soaked by the rain," Poindexter wrote, "and it would soon have sprouted."[29] But these were hearty people and they persevered in the most challenging part of the route, some showing exceptional gumption and courage. Many of the wagoners and their belongings were completely bathed in rain. Having run out of firewood, some scurried around camp looking for dry, hardwood that would readily burn. Still, they said it was no worse than the year before. [30]

Rain was not the only challenge. One wagoner, Jack Hines of Lincolnton, made too sharp a turn with his four-horse rig, and he snapped the tongue on the wagon. Committed to reaching Boone, Hines sought out a sawmill and had a new tongue cut to his specs. He rejoined the train and made his way to Boone. Two women, committed to their own ideas of authenticity, walked the entire route barefoot. Those two ladies were delighted to reach the New River on the way to Boone. As they crossed, their sore feet bathed in mountain waters, they were assured by others that they were following the route that Daniel Boone took, trekking what they called the Old Buffalo Trace.[31]

At the crossing of the New River, the would-be pioneers were greeted by a sign reminding them of the history of that spot. A new wooden sign had been erected that summer to mark the site of the original Three Forks Baptist Church. It was at that site in 1913 that the Daughters of the American Revolution had erected one of the bronze markers for Daniel Boone's Trail. The year before, during the first Daniel Boone Wagon Train celebration, that bronze marker had been moved from Three Forks to be installed near Cook's Gap along the Blue Ridge Parkway. To remind folks of the history of the original marker site, three men, T.K. Pease, Walter Edmisten, and Avery Jackson, erected a wooden sign with the same words which had been

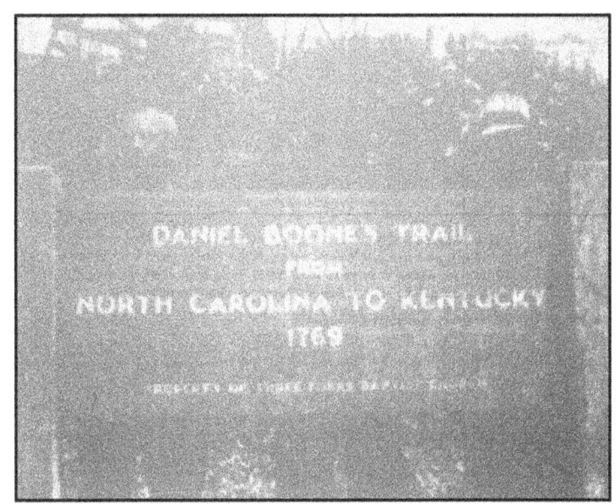


**Three Forks Baptist Church reminded the public where Daniel Boone's Trail was marked in 1913.**
from microfilm, courtesy of *Watauga Democrat*

on the bronze plaque. The wooden sign was about ten times the size of the bronze tablet.[32] (Years later and well after the wooden sign at New River had deteriorated and been removed, the relocated bronze plaque along the Blue Ridge Parkway near Cook's Gap was taken by parties unknown around 2002. Today, a granite monument marks the site of the original Three Forks Baptist Church at the ford of New River.)

## A Long Show of Horses, Queens, and Cowboys

Arriving in Boone around 3:30 on Friday afternoon, the Wagon Train camped in the valley adjacent to the *Horn in the West* parking lot. They would be there all Fourth of July Weekend for folks to come see and visit.[33] At 10 o'clock on Saturday morning, many of the wagons, riders, and walkers processed through town in a parade just as they did the year before. The parade was a major attraction in the town for the weekend and it drew another large crowd; and that crowd was encouraged to get into the act, too. A costume contest was held throughout downtown on Thursday and Friday. Those who wanted to be judged simply had to walk around downtown; the judges, under the direction

**Cute but historically curious costuming.**
from microfilm, photo by Rachel Rivers, courtesy of *Watauga Democrat*

of Mrs. Carrie Winkler, would find them. Again, what passed for "historically correct" was given a wide berth, prompting one young girl to show up dressed as a pilgrim of the 1620's Plymouth Plantation.[34]

Those wagon trainers who did walk and ride in the parade got wetter than at their crossing of the New River as more rain fell; but, they were joined in the celebration by a near-record crowd for Boone.

Thousands of people braved the weather to line the streets and watch the passing wagons and horses under the direction of parade marshal Austin Adams. The parade included a National Guard Color Guard, Mayor Wade Brown riding in a car, Miss Rhododendron, and Miss Watauga County. Another car carried the cast of *Horn in the West.* Fred Kirby of Tweetsie Railroad was there, too. The whole procession was long and slow and led by the Appalachian High School Band, wrote Rachel Rivers in the *Watauga Democrat*, "striking a cadence which promised the little people—those with a belt-buckle view of things—that a long show of horses, queens, cowboys, and wagons was on the way." But, "when the clouds finally tired of their load, and a little rain came to the street," Rivers continued, "umbrellas appeared and the horses began to dance on the rain-speckled pavement." In time, the marching band got tired (or got tired of the rain) before the parade ended and fell out; but, the mile-long caravan of wet and weary wagon trainers soldiered on to complete the parade.[35] [36] [37]

**In good weather and bad, the wagon train paraded.**
from microfilm, courtesy of *Watauga Democrat*

Those who had walked the farthest showed the most resiliency. They gathered that night after the parade and before the beginning of the performance of *Horn in the West*. Showing the stuff they were made of, they square-danced in a frolic joined by hundreds of people eager to join in the celebration.

Before the second Daniel Boone Wagon Train had come to an end, planning began for the following year. Enthusiasm prevailed. Some talked about extending the route all the way from North Wilkesboro to Boonesborough, Kentucky. "We don't know whether it will develop," said Chief Scout Ivey Moore, "but there is every reason to believe it may come about in the next few years." It would take perhaps more than a month, they reasoned, with the train making 15 to 20 miles each day. "We ought to do it though," Moore declared. "It would bring the name of Daniel Boone to the attention of the American people and show them what he contributed to our history."[38]

As Ivey Moore and America were about to discover, others shared his passion for telling the story of Daniel Boone; and, though Moore and those on the Wagon Train were unwittingly inappropriate to the period in their dress and in their reenactment, they were at least sincere. A new telling of Daniel Boone's life was about to trump their effort to educate; and, this new effort was not in the least bit concerned with sharing the story with any sense of authenticity or accuracy.

## An Insult to the Intelligence

On September 24, 1964, *Wagon Train*-watching Americans were treated (or subjected, depending on one's point of view) to *The Adventures of Daniel Boone*, a television show starring Fess Parker. The producers had hoped to reprise Parker as Davy Crockett in a television series, following his resounding success in the mid-1950s playing the folksy Tennessee bear hunter and congressman. But, the Walt Disney Company would not negotiate with them, so, the producers settled for Daniel Boone. (Would that they had dropped the whole thing!)

The series was wonderfully popular, but not nearly as popular as Davy Crockett had been. It was, however, a colossal disaster of misinformation, a perfect storm of ignorance and dishonesty preying on the trusting innocent. *The Adventures of Daniel Boone* was so terribly inaccurate that the Kentucky House of Representatives condemned its portrayal of historic events and persons. Calling the program an "insult to the intelligence" of millions, especially Kentuckians, the

***The Adventures of Daniel Boone*, starring Fess Parker, was abominably inaccurate with its history.**
from microfilm, courtesy of *Watauga Democrat*

legislature passed House Resolution 113 in March 1966. "The NBC series might be excused for 'using black-haired 6-foot 5-inch Fess Parker to play the red-headed, 5-foot 10-inch Boone.' But it is 'an inexcusable farce … to give Boone an Indian companion with a cultured Harvard accent, portray an encounter with the Inca Indians, [and] have Gov. Patrick Henry of Virginia ride into Fort Boonesboro in a horse-drawn coach … .'"[39] The series remained popular enough—inaccuracies and all—through seven seasons, completing its mission of miseducation in early September 1970.[40]

Some publicists argue that any publicity is better than no publicity, and so perhaps a renewed and broader interest in Daniel Boone could only help the cause of the Daniel Boone Wagon Train as they planned their third event for the summer of 1965. Be that as it may, from its debut in the fall of 1964, the TV program served to both inspire and misinform for many years, among all its audiences, those who participated in the Daniel Boone Wagon Train.

And the world turned:

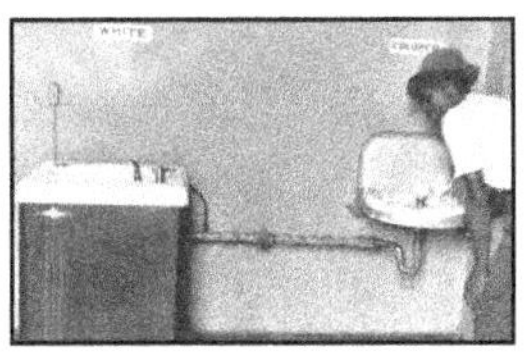


On July 2, President Lyndon Johnson signed the Civil Rights Act of 1964, outlawing racial segregation in America. Announcing in July that U.S. casualties in Vietnam had reached almost 1,400, the President sent 5,000 more advisors, reaching a total of 21,000. In early August, 1964, the bodies of three slain civil rights workers— Michael Schwerner, Andrew Goodman, and James Chaney—missing since late June, were found in Philadelphia, Mississippi. Congress passed the Gulf of Tonkin Resolution after North Vietnamese and U.S. war ships engaged, thus enabling the President to escalate the Vietnam conflict without Congress actually declaring war.

The Warren Commission reported that Lee Harvey Oswald had acted alone in assassinating President Kennedy. The U.S. Olympic Team returned from the Summer Tokyo Olympics after dominating with 90 medals including 36 gold. In November, the Democratic Johnson/Humphrey ticket defeated the Goldwater/Miller ticket by 15 million votes. The Berkeley Free Speech Movement gained momentum on the California campus demanding removal of the administration's ban of on-campus political activities. Dr. Martin Luther King, Jr. received the Nobel Peace Prize in Oslo, Norway.

In his 1965 State of the Union address, President Lyndon B. Johnson announced his "Great Society." Shortly, he ordered the bombing of North Vietnam, and the war escalated. Soon, the first combat forces landed in Vietnam. By May, 42,000 U.S. troops were there with another 21,000 sent in June.

*Ranger 8* crashed into the moon, as planned, after photographing possible lunar landing sites. In late February, Malcolm X was assassinated in Manhattan by three Black Muslims.

On March 7 in an incident which became known as "Bloody Sunday," 200 state and local troopers in Alabama, some deputized only that morning, used billy clubs and tear gas to attack over 500 civil rights demonstrators marching from Selma to Montgomery to protest voting rights discrimination. Police again clashed with demonstrators 10 days later in Montgomery. By month end, Dr. Martin Luther King, Jr. had successfully led another four-day march from Selma to Montgomery with 25,000 demonstrators; however, one participant from Detroit was shot to death by four Klansmen.

On March 23, *Gemini 3*, the first manned flight in the series, orbited earth with astronauts Gus Grissom and John Young aboard. On April 9, the Astrodome opened in Houston, Texas.

President Johnson sent 20,000 US troops to the Dominican Republic; and, 40 men burned their draft cards in Berkeley, California, as they marched a coffin to the draft board. During a subsequent demonstration, more cards were burned and President Johnson was hanged in effigy.

In the weeks before the 1965 Daniel Boone Wagon Train commemorated the crossing of the Blue Ridge in 1773, astronaut Edward White, II, during the flight of *Gemini 4*, conducted the first U.S. space walk. His fellow pioneering astronaut was James McDivitt.

Meanwhile:
Television audiences saw the premier of *The Addams Family, Flipper, and Gilligan's Island.* The theaters were filled with audiences watching *My Fair Lady, Goldfinger*, and *Sound of Music.* The radio resounded with "Rag Doll" by the Four Seasons, "Pretty Woman" by Roy Orbison,

and the Righteous Brothers singing "You've Lost That Lovin' Feeling." Roger Miller sang "Dang Me" and "King of the Road."

For more about television, movies, and music of the following 12 months, see Appendix, Popular Culture: July 1964-June 1965.

# Chief Scout Ivey Moore

Ivey Moore was quite a character. Most anyone who knew him would have agreed; and he was the one person whose name most immediately came to mind with mention of the Daniel Boone Wagon Train. He was involved in that expedition from the start, but there was more to the man and his life story than that one episode.

**Roy Ivey Moore portrayed Daniel Boone in his role as chief scout of the Daniel Boone Wagon Train.**
Photo by Larry Penley, Daniel Boone Wagon Train, Inc.

### The Guy Loved Adventure

Ivey Moore was born December 8, 1902, in Caldwell County. He moved with his parents' family to Wilkes County when he was only 4, but he already had a reputation in the family as being a wanderer and an adventurer. "I can tell you one story that is symptomatic of my father," said Dudley Moore, 80, one of his three sons, in a 2011 interview.[1]

"He was born in Globe. It's a little valley community off the side of the mountain, just down from Blowing Rock. You go to Blowing Rock and you drop down off the mountain and you get down to Globe. My father was born there. While they were living there, they had a fence around the property. My father was bad to crawl out into the yard and tunnel under the fence and go off on an adventure when he was a very small child. My grandmother took some tree limbs and stuck them in the ground underneath the fence, and they rooted and became a huge tree in later years. [Laughter.] That is kind of emblematic in that the guy loved adventure. He loved being in the woods."

The family's move to Wilkes County was made for business reasons in 1906. Ivey Moore's father, James Dudley Moore, operated a sawmill in Caldwell but moved to Wilkes because it had not yet been timbered out. Dudley Moore continued:

> "What [Ivey Moore's father] did was to uproot his family and carried them down the mountain to North Wilkesboro. They packed up their belongings in a covered wagon and pulled a sawmill to North Wilkesboro. That was quite an endeavor. If you think about trying to get a covered wagon from Globe to North Wilkesboro, you've got to traverse some hilly country to get down there. You couldn't do it in a day. It would be several days to get down there."

Ivey Moore had his own recollection of this family move. He shared in a 1974 taped interview[2] that the move had made "an indelible impression on my mind," but he declared he was not sure whether what he recalled was a memory or a dream. He was only four years old at the time. Moore said:

> "It seems that we were going someplace and we camped one night at the fork in the roads and there was a big tree there. And there was a store building across from where we were camping. And we were in a caravan of people and there were

> buggies, and a surrey, and old covered wagons at camp there. And dad picked the banjo and sang and the nigras [Negroes] sang by the campfire that night. And Jay and I—Jay was my older brother at the time, he died in 1909—was there and he and I slept in the surrey, in the bed of the floor and [Mother] and Dad slept on the ground. The thing that impressed me the most was that those nigras [Negroes] was singing and Dad was picking the banjo. He was a great one to pick the banjo and the guitar."

Ivey Moore loved the outdoors and cited that memory from age 4 as elemental to his childhood. He continued:

> "Well that was a camping activity, and I was very impressed with it. And as I grew up I made all kinds of pretend guns, went out to hunt Indians, run through the woods. Actually I was trying to be Daniel Boone, I guess, having no idea that in future years my life would be affected by something like this [wagon train]. The outcome of it was that in 1914, I joined the first Boy Scout troop in Wilkes County. … I think that was partially responsible for my becoming active in scouting years later when my boys grew up, and my love of nature and the outdoors, the study of the woods and the trees. I went squirrel hunting and I'd go out and just sit for hours and listen to nature. I loved the flowers that grew and learned the names of all of them."

**Ivey Moore, Sailor**

Dudley Moore declared, "My dad was one for leaving, always ready to go. He was endlessly looking for adventure. So, let me tell you about my father":

> "When he [Ivey Moore] was 16 years old, he ran away from

home and joined the Navy during the first world war. He served on the *USS Arizona*, the ship that was later sunk at Pearl Harbor in 1941. That would have been in 1918 when Dad ran away. He served out his enlistment, which I assume was probably three years. Then in 1942, after the Japanese bombed Pearl Harbor, he re-enlisted in the Navy. He served in the South Pacific. Of course, he was almost 40 years old then. He served as a medical assistant. He was in the Navy from August, '42 until March 12, 1945, when he was discharged. And, that ship was sunk, too." [Dudley Moore was born in 1931, so his father had left the family to go off to war.]

**Ivey Moore served in the U.S. Navy during both World War I and World War II.**
courtesy of Dudley Moore

"He was on this ship, *USS Asphalt*, in a typhoon at Saipan. (Ivey wrote 'August 1945' on the back of this photograph, but it must have been '1944.') Anyway, he was shipwrecked. This ship was basically a barge made of concrete. [It was used for storage of supplies and was towed by another ship. It had no self-propulsion.] This typhoon occurred. He and another guy were on a rubber raft in the typhoon and they were tethered to the ship. The wind got up pretty good and they tried to get loose. They had to cut the rope and all they had was a can of Planters peanuts. They opened the can and used the sharp edge of the can top to severe the rope. [The barge was driven by the winds onto a coral reef on 6 October, 1944.] My dad was shipwrecked along with several other crew members. He developed a healthy distaste for the Red Cross because they wouldn't give him any clothes. He had lost all his clothes in the storm, and he was in his underwear on the beach. He got mad at the Red Cross because they wouldn't give him any clothes. [Laughter]

"Ivey had been on another ship for awhile, the *USS Thatcher*. He was a pharmacist's mate on the ship. Pharmacist's mates were much like nurses. They assisted a doctor, if a doctor was onboard the ship. When there was no doctor, the pharmacist's mate acted on the doctor's behalf.

"Ivey was a wild and wooly man. He was an adventurer. We went places we weren't supposed to go. I drove him to Arizona in 1947. I had a broken collarbone and my arm was in a sling. And I had to drive a Studebaker automobile with a straight shift with my left hand reaching through the steering wheel. We went out there, just like vagabonds. We slept on the side of the road. We slept in a city park; we went to the police and asked, so they let us. We were pulling a one-wheel trailer. They let us pitch our tent in the park and on the side of the road going to Yellowstone. Then on the way back, when we got to Omaha, Nebraska, he had me take him to the airport and he flew to the Chicago furniture market. That left me and my two brothers, who were younger than I was—I was 15 or 16, I guess—to drive home. [Laughter] On that last day we got home about 10 o'clock at night. When we got home, we pulled in and my mother came out and said, 'Where's your father?' And I said, 'The last time I saw him was Omaha, Nebraska.' [Laughter] He was a real character, I'll tell you that.

"My mother thought she'd married a wild man. She was Freda Emily Hendren. They married October 7, 1923, in North Wilkesboro. She got used to all his "leaving." [Laughter.] My mother took care of the world. She basically did the raising of the children when my father was gone. She was the leader of the family and was a marvelous woman."

-PATRIOT

"State of Wilkes" For Over 41 Years

OUR CITY

North Wilkesboro has a trading radius of 80 miles, serving 100,000 people in Northwestern Carolina.

July 5, 1948

Make North Wilkesboro Your Shopping Center

**Father, 2 Sons Eagle Scouts**

Father, 2 Sons Eagle Scouts

Here are pictured R. Ivey Moore, center, and two sons, Jim, left, and Dudley, right, who became Eagle Scouts in the Court of Honor meeting held Thursday night in a history making event for Boy Scouts of America.—(Photo by Lane Atkinson, Jr.).

**R. Ivey Moore, Jim and Dudley Get Eagle Badges**

Large Crowd Attends History Making Event Here On Thursday Night

An unprecedented event in the history of Boy Scouts of America occurred here Thursday night when a father and two sons, R. Ivey Moore, Dudley and Jim Moore, simultaneously became Eagle Scouts.

A capacity crowd gathered at the First Methodist church in North Wilkesboro for the court of honor meeting, at which time Mr. Moore and sons reached the highest rank in the Boy Scouts organization.

According to data received from National Scout headquarters, that was the first time that a father and his sons had become Eagle Scouts on the same date.

J. B. Carter was chairman for the court of honor meeting, and the devotional services were conducted by Rev. H. M. Wellman. District Commissioner Gordon Finley led the Bible and flag ceremony.

As preliminaries to the main event Dr. John T. Wayland, First Baptist pastor, presented second class awards, which was followed by presentation of first class awards by Rev. William P. Combs, summer educational director at the First Methodist church. T. E. Story, member of the court of honor, presented merit badges.

**Ivey Moore (c) and his sons, Jim (l) and Dudley (r) all earned their Eagle Scout Awards together in 1948.**

courtesy of *Wilkes Journal-Patriot*

After the war, Ivey Moore returned to Wilkes County. He got involved as a Boy Scout leader; and, in 1948 made a little history. That year two of his sons (James and Dudley) and he all received their Eagle Scout Awards at the same ceremony. The threesome was a first in the history of the local Boy Scouts, and it would never be repeated, as the awards were later made unavailable to adults. For his later service to the Boy Scouts of America, he received its council-level service award, the Silver Beaver.

Ivey Moore's father got involved in the furniture business in Wilkes County a few years after he moved his sawmill business from Globe. In Ivey's recollections from the 1974 interview, he shared something about North Wilkesboro in the early 20th century:

"After my father [James Dudley Moore] got here [Wilkes County] and was here for some time, in 1909 he bought out the C.W. Meadows Mill Company which is located at Pore's Knob. To give you a little idea of [local] conditions at that time, there were no electric lights. There were no paved roads. There were no paved streets in the town of North Wilkesboro at the time. The fact of the matter is they didn't have sidewalks or anything. I recall the time they had sawed-off telephone poles set [in the ground] to go across the square of North Wilkesboro to step on. If you stepped off them, you went up to your knees in mud.

"Now this is kind of a bad thing, but as I recall, all the fellows would stand around there at the drugstore to watch the ladies come across walking on those poles, I guess in hopes that one of them would fall and it would stir their skirts up enough that you could see their ankles. [Laughter] Back then about the only other entertainment you had was to go down and watch the train come in twice a day. There was a hack that would go down to the station to meet the train and bring the drummers [salesmen] up to the hotel. I remember standing there one day and watching a wagon loaded with lumber mired down to the hub right there in front of the Bluemont Hotel.

"I had seen a time back in 1917 when the Yadkin River froze over and a two-horse wagon with a load of lumber and a driver going from North Wilkesboro to Wilkesboro went across the ford down there and didn't break through the ice. Now that was a pretty cold winter. I recall about October, November it started snowing and snow was on the ground well into April, almost to the first of May. We had continuous snow that winter. That was when they had so much flu and everything [Worldwide flu pandemic of 1918].

"We enjoyed ourselves until the war. And then the flu epidemic came along. Then everything was closed. No church. You could go to the store to buy your groceries, but you had to stand out in the open. We had gauze masks that we wore. You bought your groceries and then went directly back home. No loitering around, or anything, no visitation. A lot of industries came to a complete standstill when the flu epidemic hit. Many people died in those days. Too many that I knew."

**Floods**

The flu epidemic was not the only tragedy which befell Wilkes County in that decade. In the summer of 1916, when Ivey Moore was only 13, torrential rains in the upper Yadkin River valley caused severe flooding, destroying crops, livestock, warehouses, railroad tracks and claiming numerous lives. As the waters reached Wilkesboro and North Wilkesboro, even more damage was done to businesses in and near the floodplain. The crops were lost and people were deeply concerned about getting another crop planted in time to grow adequate food for people and their livestock to get through the winter.

Again in 1940, heavy rains in the Blue Ridge Mountains sent floodwaters sweeping down the Yadkin River. The August 15, 1940, *Journal-Patriot* called it "the most disastrous flood on the Yadkin in the history of Wilkes County," then added:

> "The raging torrent of the muddy Yadkin rose to unprecedented heights three to five feet higher than the high mark of the disastrous flood of July 15, 1916. Fire, adding to the

> destruction of the flood waters, wiped out Home Chair Company and the International Shoe Company tannery, two of the largest industrial plants here."[3]

Lives and livelihoods were taken away. In the two Wilkesboros, 150 homes were destroyed and eight people were killed. "The 13-room home of Lewis Triplett on Stony Fork Creek floated down the swollen stream," the newspaper reported. "Every bridge in that part of the county was either washed away or damaged to such an extent that travel was impossible. … Forester's Nu-Way Service station was completely devastated along with huge stock of gasoline and oils. Only a few animals of the zoo were saved."[4] (Forester's Nu-Way had a collection of exotic animals behind his service station. When the flood hit, some parents in the community were terrified that some of the large cats were roaming the streets. The parents made their children stay inside.)[5]

The damage sparked talk of building a flood-control dam on the Upper Yadkin River. The project was eventually secured with federal funding of a few million dollars and bonds issued by Wilkes County and by the City of Winston-Salem. Construction of the Corps of Engineers project began in September 1960 to create the Wilkesboro

**W. Kerr Scott Reservoir was completed in fall 1962 to help control flooding on the Upper Yadkin River..**

from 1964 Daniel Boone Wagon Train souvenir book

Reservoir. It was dedicated on September 16, 1962, and renamed the W. Kerr Scott Reservoir. The dedication ceremony had to be held inside the Wilkes Central High School because of rain. The dam and reservoir were completed less than a year before the Daniel Boone Wagon Train first began.

**Home Chair Company**

Ivey Moore continued his recollections of his life and times in Wilkes County:

> "As I said, my dad went into the mill business. He [James Dudley Moore] manufactured some goods for International Harvester out of the old C.W. Meadows Mill. He bought that from Mr. Meadows who was a Baptist minister out there at Pore's Knob. He did so until 1923, when he bought what was the Shell Chair Company and it became under his leadership the Home Chair Company. He operated there until the 1940 flood. We then moved to Ronda and bought out the old cotton mill down there and rebuilt it. We had 26 acres of land and 23 rental houses. It was a pretty good building that could be converted without too much expense into a furniture factory. We manufactured chairs there until 1967 or '68. Then we sold out to United Furniture Company that later merged with Burlington Industries.

"Home Chair Company was located down next to the tannery

**Employees and owners of Home Chair Company in 1939. James Dudley Moore is at right. Ivey Moore is next to him.**

courtesy of Dudley Moore

**The Home Chair Company in North Wilkesboro in flames during the August 1940 flood.**
courtesy of *Winston-Salem Journal*

[on Maple Street at Cherry Street]. There were two plants there, two two-story buildings. One was upholstery and finishing. The other was manufacturing. They had steam power and electrical power. Actually during the flood, it was a transformer on the far side of the building away from the river that caused the problem. There was a drift of four or five houses that come in there and pushed the transformer over against the plant. The transformer started burning and consequently the plant burned down."[6]

## Jesse Moore's Flintlock

Ivey Moore loved family history and shared some interesting stories about his own ancestors who came to the Wilkes County region before the Revolutionary War, in the times of Daniel Boone:

"We knew we weren't going to move out of Wilkes County. ... My dad lived and died here, from 1906 to 1943. This has been home to us although we have a soft spot in our hearts for Caldwell County due to the fact that my third-great grand-

### Rebuilding Home Chair Company

"After the fire was over we saved some of our supplies," Ivey Moore recalled. "It was a funny thing, that no matter how swift the water was, all the barrels of finishing materials and shellac we had out there, all rolled around in the river until they come to a little small branch and then they dropped down and the water then flowed over them. We got mules and dragged the barrels out, put them on the truck and took them back. They weren't damaged in any way. But we found out that some of the people, back when bootlegging and liquor-making was so prevalent around here, had found out those barrels were down there. They'd go down and pour out the varnish and shellac and everything, take the barrels and make a still out of them. So we found out that we had to work pretty quick to beat the bootleggers to the barrels. [Laughter.]

"The 1916 flood had washed the tannery away as well as damaged my father's plant. I think the damage was about $90,000 and back then that was a lot of money. No insurance at all. And in the 1940 flood, he had a $256,000 loss. We salvaged and recovered a lot of the materials; and, as the plant burned down, the water kept the heat from damaging all the machinery. Consequently, when [the 1940 flood] was all over with and all the machinery was thrown in there together, it looked like a total loss. But dad got the machinery out, put the calipers on it and put the levelers on it. Only one machine was seriously damaged, so he had them all reworked and in six months' time they were back in operation [at Ronda] after the plant burned down."[7]

father [Jesse Moore] settled up there in the year 1762 in a town known as the Globe. Ol' Jesse was about 30 years old and he had five children when he came here. He brought an old rifle with him to North Carolina. That rifle has been handed down through the family for years and years and years and it finally got around to me. That's the rifle that I carried on the Wagon Train. It's a flintlock, one of the earlier flintlocks, one of the first. It was a Gordon. It had a short barrel. The old Kentucky rifle had a long barrel, a tremendously long barrel.

"That Gordon [gun] came down to me when my father died. It was Jesse Moore's gun. It was not a rifle. Incidentally, Jesse's son, Daniel, used that gun in the Revolutionary War at the battles of Cowpens and Guilford Courthouse. ... The remarkable thing is they came from Amherst

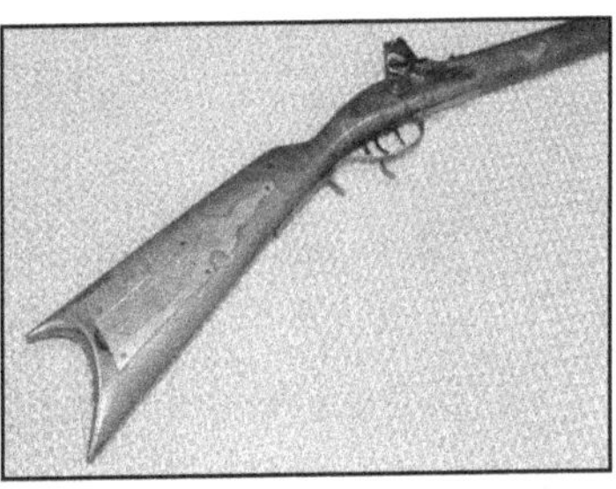

**Dudley Moore holds the family flintlock during a 2011 interview. A painting titled "The Ivey Moore Rifle" by artist Ward Nichols hangs on the wall. At right, the patchbox on the stock is engraved with dates and battles giving a history of "The Jesse Moore Rifle."**

County, Virginia. Both of them went back to Amherst County and married sisters. That was in 1786 and 1788. You can imagine going all the way to Amherst County, Virginia, and then coming back. That made for a long honeymoon.

"They didn't worry too much about going great distances. My third-great grandfather, Jesse, heard that they had some new, steel plows over at Salisbury. It was the spring of the year and he was anxious to get one. He had five slaves he had brought from Virginia and they were good to plowin' up there, so Jesse just lit out and walked all the way to Salisbury, bought himself a plow, put it on his shoulder, and carried it all the way back to the Globe. I guess that was 80 to a hundred miles the way he had to come."[8]

**Daniel Boone**

Ivey Moore had personal historical reasons for wanting to be involved in the Daniel Boone Wagon Train and as chief scout he had a bird's-eye view to see it work well and otherwise. He explained:

"There is no direct line from me to Daniel Boone, but through marriage there is, through Daniel Moore. He had a daughter named Elizabeth, who married Israel Boone who was the son of Jesse Boone who was the son of the original Israel Boone, a brother to Daniel Boone. And so, by marriage, that makes me the fourth great nephew of Daniel Boone. That's probably why I was elected to be "Daniel Boone" on the Daniel Boone Wagon Train.

"Now when we started the Daniel Boone Wagon Train, Clyde Green and I got together on the thing and we decided we would do this in authentic dress and style. Had we gone ahead and stuck to the original plan and carried this thing out to its completion, and had we been careful about screening our people, we would have been better off and we would have had something from a historical standpoint that would have been a great attraction to people across the United States. People would have come here to see this wagon train. But it didn't work out that way at all. So it's unfortunate that it doesn't have the popularity that it had back when we first started it. We had hopes that we could keep it that way, but it seems that when those cowboys came in, they took over. The first thing we knew there were 45s and hip-hip-hoorahs, and cowboy hats and things like that. And that was about the end of it.

"Another thing, we had to have such rules as 'no whiskey,' of course, and that was infringed on considerably. And another thing was 'no profanity.' Well, we had an old fellow with us on the train down there and he was awful bad to cuss. He was quite a character, too. Well, he was out there trying to get his mules working and he wasn't speakin' no Sunday School words. He was trying to get those mules to do what he wanted them to do. Well, I went up to him and I said, 'Now look

**Ivey Moore thought that too much "cowboy" influence contributed to the problems and demise of the Daniel Boone Wagon Train.**

from microfilm, courtesy of *Watauga Democrat*

here, hoss. We got a lot of people on this train, a lot of girls and scouts and young boys. And you signed that agreement not to use any profanity on the train. And I've told you once before and I'm havin' to tell you again. You're going to have to stop.' Well, he spit his juice out to the side and said to me, 'How the hell do you expect my mules to understand a word I'm sayin' if I don't cuss at 'em?' [Laughter]"[9]

**Nagagamasis Lake**

Moore loved nature, he declared, and he made some special opportunities to enjoy it in one particular, out-of-the-way place. Dudley Moore recalled his father's favorite fishing spot in Canada:

> "Ivey enjoyed the wilderness," Dudley Moore declared. "We opened the trout season in Virginia many years. We'd go to Virginia and camp out in Taylor's Valley and we'd open the trout season every year when I was around. I took my son there several years and then the daughters wanted to go. So we went out there. My wife slept in a tent. They hated it and we never went back. [Laughter]
>
> "In his later years, my dad spent every summer—six weeks to two months—(up to a few years before he died) in a place called Nagagamasis Lake [in Nagagamasis Provincial Park, Ontario, Canada]. He and a friend of his, Doctor T.L. White, he was the dentist in North Wilkesboro, would get in my dad's car—a van of sorts— and put a canoe on it and drive to Nagagamasis Lake. [The lake is about 120 miles northeast of Lake Superior.] They would spend a good part of the summer camped on the side of that lake until they returned to North Carolina, living off the fish they caught. I drove there one time. I took my son and my sister's son to Nagagamisis. We

**Ivey Moore loved to fish in Canada each summer, especially at Nagagamasis Lake in Ontario.**
courtesy of Chris Crooks

went up there and lived in a tent for a week or so and I would imagine that would have been in the late 1960s."[10]

### Daniel Boone Trail

Ivey Moore was one of the folks who most adamantly championed the creation of a heritage trail in honor of Daniel Boone. He and Thomas Ferguson were stalwart champions of the effort for years. In 1975, on the 200th anniversary of Daniel Boone's marking of Boone's Trace through the Cumberland Gap and on to establish Fort Boonesborough, Ivey Moore and seven other men walked the 368-mile route from Wilkes County, North Carolina, to Fort Boonesborough, Kentucky. They participated in bicentennial celebrations at several towns along the way. They completed the walk between April 10 and May 10.[11] They took with them a stone from the fireplace of the Boone cabin on Beaver Creek near Ferguson. They also carried some walnuts dropped from Wilkes County trees to be planted at Fort Boonesborough; the new trees would be so marked. Moore later referred to this undertaking in support of having a national Daniel Boone Heritage Trail marked. He spoke before a Congressional subcommittee, dressed in his buckskins and he carried his Jesse Moore heirloom flintlock into the hearing—a courtesy extended to few people.[12]

### Civic Servant and Showman

Ivey Moore had a longtime interest in history. He had a hand in organizing the Wilkes Historical Society and served as the first president of the Wilkes Genealogical Society. The Bicentennial celebration in Wilkes County was dedicated to him as "a goodwill ambassador and a one-man crew in promoting Wilkes County." He was also responsible of organizing Little League Baseball in Wilkes County and served as the first president.

Ivey Moore was a bit of a showman and something of a publicity hound. "My dad was an amateur magician," recalled his son Dudley. Ivey Moore apparently put his showmanship to good use performing magic on the steps of various schools to help raise money for those schools' libraries.[13] He also helped raise money for lighting Memorial Park.

His services as "Daniel Boone" were called upon often. He appeared at the Dixie Classic Fair in Winston-Salem to promote the Northwest Development Association, and he was part of the honor guard for Gov. Dan Moore on a promotional tour of Florida for the Travel Council of North Carolina. Another time, he appeared on behalf of the Travel Council for a week at the Canadian International Exposition in Toronto; and, the Daniel Boone Wagon Train got some national publicity when Chief Scout Ivey Moore appeared on television in 1964 as a contestant on the

**Ivey Moore volunteered at travel shows to promote North Carolina.**
from newsprint, courtesy of *Wilkes Journal-Patriot*

CBS panel show, *To Tell the Truth.* [14]

"Ivey loved to have his picture made," said his son Dudley. His picture appeared in the history textbooks used in North Carolina public schools for elementary grades. In 1969, he was involved with creation of a picture book, *Sense of Discovery, the Mountain,* by Nancy Roberts with photos by Bruce Roberts. He portrayed a "stranger in buckskins" who acquainted a little girl with nature to be found on one mountain. Many folks agreed that if a camera was around, Ivey Moore was looking for a way to be in front of it.[15]

"Ivey lived as full a life as anyone I have ever known," wrote Dudley Moore to columnist Jerry Bledsoe of the *Greensboro Daily News* in January 1984 a few days after his father's passing on the 18th. "The man left a mark and gained a bit of immortality. Somehow that makes losing him a little easier to bear."

Wilkes County's Ivey Moore was indeed quite a character.

**Chief Scout Ivey Moore**
photo by Jim Keith, courtesy of *Winston-Salem Journal*

# Daniel Boone Wagon Train, 1965

We all like to repeat our successes when we can, so staging another Daniel Boone Wagon Train, the third, seemed a natural. It was championed by all the community leaders, of course, and the prospect of an economic development opportunity made it more interesting. In June 1965, the editor of the *Journal-Patriot*, Dwight Nichols, laid out the possibilities for a "vacation-type wagon train" experience that could wind its way through the back roads of Wilkes and Watauga counties offering paying customers the opportunity to do something "pioneer style." The tourist and recreation industry seemed ripe for it and the Blue Ridge Mountains offered all the attractions that would reward those who wanted "to get away from it all." "Nature has endowed this area with wonderful resources," he wrote. "It is up to the people now to put them to good and profitable use."[1]

Some honest interest had been expressed by the public in such a "vacation wagon train," but it was prompted by an inadvertent mistake in the national press. The April 3 issue of *This Week Magazine*, distributed nationally, had mentioned the Daniel Boone Wagon Train in its article about "Off-Beat Vacations." Fifteen-hundred people wrote to Ivey Moore wanting to sign up to ride on the Wagon Train. A committee considered the matter and decided against commercializing the Daniel Boone Wagon Train. But private interests picked up the oppor-

**A "vacation wagon train" seemed attactive to some.**
from newsprint, courtesy of *Winston-Salem Journal*

tunity and the first vacation wagon train took place in July, after the third and official Daniel Boone Wagon Train was completed.[2]

## Creaking and Rumbling

The '65 Daniel Boone Wagon Train (not the commercial venture) began, as it did in '64, with a gathering of wagons at Memorial Park in North Wilkesboro, a parade through town, and a departure on Tuesday morning for the first night's camp at Ferguson. The Stone Mountain Boys provided the music for what was called a "hoedown" at Midtown Plaza on Monday evening. Some rainy weather had kept the early registration down to about 40 wagons, but Ivey Moore was confident they would have a full complement of 80 when they departed. A new addition to the wagon train for '65 included an "authentic" Indian village, which would travel with the wagon train and be set up at each campsite. It was organized by the Wahissa Lodge, Order of the Arrow, Old Hickory Council, Boy Scouts of America.[3] Some of the scouts were from West Wilkes High School. The scouts performed authentic Indian dances at the campgrounds at Memorial Park before the wagon train's departure. [4]

"The Daniel Boone Wagon Train creaked and rumbled its way through the Wilkesboros Tuesday morning on the annual trek to Boone," the *Journal-Patriot* reported. "Some folks didn't get to see the train parade. Chief Scout Ivey Moore had billed the train to leave at 9 a.m., but Wagon Master Dewitt Barnett had other ideas. He ordered the train out at 8:30 a.m. from Memorial Park while prospective parade viewers were making their way to the downtown North Wilkesboro streets."[5]

The *Journal-Patriot* continued, "Before leaving, train riders had spent three smelly, sweaty days encamped at Memorial Park in an atmosphere that resembled a carnival, horse show, and circus combined. While 'injuns' whooped it up inside the ball park, Optimists hawked concession goodies; ladies in calico and gingham and gents in buckskins and beards paraded by to the tune of braying jackasses and neighboring horses. The smell of frying hamburgers mixed with the more pungent odor of horses, sweat and campfire smoke."[6]

Whether the *Winston-Salem Journal* viewed covering the Daniel Boone Wagon Train as "boot camp" for new reporters or as punishment of some sort is unclear; but for the third Wagon Train, the *Journal* assigned yet a third different reporter. His challenge was to find a new way to make exciting the coverage of an event that was trying every way it knew how to be exactly what it had been the year before. But Joe Goodman was up to the challenge.[7] He tried writing really good copy:

> "Ferguson—The Daniel Boone Wagon Train never really sleeps. Some of the old folks might bed down early, but everything else seems to have wound itself up during the day and is just getting started good after nightfall. Somewhere

down the line of wagons, somebody's piping away on a harmonica. An old timer is chuckling at one of his own jokes. The gigantic oxen, their forelegs tucked under their bodies, have bedded down and are munching their cud. Occasionally they rumble a long 'moo,' seemingly in answer to the horses' whinnies.

"The whole picture is an anachronism, not belonging to this century of satellites. But a wagon train doesn't stay asleep long. It's hard to tell which comes first, the light gray predawn, the bedlam of awakening birds or the giggles of the girls who seem never to sleep. But by 4:30 a.m. the camp is in an uproar again just as it was at midnight. Even to the most dedicated sleeper, the uproar can't be denied or ignored.

"Trace chains are jingling as enormous draft horses are led—clop, clop—to the creek for their morning water ration. Coffee pot lids are clanking open, then closed. So, apparently doomed to the fate of never getting intimately acquainted with your sleeping bag, you haul out of bed lest you miss something."[8]

**Red, White, and Blue Tahitian Design**

On Tuesday, June 29, 1965, the Daniel Boone Wagon Train began with a parade through North Wilkesboro with the Order of the Arrow Boy Scouts portraying "Indians" in whatever fashion they deemed appropriate. The influences of television and movies were evident. Their portrayals were decidedly from the latter 19$^{th}$ century and from the Plains—complete with tipi (tepee), not the 18$^{th}$ century Cherokees and Shawnees (Shawanoes) whom Daniel Boone encountered. Still, the young men were sincere and earnest in their efforts.[9]

Goodman also chose to write about some of his fellow travelers to pique reader interest. People had come from as far away as Myrtle Beach and Cincinnati and others from as close by as Thurmond and Deep Gap. Everybody had a special reason for being there. Goodman tried to share the better stories. There was a man who sent his wife packing for home because she'd tried to serve him canned biscuits and instant coffee. (One suspects she was glad to go.) Another was Ruth Stanley, a great-great-grand niece of Daniel Boone and the state's only female licensed prospector, carrying a loaded Derringer pistol and leading a jackass named Abraham. But if those weren't interesting enough, Goodman knew for sure what would sell more papers. This was America in transition from the sexploitation of Marilyn Monroe to the future consideration of the Equal Rights Amendment, and Goodman knew what his editors wanted. So he went for it. At great length in one account, he anticipated the opportunity for all to witness "Miss Sandra Laughlin, an airline stewardess from Cleveland, Ohio" and a charm-school graduate taking a dip in a cool mountain creek in her "bikini with a small red, white, and blue Tahitian design." If the prospect of that photograph did not keep the newspapers rolling off the presses, then maybe mid-1960s American males were not as red-blooded as everyone had thought.

**Willard Watson talks with licensed prospector Ruth Stanley and burro, Abraham.**
from newsprint, courtesy of *Wilkes Journal-Patriot*

The wagon train experience had taken on a life of its own. It had become somewhat less about Daniel Boone and his times and something more about the people who were making the effort to have a special experience.[10] But it was not a unique experience. On July 1, "the nation's oldest annual wagon train" got underway near Andrew, North Carolina. Continuing a trek begun in 1957, wagon trainers crossed through the mountains from Tennessee to North Carolina to call attention to the need to build better roads through the Forest Service lands.[11]

About 60 wagons rolled out of North Wilkesboro when the Daniel Boone Wagon Train finally started. They were joined by "countless" horseback riders and, with special note, a 15-year-old young lady bringing up the rear and leading a goat.[12]

The days were long and hot, as they had been the two years before. The camp at Ferguson had been moved from the Tom Ferguson farm to the school grounds in 1965.[13] The camp, regardless of its location, was a welcomed respite from the first day's excursion. "Happiness is planting your scorched carcass in a cool mountain stream after a day

**As in the past, the first day out was long and hot.**
from 1964 DBWT Souvenir Booklet

on a wagon train," wrote Goodman. "It's walking, jolting in a wagon or chafing in the saddle all day, then seeing that mountain water ripple in front of you. Even the horses feel it. Their ears perk up and their straggling pace becomes a prance as they sense the nearness of water."[14]

The people varied in their responses, some splashing their faces or wading in up to their ankles. Others were a bit more energetic. The prospector lady "dashed fully clothed, snake-proof boots and all, into the Yadkin River, then splashed, stroked, and then finally floated, vowing she wouldn't stop until she reached Elkin."[15]

**Two Acres of People**

The second day began earlier than some had hoped with the too-soon crowing of roosters at 4:15 a.m. Richard Horn of Winston-Salem had brought them along as his alarm clock. A brief rain shower early in the day cooled things off a bit and kept the dust down. Still, by the time the wagon trainers reached Darby, they were ready again for a dip in the creek. This time, the male wagon trainers and Goodman's teased readers were treated at the swimming hole on Elk Creek in Darby to the appearance of Miss Laughlin in her "red, white, and blue Tahitian print bikini."[16] The readers were also titillated by Goodman's recounting his horse-riding experience and the detailing of his saddle sores. "The first couple of miles weren't bad. Then a crease in the seat of the pants became noticeable … . A fold of cloth in an undergarment fixed and made permanent by a

**The "red, white, and blue Taitian print bikini" at Dugger Creek.**
photo by Joe Goodman, courtesy of *Winston-Salem Journal*

pair of tight blue jeans. Try everything—stand up in the stirrups, shift from one side of the posterior to the other, but the crease could not be avoided. Nor could the blister."[17]

Despite the soreness of seats and feet, the campsites at Ferguson, Darby, and Triplett were filled with people entertaining themselves with a frolic. That would have been the proper term from the 18th century, but the Daniel Boone Wagon Train had lost its way in history. The reporter called it a "hoedown" and it was a big one each night. Added to the few hundred folks on the wagon train, another 3,000 to 4,000 folks (three times that number by one estimate) came to visit the camps at Ferguson and Darby.[18] "They were best measured in acres," Goodman wrote. "A surveyor might gauge it at two acres of people, elbow to elbow, back to belly button, either looking or bobbing up and down to the music." He added, "The string music is broadcast across the pasture with newfangled amplifiers. And there is a little of the Charleston and twist in the dance steps. But all the frontier essentials are there—the feet slapping on the hard dirt, the 'hoo-hah's' shouted with the head held back, the loose bib overall strap flapping behind the dancer."[19] The ladies in Darby declared they served 1,200 barbecued chicken dinners and sold "hundreds and hundreds of hotdogs." They ran out of food at 11:00 p.m.[20]

**Misty Gray Peaks**

Press coverage of the trip continued to offer vignettes from the lives of the wagon trainers. Chief Scout Ivy Moore had a chipped tooth, but no doctor or dentist was on the trip, not even a veterinarian. So, Moore did what his ancestor would have done, sort of. He handled it himself. He filed down his own tooth, but with the aid of a modern fingernail file. Another couple piqued Goodman's curiosity. Spencer and Doris Miller were back on the trek again this year, but with 20

**Spencer and Doris Miller, parents of 20 children, yoked their oxen for another day's journey.**

photo by Frank Jones for *Winston-Salem Journal*, courtesy of Forsyth County Public Library Photograph Collection, Winston-Salem, NC

children this time. "What's it like to rear 20 kids?" Goodman asked. Mrs. Miller's considered response revealed a good bit. "Not much different from raising 10," she said.[21]

"Not much different" might have referred to rearing her children, but not to the miles covered by the wagon train. The miles on the route from Darby to Triplett were known to be the most grueling, a big challenge to the livestock as they climbed up Jake's Mountain. But the trip was not without its aesthetic rewards to those who would make the trip. "As usual the wagons moved out at 8:30 a.m. led by the horsemen," Goodman wrote. "In one place the road was littered with cherries from the trees that arched overhead. And the dense forest canopy allowed only splotches of sunlight to filter through to speckle the wagon tops."[22]

But this year another obstacle presented itself—photographers. Along the most scenic stretch of the wagon train, photographers descended on the wagon train imploring Wagon Master Barnett to halt the climb for photographs. As the animals rested in the shade, the photographers dragged some of the more interesting-looking people off to the side for pictures. Ivey Moore was a popular subject, dressed in his coonskin cap and buckskins, and swinging around his tomahawk.[23] Barnett would have been a good one to photograph as well. On this day, he had the look of man who had faced danger and got away with

**The wagon train climbed slowly toward Jake's Mountain and the "misty gray peaks."**
from 1964 DBWT Souvenir Booklet

it. The night before, at Triplett, they discovered "a big copperhead" behind Barnett's tent. That report coupled with lesser sightings along the way probably prompted a more thorough checking of bed rolls across the camp that night than had ever been undertaken before.[24]

Most of the people walked up Jake's Mountain to Cooks Gap just to spare the animals the task of pulling the extra weight. "Suddenly, as you labored up hill," Goodman wrote, "you realized that the sweat on your back had turned ice cold. You looked back, saw the misty gray peaks to your right and knew you were near the summit of Jake's Mountain—Cook's Gap. Once over the top, the wagoners had to ride the brakes, pressing blocks of wood against the steel tires that encircled their wagon wheels."[25]

As the wagoners approached the camp at Perkinsville, they forded the New River. This was a spot that attracted photographers wanting to capture a classic pioneer scene; and, Herman Wilcox reported that *Life Magazine* was planning to do a story on the Wagon Train, too.[26] He had words of praise as well for all the regional media as well as *Look Magazine* and United Press, all of whom were covering the Wagon Train that year. Wilcox was especially pleased that an audio tape of sounds along the train as well as documentation of the Wagon Train's origins was being prepared by WATA Radio Station for broadcast by *Voice of America* through the United States Information Agency. "The production will include interviews to record the background of the formation of this event, the assembling of the 'Train' at North Wilkesboro, the actual start of the train, the click of the wheels, the beat of the hoofs, the command of the Wagon Master, the supervision of the Chief Scout, the bawl of the oxen, the bray of the mule, the camp ground activities, etc." Wilcox declared this would give our area "World Wide recognition."[27]

The camp at Perkinsville was on 15 acres made available by Clyde R. Greene, President, Daniel Boone Wagon Train, Inc. The wagons circled up and a campfire was lit in the center for a pow-wow. The Boone Worthwhile Woman's Club served food and drink to the wagon trainers and visitors, while 30 to 40 "Indians" entertained the crowd with their dancing.[28]

**Order of the Arrow dancers performed for the crowds.**

from newsprint, courtesy of *Wilkes Journal-Patriot*

That night many of the wagoners went to see *Horn in the West.* There they and the audience enjoyed more dancing of the costumed dancers from the Wahissa Lodge of the Order of the Arrow. They performed a snake dance as part of their repertoire, holding a near 7-foot-long black snake in their mouths. When the wagoners returned to camp, they found underway a frolic and square dance which had been going on for some time, joined as it was by the sizeable number of visitors who came out to see the wagoners' camp on this Fourth of July weekend. But some of those who had made the trek had already loaded up and left Boone, even before the parade on Saturday. They might have been glad they did. Some of the visitors at the camp got good and rowdy. There were drunks, deputy sheriffs, bloody noses, domestic squabbles, and noise well after most of the other wagoners had turned in for the night.[29]

The Wagon Train processed through the streets of Boone, just as it had before with a thick host of spectators lining the streets. The parade began at 1:00 p.m. with Spencer Miller and his family filling the lead wagon.[30]

### Vacation Wagon Train

After the Daniel Boone Wagon Train, Inc. declined to operate a "vacation wagon train" for paying customers, the opportunity lay open to others. James H. Richardson and Claude B. Minton decided to give it a try as a private venture. Together they owned 12 wagons. "From the

**Arnold Cooper's "mule-powered" wagon rolled through the streets of Boone.**

from microfilm, courtesy of *Watauga Democrat*

response we've had so far," Richardson had said at the camp in Perkinsville, "I have no doubt that it will be a success." The 30-mile vacation wagon train included a visit to the grave of Tom Dula (of recent fame from the 1958 Kingston Trio song, "Hang Down Your Head Tom Dooley") and plenty of time for swimming in the creek at Darby. It started in Ferguson and ended in Triplett on a return trip after a visit up to Cook's Gap. Vacationers would bring their own camping gear, including tents, and their own food. Stringed instruments were welcomed and square dancing would be held. The two entrepreneurs planned weekly departures from mid-July through mid-September. The first of the vacation wagon trains departed Ferguson on July 14.[31]

And the world turned:

On July 14, United Nations Ambassador Adlai Stevenson, a three-time presidential hopeful, died in London at age 65. On the same day, *Mariner 4*, which had been launched in late November1964, passed by Mars and sent back the first close-up pictures of the Red Planet.

President Johnson announced plans to double the draft quota and to build troop strength in Vietnam to 125,000. Two days later, he signed the Social Security Act of 1965, establishing Medicare and Medicaid. A week later, the President signed the Voting Rights Act outlawing literacy tests and the like used in the South to disenfranchise black voters.

In mid-August, race riots, sparked by residents opposing police action during an arrest, broke out in the Watts neighborhood of Los Angeles, California, killing 34 people.

Looting and fires did $40 million in damage over six days.

On August 15, a near-riotous crowd at Shea Stadium in New York City deliriously greeted The Beatles in the first performance of their second US tour. Record attendance and record receipts encouraged the era of large venue concerts. *Gemini 5* was a test of astronauts Gordon Cooper and Pete Conrad to endure space travel for one week. On September 9, the city of New Orleans was tested by Hurricane Betsy, causing 76 deaths and the first to rack up $1 billion in damages.

In mid-September, most of New York City's major newspapers went out on a three-week strike. in January, bus and subway transit in New York City would be paralyzed for nearly two weeks by a strike.

In October, Pope John Paul VI visited New York, speaking to the United Nations. In November, the U.S. began flying refugees from Cuba after Fidel Castro had said any who wanted to leave Cuba could do so. On November 9, the Northeast Blackout of 1965 struck, leaving several northeast states without power for more than 12 hours. Two pacifists emolated themselves at The Pentagon and at the United Nations to protest the Vietnam War. Tens of thousands of protesters picketed the White House.

In December, *Gemini 6* and *Gemini 7* performed a controlled rendezvous in Earth orbit to within one foot, but did not dock. Astronauts were Walter Schirra, Jr., Thomas Stafford, Frank Borman II, and James Lovell, Jr.

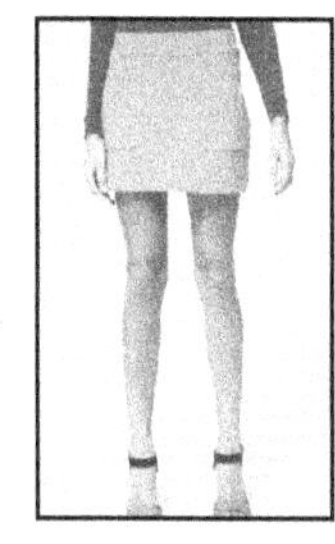

The miniskirt arrived in America in 1965, with its hemline several inches above the knees.

In January 1966, President Johnson appointed the first African-American cabinet member, Robert Weaver, Secretary of Housing and Urban Development. Another 8,000 U.S. troops landed in Vietnam, making a total of 190,000.

On March 4, Beatle John Lennon spared controversy by commenting in an interview, "We're more popular than Jesus now."

In early March at UNC-Chapel Hill, the Speaker Ban law of 1963 was tested when activist students invited banned speakers Frank Wilkinson and Herbert Aptheker to address students on campus. After being denied use of a building, the students gathered on the old quad at the "Governor Dan Moore" wall separating the campus from town property and listened to the speakers who stood on the public sidewalk along Franklin Street.[32]

In March, *Gemini 8*, with astronauts Neil Armstrong and David Scott, docked in space with a target vehicle, becoming the first to do so; however, in the process they experienced a life-threatening, in-flight emergency which caused them to abort the mission. On June 2, unmanned *Surveyor 1* made a soft landing on the moon three months after the Soviets accomplished the same. The "Space Race" continued.

Protests against the Vietnam War broke out across the country, in San Francisco, Chicago, Boston, Philadelphia, and Washington, D.C. Troop strength reached 250,000 that spring.

In June, the Supreme Court ruled in *Miranda v. Arizona*, leading to the police practice of "reading their rights" to suspects under arrest. At month's end, the U.S. began bombing Hanoi and Haiphong in North Vietnam; and, the National Organization of Women was founded in Washington, D.C.

Meanwhile:
More color programming replaced black & white television shows and audiences welcomed *Lost in Space, I Dream of Jeannie*, and *Get Smart* among their favorite shows. *Doctor Zchivago, Thunderball*, the fourth James Bond movie, and *Alfie*, with Michael Kane, entertained theater audiences. On the radio, America met Sonny and Cher with "I've Got You Babe," was enthralled by the Beatles singing "Yesterday," and stood tall whenever they heard Staff Sergeant Barry Sadler sing "Ballad of the Green Beret." "Is It Really Over?" was a posthumous country hit for Jim Reeves.

For more about television, movies, and music of the following 12 months, see Appendix, Popular Culture: July 1965-June 1966.

# Daniel Boone Wagon Train, 1966

The fourth annual Daniel Boone Wagon Train was eagerly anticipated. In May, Chief Scout Ivey Moore spoke to the Chamber of Commerce in Boone, updating them on the plans and the interest expressed by new participants. "There is tremendous outside demand from the United States and foreign countries," he said. "Some wagoners have agreed to take passengers and a party of 40 or 50 is coming from Ohio." He shared that 83 wagons had already signed up and he was hoping participation would reach 1,000.[1]

**Television Father**

The event itself was preceded by another announcement, as well, on June 2, that actor Fess Parker, who then played "Daniel Boone" on the 20th Century Fox television program, *The Adventures of Daniel Boone*, would be coming to Boone, North Carolina, that August to appear at performances of *Horn in the West.* On May 26, Parker had been recognized as Television Father of the Year by the National Father's Day Committee. He attributed the recognition to both his real family (he had two sons) and his television family. The television family, however, was an appalling fiction, leaving out more of Boone's children than it included and switching around birth orders to create appealing stereotypes for a modern American audience. Still, in 1966, people in Watauga County were excited to have this television and motion picture star coming to town, in what Parker acknowledged as "real Daniel Boone Country."[2]

### Get You a Wagon Train

As the time of the Wagon Train approached, its planners found themselves surrounded by a host of other competing activities. The Cove Creek Horse Show, the Rhododendron Festival, the season opening of Tweetsie Railroad, and the Grandfather Mountain Highland Games and Gathering of Scottish Clans all competed for the attention of visitors to the Boone-Blowing Rock-Linville triangle. But the Daniel Boone Wagon Train and the season opening of *Horn in the West* had their own special appeal and created their own excitement in the public. And the Daniel Boone Botanical Garden, dedicated in 1963, was just about to open to the public, with its Squire Boone Cabin, a gift from Miss Nancy Beyer of Blowing Rock.[3]

**Miss Nancy Beyer donated the "Squire Boone Cabin" to the Daniel Boone Botanical Garden in 1963.**
from microfilm, courtesy of *Watauga Democrat*

The Daniel Boone Wagon Train got under way in North Wilkesboro on June 27 as arriving participants prepared for the usual parade through the streets of the city and a party of square dancing and string music that night.

Ivey Moore, again serving as chief scout, said as the event began that he expected about 90 wagons and 800 people to participate. He counted 75 wagons and 500 people on the day before the march, as people continued to arrive.[4] One of the new arrivals was Farnum Gray, the latest reporter sent by the *Winston-Salem Journal* to be treated to the rigors of the Daniel Boone Wagon Train.

"Dan'l Boone thought he had problems," wrote Gray, "… but Boone's contemporary counterpart, Ivey Moore of North Wilkesboro, thinks his problems in re-enacting the trip are just as big. 'If you want something that'll run you absolutely nuts, get you a wagon train,' Moore said." While Gray was interviewing Moore, someone ran up to tell him that a horse had been spooked, had broken loose, and had kicked in the side and back of a late model Lincoln Continental. And that was just the beginning of the troubles that would follow.[5]

**Its Unsung Heroes**

"Thousands of spectators lined B Street in North Wilkesboro," the *Wilkes Journal-Patriot* reported. "Long before the train put in an appearance, people were lined three and four deep on each side of the street. Some sought roof tops for vantage points. Under a scorching sun the train moved into town just after 3:45 p.m., almost on schedule. In the

**The Daniel Boone Wagon Train and the Blue Ridge Wagon Train were popular attractions in North Wilkesboro during the 1960s.**

courtesy of *Wilkes Journal-Patriot*

train, led by Chief Scout Ivey Moore, were horse, mule, and oxen drawn wagons, hundreds of horseback riders on prime horse-flesh, ponies ridden by children, 'Indians' walking in the train and 'Indians' on horseback. It took about a half hour for the two-mile long train to pass."[6]

"Dan'l might have removed his buckskin shirt to ride a horse in such smothering heat," wrote Gray. "But Ivey had to make it a good show. He wore a coonskin cap, a gray beard, a buckskin suit, and moccasins with Indian-bead decorations, and carried a muzzle-loading rifle made in 1720." Gray also reported some participants in the wagon train that he recognized as not quite in line with the theme. One wagon was pulled by four tiny, matched ponies. Another rolled on pneumatic tires and was pulled by a tractor. One of the horsemen was dressed as a circuit-riding preacher complete with "black tails, string tie and top hat." Gray also put his finger on an issue that would begin to rankle the purists in the group by the end of this wagon train. "The parade included many horse fanciers," he wrote, "concerned not so much with re-enacting history as showing their well-groomed mounts."[7] And striking a humorous note, he added, "With its horses, ponies, mules, and oxen the parade left a massive chore for its unsung heroes—the North Wilkesboro street cleaners."[8]

"At Midtown Plaza and Memorial Park Monday night a horde of people descended to square dance and view the encamped train. It is estimated, that some 10,000 people were on hand, jamming the Plaza and creating a traffic jam of record proportions."[9] The Daniel Boone Wagon Train had become an event with its own reputation and expectations. People knew it was an occasion for a good parade, a little history, and some great parties.

A week before the celebration of Independence Day, Dwight Nichols, editor of the *Wilkes Journal-Patriot* shared with his readers a sense of the importance of the Daniel Boone Wagon Train to society at-large, reminding all his readers:

> "Americans have a great heritage. This country was hewn from the wilderness by brave and good, God-fearing men and women. … When the Daniel Boone Wagon Train rolls and the modern day people appear in pioneer dress, give a thought to the people who played the original roles as pioneers and who braved hazards and hardships to form the greatest nation in all the history of the world."[10]

Some of the rules Ivey Moore shared with the wagoners at their organizing meeting were the same as before: no intoxicating beverages allowed. Hoping to retire the grumbling of the horsemen who felt slowed by the pace of the wagons, Moore declared that the "riders who want to run their horses will be invited to go to the front of the line and ride hell-bent for Ferguson."[11] He would come to regret offering that flexibility.

The successful wagon train had attracted more participants for this year's experience, many coming from hundreds of miles away. "Typical of these are a group from Lima, Ohio, who have traveled 546 miles, bringing with them six horses, four trailers and five trucks," reported the *Journal-Patriot.* "Wagon train veterans, they rode in the Telico Plains-Andrews Wagon Train three years ago where they learned of the Daniel Boone Train." These folks were members of a riding group called the "Sheriff's Posse." Indeed, among all the participants, the horseback riders far outnumbered the wagoners.

The wagon train stretched out about two miles along NC Hwy 268

**The Sheriff's Posse, a riding club from Ohio and like many of the horseback riders, rode to show off their horses.**

from newsprint, courtesy of *Wilkes Journal-Patriot*

running from Wilkesboro to Ferguson. It was a hot day, but the wagoners persevered. They covered 16 miles in six hours.[12] Some of the horseback riders withered more quickly having started out as if they were riding in a horse show. But some of the spectators used the train to their advantage. One resident, L.C. Matherly, stood by with a wheelbarrow and shovel, ready to clean up after the horses, ponies, steers, and oxen. He planned to put the droppings on his garden.[13] In the early afternoon, the wagons began to arrive at the campsite, and Moore agreed with one of the folks who had been on the other trips that this one, so far, was the best yet. Others disagreed. Some wanted fewer rules and others wanted more. It seemed that *Winston-Salem Journal* reporter Farnum Gray had stumbled onto a fight.

**Old-Time Style**

Willard Watson, a cousin of some distance from musician Doc Watson, he said, was the spokesman for the traditionalists, as Gray captured it: "'This modern stuff has crept into the wagon train and we've got to get it out,' declared the 61-year-old man from Deep Gap. 'I'll fight it,' Watson emphasized, adding apparently from experience, 'and there ain't nothing alive I'm afraid of but a fightin' boar hog. Now, I'm afraid of that.'"[14]

"'It's just my nature to like the old-time style,' Watson said. 'I wouldn't give a nickel for an electric stove.'" He was particularly put off with the dancing that was allowed. "For a good dance, you need six couples; you do the grapevine swing and the four circle. The grand star is the hardest thing in it. There ain't none of these youngsters can do a grand star. They're good on the twist stuff, but that won't stand up. This hootenanny stuff has already gone out."[15] (*Hootenanny* was an ABC Television production featuring folk artists in live concerts recorded on college campuses. It aired from April 1963 to September 1964, when it was cancelled due to the sudden appearance and popularity of The Beatles and a major shift in American popular music.)[16]

Adding a plug for his cousin's type of music, Watson added, "The old-time strumming music with the guitar, fiddle, and banjo—ain't nothing that'll linger like that." He added that he thought all the women on the wagon train should have to wear the long dresses and bonnets. He was not in favor of the shorts and tight pants the women wore. It was too "citified," he said.[17]

Ivey Moore listened diplomatically to Watson and then laughed when he said with reference to Watson's own violation of his supposed code, "His idea of authenticity is that damned Mexican hat he wears." Then Moore added his own perspective, saying that some of the folks "go in too much for cowboy stuff." The horse riders dressed like cowboys, rode western saddles, and some even carried 45-calibre pistols strapped to their hips.[18] A definite rift was forming between at least two factions in the wagon train, Gray reported. But there were other problems to address and those were more immediate.

**Three Inch Dust**

At the Ferguson campsite, six men came fishtailing through the camp in a '65 Pontiac station wagon and menaced one sleeping fellow whom they tried to jerk from his vehicle. Moore had to chase off the ruffians three times. One of the scoundrels weighed about 215 pounds, the "small, wiry" Moore reckoned, declaring, "But that tommyhawk [tomahawk] would have made the difference." Moore carried that authentic weapon with him always as part of his Daniel Boone costume.[19] But that evening, all went better for a while as an estimated 10,000 visitors[20] descended upon Ferguson to visit the camp, to eat barbeque chicken, and to join in the square dancing.

"A carnival-like atmosphere prevailed," reported the *Wilkes Journal-Patriot*, "Cotton candy was for the asking, candy apples were available and there was at least one novelty stand selling authentic mountain trinkets made in Japan. While Hawaiian music blared from a stereo, a rock and roll combo banged out melodies to twist by."[21]

That "rock n' roll" group, which started off the evening's music, soon lost its audience to a performance nearby that would have made Willard Watson proud. Taking to some mountain music, "couples did a sort of ragged square dance to music by three guitars (none electric), a banjo, a fiddle, and a pair of clicking spoons."[22] "The dance scene moved to the ball field where partners were swung in three inch dust."[23] Everyone had a good time until five drunks surrounded the microphone and began singing country hymns. The audience moved on and the wagon trainers eventually retired for the night, preparing for their next day's journey.[24]

For reasons of patriotism, recreation, and fundraising, the communities along the route looked forward to the annual event. At Ferguson, the community development club declared it had sold 1,200 chicken dinners by 8:00 p.m. and people were still coming. "Women-folk were manning the kitchen and serving line in a manner reminiscent of military life," the *Journal-Patriot* observed. Tom Ferguson spoke to the matter of the historical marker the community wanted to erect for the Boone Cabin Sites along Beaver Creek and the Upper Yadkin River. "They [the authorities in Raleigh] don't believe we have enough documentary evidence to substantiate a claim that Daniel Boone had a cabin near here. Maybe if the people from Raleigh came up here and saw these thousands of people visiting the wagon train which commemorates Daniel Boone's stay in this part of the country, we'd get a marker."[25]

On Wednesday, the wagon train departed Ferguson at 8:30 and made its way to Darby. That's where the trouble came to a head. The horse riders had driven ahead that morning, parking all their trucks and trailers in the best camping spots. They were taking up the shade that the wagoners needed for their livestock. One fellow had roped off a quarter acre saying he had five wagons

**In 1975, the Ferguson community did place a private marker on NC Hwy 268 for the Boone Cabin sites along Beaver Creek.**
**Tom Ferguson is on left. Ivey Moore holds his family rifle.**

courtesy of Edith Carter

and 21 horses coming. Moore was suspicious, but he could not call the man a liar. There was nothing he could do; he could not get them to move. So, four of the wagoners left the wagon train and drove on toward Triplett with plans to spend the night at the old Allis Hodge place about half way there. All four wagoners were from Lenoir: Tom Winkler, Allie Greene, Hoy Moretz, and Roby Moretz.[26] They were protesting the Daniel Boone Wagon Train being taken over by the horse riders.[27]

Jack Hines of Lincolnton decried the turn of events, noting that the event was popular because of the wagons, not the horses. "The wagon people have got to have a place when they get there. [The wagon train has] got so big now that the one's that didn't help start it are takin' over." John Dawson, the president of the Daniel Boone Wagon Train agreed with the wagoners, "Our problem is the horseback riders. … We tried for an hour to get the trucks to move and there's no way you can do it." But tempers ran hot, with one of the complaining wagoners blaming Ivey Moore and insulting him. Moore got so angry he slammed his tomahawk into one of the wagons.[28]

Hot tempers cooled off a bit during the evening as a throng of visitors came to the campsite at Darby. "We sold 1,300 [barbeque] chickens last year," declared John Dawson, the unofficial "mayor," of Darby. "Made enough to put aluminum siding on the church." In 1966, business was even better. "By 9 p.m., 1,700 chicken dinners had been sold and folks were still lined up" the *Journal-Patriot* reported. "From the clouds of dust rising, there must have been 17,000 there."[29]

The music and the dancing continued as it had the night before, much to the delight of Robert Lee Cloer from Lenoir. At 97, he was likely the oldest person there and declared Darby "a wonderful place to be."

During the evening, the wagon train leaders planned better for the next campsite. They rode ahead to Triplett the next morning to reserve the best spots for the wagoners. They found six of the wagons already there. Two wagons, driven by Daniel Lewis and Rollen Shirley of Deep Gap, had left Darby at 3:00 a.m. and were joined by the four wagons camped at the Hodges' place. As the horsemen arrived with their trucks and trailers at 7:00 a.m., the wagon train leaders directed them into an open field. The shaded campsites were reserved for the wagons and the livestock. "We helped get the train started," said Hoy Moretz, one of the rebelling wagoners, "and if it wasn't gonna be run for the wagons anymore, we were gonna bust it up." Ivey Moore was glad to see the wagons get first choice on the camping sites and he said that everyone on the train should wear "Daniel Boone clothes not this Western stuff." He then announced that he would not be on the train the next year.[30]

The trek from Darby to Triplett was nine miles and a pretty good climb. The heat was intense, so the drivers had to rest their teams

**The climb from Darby to Triplett was the most scenic on the trip.**

from 1964 DBWT Souvenir Booklet

often. "The travelers ate a lot of dust as they wound over the narrow unpaved road through the Blue Ridge Mountains," reported Gray. "It was the most picturesque stretch so far."[31]

The party at Triplett was another success as far as the participants were concerned. Good food, good crowds, lots of music and dancing, but for some of those who had the task of marshaling all this energy into a good time for all, it had become a bit too much.

"I am through," Chief Scout Ivey Moore declared again on Friday. "Too many headaches. Too much money out of my pocket. Too many people cussing me out," he said. "I may ride in the thing next year, but I won't be the chief scout." At 64, Moore did not need nor want the trouble. DeWitt Barnett predicted that Moore would return. [32]

**Another Parade**

Despite Moore's dispirited assessment of the fourth Wagon Train, the folks in Boone were still excited about its pending arrival. "They're on the way for the fourth year!" wrote Rachel Rivers in the *Watauga Democrat,* "Waving at folks who line the trail from authentic covered wagons, stopping to water the thirsty horses, mules, and ponderous oxen who pull and carry the gay procession more than 30 miles. … Friday the big Train will pull up through Cook's Gap and follow Deerfield Road to the Boone Camp on Blowing Rock Road. The big field across from the construction site of Holiday Inn is where the flames of the Boone Camp will blaze."[33]

The merchants had decided that having such a crowd of people coming to town was a good enough reason to put on a sale. They created Wagon Train Days and in the merchandising and marketing manner of the 1960s implored in the guise of a newspaper article: "Visitors in the

**The Daniel Boone Wagon Train camped outside Boone along Blowing Rock Rd.**
from microfilm, courtesy of *Watauga Democrat*

city are asked to get acquainted with our friendly merchants and the courteous sales people, and to partake of the harvest of bargains which have been made available to them."[34]

The wagons had arrived in Boone a little earlier than planned, which gave everyone a chance to rest and relax a little just before the crowds of admirers descended on them. "Cotton candy, popcorn, and candied apples added just a smidgen of the carnival touch, but the campfires and skilletsful of slicked potatoes took spectators back to the pioneer era the Wagon Train is set up to revere."[35]

J.B. Greene was Boone's parade marshal in 1966, replacing Walt Edmisten who was out of town. That year they allowed those horseback riders who were not attached to the Wagon Train to join in the parade at the tail end; but, they insisted that "no stallions" were allowed. Some of those spirited and unruly creatures had nearly injured some spectators along the parade route the year before.[36]

Rachel Rivers reported the parade for the *Watauga Democrat*:

"Except for the glint of silver on one of two saddles, the Daniel Boone Wagon Train Saturday presented the most authentic parade in its four-year history. And it was spectacular!

"A blue-eyed blonde came ariding sidesaddle, wearing a flowing gown that set off her black horse handsomely. And the bare-chested Presnell Boys from Beech Mountain were comical as usual and yet deadly serious about the mission of folks hitting the trail with the Wagon Train.

"It was either Perry or Hoover [Presnell], who during a brief halt of the parade, whipped out a gigantic antique pipe, lit it dramatically, sucked through his teeth and whooped 'Giddap' and the mule team dropped into the harness and started the wagon rolling again.

"Pretty women in old time dresses and bonnets complement-

**The wagon train paraded through Boone, drawing a throng of spectators along the route.**
from microfilm, courtesy of *Watauga Democrat*

ed the Presnell rig, and a gentleman with a fretless banjo picked a happy tune from the back of the wagon, and the procession moved westward along King Street.

"There must have been 10,000 folks downtown for the parade."[37]

After the parade the crowd dispersed and the wagon trainers said their good-byes to those whose company they had enjoyed during the week. Many made promises to each other to come again the next year.

And the world turned:

As the 1966 Wagon Train was in progress, the President announced plans to begin bombing Hanoi; troop strength in Vietnam was announced as 285,000.

Richard Speck murdered eight student nurses in their dormitory in Chicago; and two weeks later, sniper Charles Whitman shot students from the tower at the University of Texas after killing his mother and wife. Race riots erupted in Chicago in mid-July and expanded to other cities: Baltimore, San Francisco, Cleveland, Omaha, Brooklyn, and Jacksonville, Florida. In September, rioting erupted for two days in Atlanta. A week later a mob of whites attacked black students attempting to integrate schools in Grenada, Mississippi.

Congress passed "urban renewal" legislation leading to 70 demonstration projects across the country costing $900 million.

In October, nearly 200 years after Daniel Boone had first made his way through the Cumberland Gap and later marked Boone's Trace into Kentucky, President Johnson created the 12th cabinet-level department: Transportation. It began operating April 1967.

In November, the first black Senator elected since Reconstruction, Edward Brooke, won in Massachusetts. In December, Walt Disney died, while working on the last animated feature under his direct supervision, *The Jungle Book*.

For two weeks in January 1967, the U.S. engaged in its largest offensive effort in Vietnam to date. Total US troops in South East Asia numbered 380,000. Casualties to date numbered over 6,600 killed and nearly 38,000 wounded. Meanwhile, at Golden Gate Park, San Francisco, the "Human Be-In" set the stage for "The Summer of Love."

The Green Bay Packers, led by Quarterback Bart Starr, beat the Kansas City Chiefs to win the first Super Bowl, January 15, 1967.

In late January, fire erupted in the oxygen-rich atmosphere of the capsule of *Apollo 1* during ground testing at Cape Kennedy, killing three astronauts: Gus Grissom, Edward White, and Roger Chafee. In April, the first Boeing 737 flew its maiden voyage, and lunar probe *Surveyor 3* landed on the moon, taking subsurface soil samples for photographing. Boxer Muhammad Ali refused military service, and Expo 67, the Montreal World's Fair, the most successful of the 20th century, opened.

In May, Tennessee's Gov. Buford Ellington repealed the "Monkey Law," which had remained on the books since 1925 making it illegal to teach the Theory of Evolution. In June, the Supreme Court, under *Loving v. Virginia*, ruled as unconstitutional laws in 16 states banning interracial marriage.

From June 5 to 10, Israel and Soviet-backed Egypt (then United Arab Republic) and Soviet-backed Syria engaged in what became known as the Six Day War. Israel captured Sinai, Gaza Strip, Golan Heights, and East Jerusalem. The war consolidated the special relationship between the United States and Israel.

Race riots erupted in Tampa, Florida, and Buffalo, New York. Meanwhile, President Johnson met with Soviet Premier Alexei Kosygin in Glassboro, New Jersey, for a three-day summit. On June 29, actress Jayne Mansfield died at 34 in an automobile accident in Slidell, Louisiana.

Meanwhile:

*Mission: Impossible* and *Star Trek* first began to gather their loyal television fans, as did *The Monkees* and *The Newly Wed Game.* At the movies, *A Man for All Seasons* and *Who's Afraid of Virginia Woolf?* appealed to thinking audiences; *Casino Royale* and *The Russians Are Coming, the Russians Are Coming* entertained. "Wild Thing" and "Good Vibrations" were among the popular tunes, and on the country charts, "Don't Come Home A Drinkin' (With Lovin' on Your Mind)" was a big hit for Loretta Lynn.

For more about television, movies, and music of the following 12 months, see Appendix, Popular Culture: July 1966-June 1967.

# Daniel Boone Wagon Train, 1967

Ivey Moore would quit the Wagon Train. He had declared that much for sure at the end of the fourth one. "Too many people cussing me out," he had said. So, what lay in store for those who flocked to the Daniel Boone Wagon Train in 1967, its fifth edition?

First off, Ivey Moore was back, just as Wagon Master DeWitt Barnett had predicted. Moore was in full bloom, too, declaring that he supposed he would return, "if it meant that much" to people. His enthusiasm for the Wagon Train was described by one reporter as an "addiction," but it was probably the attention that he craved the most. Moore had scored a bit of a public relations coup after the last wagon train. John Steinbeck's new book, *America and Americans,* had come out in October, and Ivey Moore's picture was one of five photos on the cover. Tribute was also given to him inside the book. North Wilkesboro's own Ivey Moore on the cover of a book by the celebrated John Steinbeck! How could he not continue his role as "Daniel Boone" with that kind of notoriety? And, to boot, his annual vacationing in the wilds of Canada had landed him a principal role in a new travel film to be shot over the summer by

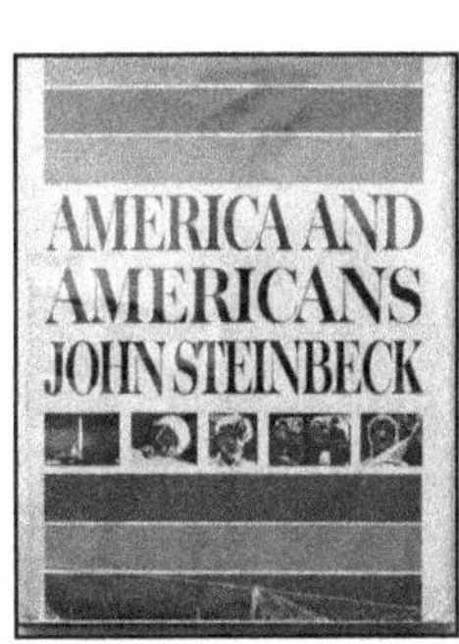


**Ivey Moore's picture appeared on the cover of John Steinbeck's 1966 book about Americans.**

the Ontario Department of Tourism. In the movie segment, he would be teaching two young boys some of the tricks of living in the wilderness, a role perfectly made for a "Daniel Boone."[1]

**Garden Spot of the World**

"The Train gets better every year," Moore declared as the event approached and he continued his work as registrar, work he had to complete before he got to the fun part, being chief scout. It certainly was becoming a more popular activity for the folks of northwest North Carolina, too; they were expecting 80 wagons. It was attracting people from farther away, too. This year, they announced participants coming from 25 states, including Connecticut, Missouri, Massachusetts, Pennsylvania, Maryland, Ohio, California, Kansas, Georgia, Iowa, Virginia, and Florida.[2] [3]

And that created a great opportunity for promoting the region. U.S. Rep. James T. Broyhill, 9th Congressional District, was the principal speaker at the send-off ceremonies in North Wilkesboro. He declared, "The Wagon Train is helping put the section on the map."[4] The audience was reminded during Broyhill's introduction that he got more votes each time he was elected. Not taking such popularity for granted, Congressman Broyhill spoke briefly, declaring with a smile that he would not filibuster as his Senate colleagues did, but invoke the House of Representatives' five-minute speech rule.[5] "Our Northwest section need take a back seat to no place," he said. "We regard it as the garden spot of the world—beautiful scenery, wonderful people, a place that is growing and which attracts more and more people."[6]

**Rep. James T. Broyhill**
courtesy of *Wilkes Journal-Patriot*

**If I Live To Be 100**

The event had, indeed, attracted more people including some folks of note. Three descendants of Daniel Boone's family were featured participants in the 1967 Daniel Boone Wagon Train. Mrs. Florine Thompson Norby came from Prescott, Kansas, specifically to portray Rebecca Boone, Daniel's bride, in the Wagon Train. Dressed in buckskins, she mounted up in a saddle and rode following Chief Scout Ivey Moore. To make sure everyone got the point, she draped a sign off the saddle that read "Rebecca Boone." She was a fifth-great granddaughter of Edward Boone, Daniel's brother, and served as the historian of the Boone Family Research Association of Missouri. "It is a real thrill," she said, "to see the site of Daniel's cabin and to travel beside Elk Creek, which we know he followed to cross the mountains." [7] [8]

Ivey Moore met Mrs. Norby at the Smith Reynolds Airport when she flew into Winston-Salem. He was dressed in his buckskins and decked out as "Daniel Boone." His appearance raised a lot of curiosity among airline passengers and those waiting for planes to arrive. But they must have been really perplexed when Mrs. Norby deplaned from her flight also dressed as a pioneer, in her own buckskin outfit.[9]

Mrs. Florine (Fred) Norby recounted her ancestor's 1779 departure from North Carolina that was not unlike the 1773 event the Wagon Train purported to celebrate. She "is the great-great-great-great granddaughter of Charity Boone and Francis Elledge," the *Wilkes Journal-Patriot* reported, "who left North Carolina in 1779 for Kentucky with their first born in a basket tied to the back of a pack horse. They were in the train of 22 pack horses and rode two of the riding horses that served as mounts for her parents, brothers and sisters. [Charity] was the daughter of Edward Boone and Martha Bryan Boone. Brothers were George and Joseph and sisters were Mary, Jane and Sarah."[10]

**The basics for joining a wagon train.**
from microfilm, courtesy of *Winston-Salem Journal*

Mrs. Norby mentioned no wagons and emphasized the use of packhorses in her historically correct telling. Because Edward's wife was a sister to Rebecca, Daniel's wife, the two Boone-Bryan couples were double in-laws; brothers had married sisters.

Mrs. Farris Goe Buckels came from Houston, Pennsylvania; she was a direct $10^{th}$ generation descendant of Daniel Boone, she said. "This is the most wonderful thing I've ever done in my life," said the 71-year old. "If I live to be 100 I shall never forget one minute of it."[11] "Daniel Boone was a daily subject in our house," Mrs. Buckels declared. She told of sitting at the skirt of her grandmother, Mary Francis Howard Goe, in Old Landing, Kentucky, and asking, "Granny, tell me about Daniel." Mrs. Buckels was born there in 1896.[12]

Sounding much like a politician or a tourism promoter, she added, "This trip—the beauty of the scenery, the kindness of the people, and the spirit of adventure—embodies the things which make life worthwhile."[13] Mrs. Buckels described her toe-length black dress as one she'd made from a pattern she'd used years ago for a traveling dress. She and her husband had left Clay County, Kentucky, for Pennsylvania with a 9-month-old baby. She and her husband rode by wagon for 25 miles before they could get on a train. "Steers are nothing new to me," she said. She drove an oxcart in the wagon train. "If I didn't live so far away," she added, "I'd make my own wagon for the trip."[14] [15] [16]

Mrs. Beulah Slagle, a descendant of Israel Boone, another of Daniel's brothers, came from Marion, Virginia.[17] Israel Boone died of "consumption," (that is, tuberculosis) in 1756 in Rowan County (today's Davie County). Daniel and Rebecca raised Israel's two surviving sons, Jesse and Jonathan. Those sons grew up and helped establish the Three Forks Church on the New River.

## Orderly and Well Behaved

The events in North Wilkesboro surrounding "Pioneer Days" and the departure of the wagon train had added a few items to the agenda. A luncheon was held at the Elks Lodge to host Congressman Broyhill, the three Boone descendants, the Wagon Train officials including John Dawson of Darby, president of the Daniel Boone Wagon Train, Inc., and the local elected officials including George Weibel and G.C. Bumgarner, mayors of North Wilkesboro and Wilkesboro respectively. The merchants also got more involved, declaring special sales and discounts during the gathering. With all those people coming into town for the parade and the square dance down at Midtown Plaza, it seemed a shame not to entice some of those folks into doing a little shopping.[18]

The afternoon parade through North Wilkesboro was well attended with people lining B Street "four and five deep," the *Journal-Patriot* reported. The evening square dance had become so large, that a second location was set up to attract and entertain visitors so as to split the crowd. The Carolinians performed at the Roses store parking lot. The Brushy Mountain Boys performed at the traditional site, Midtown Plaza. Several thousand people came to the "big hurrah" and the North Wilkesboro police described the crowd as "orderly and well behaved."[19]

Another change was new this year, too. Feeding so many people had just about overrun the capacity of the communities of Ferguson, Darby, and Triplett. This year, a Holly Farms barbecue trailer would take care of the chicken. The communities would handle the accessories, sandwiches, and drinks.

But another change would make all the difference in the success of the event. A new rule stated that no trucks or cars or trailers could enter the campsite until after the wagons and riders had established the camp. Then a truck would shuttle any wagon trainers or riders back to get their cars and trucks, if they had them. This new rule prevented the conflict between horseback riders and wagoners that nearly spoiled the event the year before from becoming an issue.[20] Wagon Master DeWitt Barnett also announced there would be no horseback riding through the camps. "Those who want to have fun on the train can have fun, but it is necessary to give and take to get along."[21] All in all, this year's Wagon Train was shaping up to be a good one.

**Voice of America and An Unforgettable Lark**

So far, each Daniel Boone Wagon Train had been better than the one before; but, would this one continue the tradition, especially since there was photographic evidence of just how grand the wagon train was the year before? Filmmaker LeRoy Crooks had come from Florida the year before to create a color travelogue movie called *Appalachian Trails*. He had joined in the Daniel Boone Wagon Train and included excerpts of the 1966 Wagon Train in his movie. Ivey Moore was encouraging folks to come see the movie at the North Wilkesboro YMCA during the weekend all the wagoners were gathering for the 1967 Wagon Train. Crooks featured scenes from the Wilkesboro parade and from the campsite party at Darby. He featured shots of wagons, livestock, and horsemen and included the final parade in Boone. For good measure, he included some night shots of the performance at *Horn in the West.* He claimed that 50,000 people had seen the film during the last 12 months.[22] Crooks traveled the entire wagon train with his family in '66, and Ivey Moore befriended the whole family, inviting them to join him on some of his fishing expeditions into Canada later on.

Whether the taping project by WATA in 1965 had prompted a repeat or whether *Voice of America* was just then getting around to the project, a team of folks came to Watauga County in 1967 to tape interviews and record sounds of the Daniel Boone Wagon Train and *Horn in the West.* Miriam Rabb, the travel editor for *State* magazine, arranged for the creation of a 30-minute program. They interviewed Glenn Causey, who played Daniel Boone, Charles Elledge, who played Reverend Sims, and Bill Ross, who played Dr. Stuart in the outdoor drama. Ross had performed his role in every show since the beginning, never having missed a performance in 15 years. Clyde Greene was interviewed about the Daniel Boone Wagon Train. The producers said the program, *Daniel Boone Country*, would be broadcast on morning English shows and they expected it to be "interpret-

**Reverend Sims and Widow Howard in a scene from *Horn in the West.***
from microfilm, courtesy of *Winston-Salem Journal*

ed into many foreign languages," too. As one would have expected, Herman Wilcox was really the person behind all this promotion.[23]

Mixed in with the celebrity participants were folks who were returning and others who were joining for the first time, reported the *Winston-Salem Journal*:

> "It is an unforgettable lark for many a youngster. Oscar Hill of Asheboro, who drives a double team of draft horses, was along with his six-year-old son, V.F. The boy made the trip two years ago and his eyes were still bright with that memory. There is music with the train. Stanley Hicks of Vilas, Rt. 2, a homemade banjo maker, was strumming away at lively mountain tunes for hours before parade time. Playing with him—"I'm just trying to learn"—was Adam Lamb of Burlington, who had bought one of Hicks' instruments.
>
> "First wagon in the parade was that of J. Ernest Finch [Smith?] of East Bend, drawn by a yoke of black Holstein steers. Not far behind was another oxen-drawn wagon, entered by Claude White of Harmony. Riding with White is Charles Earnhardt of Spencer—with a fine red beard."[24]
>
> "The youngest traveler to ever ride with the Daniel Boone Wagon Train—out of some 2,000 participants—is 6-month-old Davie Keifer. He is making the trip with this parents Mr. and Mrs. Henry Keifer of Bremen, Ind., and brothers, John, 9, and Jim, 6."[25]

**A Little Bit Old Timey**

The wagon train pulled out from Memorial Park in North Wilkesboro on time at 8:00 a.m., taking 30 minutes to get the last wagon in motion behind those in line ahead of it. They had 80 wagons registered, but only 64 pulled out for the wagon train. The others must have come just for the parade through North Wilkesboro over the weekend.

The 600 to 700 wagon trainers made good time to Ferguson, arriving earlier than expected. They covered 16-and-a-half miles in just five hours of travel plus an hour stopped for lunch. They arrived at 2:00 p.m., being about an hour earlier than the years before. "Today was the nicest day we've ever had," declared one veteran wagon trainer. "It was a cloudy day," Moore added. "The people and horses did not get as tired as usual, and I guess that's why we made better time."

The less-tired participants themselves had plenty of spirit for partying at Ferguson. "It was swing your partner and promenade at Ferguson Community Tuesday Night," reported the *Journal-Patriot.* "Dancers, as many as 200 couples at one time, raised clouds of dust as they circled to tunes provided by the Carolina Opery [*sic*?] from Lenoir. When folks weren't dancing, they were lining up for barbeque chicken plates or touring the camp ground to see and visit with Wagon Train riders and view the wagons and stock."[26]

People joined in the Wagon Train for lots of different reasons and came from varied backgrounds. *Winston-Salem Journal* reporter Jeanette Reid captured a few of them. "Ask any 50 of the 700 now traveling with the Daniel Boone Wagon Train and you will get at least 49 different answers. Two might say the same thing, 'Because it's fun.' The people range from a Pennsylvania Lutheran minister to a Winston-Salem lab technician, from a Stokes County farmer to an Elkin retired mail carrier, and from a 6-month old baby to several retired people in their 70s." They shared: "Because every time I saw a Western on TV, I wondered what it would be like"; "It's an altogether different type of life

**People joined the wagon train for lots of reasons.**
from 1964 DBWT Souvenir Booklet

than what we're used to"; "It brings back kind of old remembrance; I was raised with a mule and horse"; and, "to bring the grandchildren." And Mrs. J.F. Lane, 74 of Elkin, covered all the reasons, "I came because I'm still a little bit old timey. I like to get out. I love the mountains and I appreciate Daniel Boone."[27]

**Like Everybody Knows You**

In the fifth year of the Daniel Boone Wagon Train and despite its continual hype promoting inappropriate buckskin clothing and coonskin caps and anachronistic western garb, one participant had bothered to do some research beforehand. The Rev. Jesse E. Wolfe, a Lutheran minister from Jacobus, Pennsylvania, had researched something of note about women's clothing of Daniel Boone's era. He was traveling with his wife and two daughters. He had correctly discovered that calico dresses were not prevalent in the late 18$^{th}$ century. "The women," he said, "wore solid colors because they dyed the material with native dyes such as bark and pokeberries."[28] One doubts that news made much of a dent in the character of the celebrations. The Daniel Boone

Wagon Train rolled on just as it was, just as it had been, and just as it wanted to be.

And it rolled on as a mobile party. "At night, [the Wagon Train] is a county fair, an old-time reunion and a family camping [trip] all rolled into one shindig," wrote Jeanette Reid:

> "The smell of hay and livestock give the first impression of a county fair. Then comes the cotton candy eaten by little girls in calico dresses or western jeans. Next is the aroma of hot dogs, country ham and pop corn, plus candy apples for atmosphere. Mountain women operate a booth with home-made items for sale—aprons, pin cushions, rag dolls and old-timey bonnets which are perfect for covering up a fallen bouffant hair-do.
>
> "Entertainment last night at the Triplett campground was square dancing to lively country music by a Watauga County foursome … with a good country twang. … An estimated 400 people filled a freshly mowed field with their square dancing. … For intermission some fellow from Kentucky or Tennessee—nobody knew his name—grabbed the microphone and entertained with imitations of bird calls, hounds, and car races. After dark, many of the people gathered to view slides of the first wagon train in 1963. It had 19 wagons and 150 people compared with 75 wagons and 700 people this year. … People, both spectators and participants, are always filtering through the campground. The wagon train never really sleeps. … The wagon train is also like a reunion, even the people who are making their first trip. As an Iowa dairy farmer, Charles Lubbert, said last night, 'You feel immediately like everybody knows you, and that makes you feel at

home with everybody."[29]

At Darby, the wagon trainers were greeted by Charlotte TV personality Fred Kirby of WBTV, who provided some of the evening's entertainment.[30] At all the sites, participants and the throngs of visitors were entertained as well. "There also was plenty of country and mountain music, with square dancing and an occasional modern type dance," the *Journal-Patriot* reported.[31]

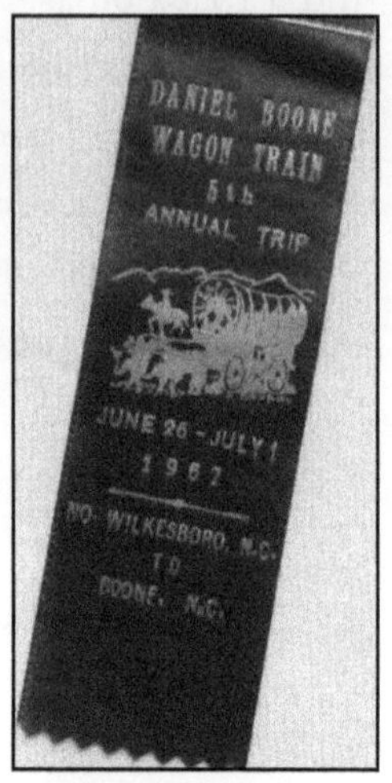


**Wagon train participants wore ribbons such as this one from 1967.**
courtesy of Betty Greene Koontz

When the wagon train reached Boone, Chief Scout Ivey Moore declared the 1967 version the best wagon train ever. They had started with 80 wagons and then it dropped to 64, but by the time they reached the end, they were back to 78. Moore credited the stricter rules with keeping down trouble and the weather with letting the participants get to the campsites earlier so they had more time to visit among themselves and to enjoy each other's company. The participants had become a family in their short time together and most were sorry to see the Wagon Train and the good times come to an end. More than a few shed tears when it came time to depart for their respective homes.[32]

### The Extravaganza of Frontier Days

"More colors, more action, more fun that ever is the offering for camp visitors and parade goers," touted the *Watauga Democrat.* The parade from the campground began at 9:30 a.m. on Saturday, July 1, reaching downtown at 10 o'clock. Helping lead the parade was the recently crowned Rhododendron Queen of North Carolina, Miss Elizabeth Ann Bailey of Concord.[33]

An editorial in the *Watauga Democrat* praised the successful 1967 Wagon Train, but demonstrated so clearly that some of the organizers, participants, and civic champions of this event had lost any sense of what history they were supposedly commemorating:

> "The Wagon Train parade Saturday was perhaps the finest that ever wended up King Street. At least it's a good bet that more people came to town that day than had ever come to attend any other Street-long exhibition. … The people were in a holiday mood, gay and happy, as the horses and wagon and ponies, and great rangy oxen pulled their wagons and carts along the avenue. There were covered wagons, one-horse and two-horse; mules and horses, and plenty of men and women riding animals of all sizes and colors in the extravaganza of frontier days. The women occupying the wagons, or many of them, wore the long dresses common in the old days and the sun bonnets their grandmothers use[d] to make. The horsemen wore cowboy outfits and jeans and the like, and there was excitement and good fun for all as the oxen plodded, the horses pranced and the draft animals poked along with their rattling burdens.
>
> "One could sort of shut his eyes to the people along the street and well imagine that the folks were headin' west to face the Injuns and the wild beasts of the wilderness and to establish frontier settlements. One could well see a tanned horseman as a tough trailman who was aimin' to face Wild Bill Hickock at Dodge City.

> "The Wagon Train is good. It's authentic and wholesome, composed of good folks who find a hearty welcome here, and more and more people are looking forward to the unique caravan."[34]

The parade in Boone at the end of the 1967 Daniel Boone Wagon Train could well have been to celebrate another historic event that day. It seems the General Assembly had acted the week before to change Appalachian State Teachers College henceforth to Appalachian State University.[35] The occasion was headline news in Boone and a great source of pride for the county and the whole state. One can only hope that the students there got a better history lesson in the classroom than was offered on the streets and sometimes in the newspapers. None doubted that had Dr. Daniel J. Whitener, the school's late, beloved dean, lived into the later years of the Daniel Boone Wagon Train, a critical eye on historical appropriateness and accuracy most certainly would have been cast. His influence was sorely missed.

And the world turned:

> In July 1967, the most extensive railroad strike in U.S. history affected 95% of the nation's railways.
>
> A week-long race riot erupted in Detroit, becoming the bloodiest and most destructive in the riot-filled year. In Detroit, 41 were killed, 2,000 injured, and 5,000 left homeless. Damages were estimated up to $400 million. This incident was preceded by other destructive riots: a six-day riot in Newark, New Jersey, and another two-day riot in Minneapolis, Minnesota. Rioting followed in Milwaukee, Wisconsin, for two days leading to a 10-day shut-down of the city.

On July 29, fire erupted on the deck of the *USS Forrestal,* killing 134 crewmen; it was the worst U.S. carrier fire since World War II. Navy aviator John McCain, later U.S. Senator and 2008 Presidential candidate, was almost killed in the explosion. In October, while on a bombing mission over Hanoi, McCain was shot down, suffered two broken arms and a broken leg in the crash, and was captured, taken as a prisoner of war.

In August, Thurgood Marshall was confirmed as the first black justice to sit on the Supreme Court. As chief counsel for the National Association for the Advancement of Colored People (NAACP) in 1954, he had successfully argued the landmark case, *Brown v. Board of Education,* which struck down the tenet of "separate but equal" and set in motion the racial integration of America's schools.

In October, space probe *Mariner 5* passed by Venus, discovering no oxygen on the planet; and, the controversial musical, *Hair*, opened off-Broadway. *Surveyor 5* landed on the moon to test soil samples. For two days in Washington, D.C., 35,000 demonstrators protested the Vietnam War.

In November, America elected black mayors in large cities and sent the first 20th-century black representatives to Congress from Louisiana, Mississippi, and Virginia.

On November 7, the Corporation for Public Broadcasting was established when President Johnson signed the Public

Broadcasting Act of 1967. *Apollo 4*, a test spacecraft, was launched to test the Saturn V rocket.

President Johnson and the Pentagon consciously began sharing more positive and optimistic reports about the progress of the war in Vietnam in an effort to build public support. U.S. Secretary of Defense Robert McNamara resigned to lead the World Bank, ostensibly because the President rejected McNamara's plans to scale down U.S. involvement in the Vietnam War.

In December, anti-war "Stop the Draft" protests took place across the country. Demonstrations lasted four days in New York City. On December 15, the "Silver Bridge," an eye-bar chain suspension bridge built in 1928 at Point Pleasant, West Virginia, collapsed into the Ohio River, killing 46. (See movie *The Mothman Prophecies*, 2002.)

At year's end, Princeton professor and theoretical physicist John Archibald Wheeler first used the term "black hole."

The Green Bay Packers won Super Bowl II. On January 21, 1968, a U.S. B-52 Stratofortress bomber crashed in Greenland discharging radioactive material from the four hydrogen bombs in its payload. Later in January, North Korea seized the U.S. Navy intelligence vessel *Pueblo* and 83 crewmen in the Sea of Japan. They were held for 11 months.

From January 30 through February, North Vietnam launched a major attack during an agreed two-day period of "cease-fire" to observe the Tet Lunar New Year. The attack by

80,000 Viet Cong against over 100 villages spread throughout South Vietnam was thereafter known as the Tet Offensive. It was the largest aggression in the war so far by either side.

Before Valentine's Day, civil rights disturbances occurred in Orangeburg, South Carolina, at the University of Wisconsin-Madison, and at the University of North Carolina-Chapel Hill. In Florida, teachers initiated the first statewide teachers strike to protest inadequate funding of education by resigning together.

In mid-February, a federal district court in Greensboro took only 10 minutes to declare North Carolina's 1963 Speaker Ban Law unconstitutional because of its vagueness.[36]

Dozens of civilians in the village of My Lai were massacred by U.S. soldiers on March 16, but this tragedy remained unknown to the America public for a year-and-a-half. Congress moved away from the gold standard, no longer requiring a reserve of gold to back the country's currency. Students at Howard University staged sit-ins and rallies and took control of the administration building, shutting down the university to protest the war; they also demanded an Afro-centric curriculum.

On April 4, during a strike by city sanitation workers in Memphis, Tennessee, the Rev. Dr. Martin Luther King, Jr. was shot and killed by a lone sniper as Dr. King stood on the balcony of the Lorraine Motel. Two days later the Oakland, California, police engaged in a shootout with Black Panthers in a confrontation that has remained controversial.

Student anti-war protesters at Columbia University in New York seized control of five buildings. Black students at Boston University took over the administration building demanding a stronger emphasis on black history. The musical *Hair* opened on Broadway. The nuclear-powered submarine, USS *Scorpion*, sank 400 miles southwest of the Azores with the loss of 99 men.

On June 1, humanitarian Helen Keller, blind and deaf since infancy, died four weeks shy of her 88th birthday. On June 5, Robert F. Kennedy, Democratic Presidential candidate, former U.S. Attorney General, and brother of the assassinated President, was shot and killed in Los Angeles at age 43 by a lone assassin.

Meanwhile:
Television welcomed *The Flying Nun* with Sally Field and *Ironside*, a reprise role for *Perry Mason's* Raymond Burr, as 25 million households tuned in to watch the final episode of *The Fugitive*. *Bonnie and Clyde, Cool Hand Luke*, and *Planet of the Apes* drew audiences to the theaters but Stanley Kubrick's *2001: A Space Odyssey* filled the seats. The Doors singing "Light My Fire" and the posthumous release of Otis Redding's "Dock of the Bay" dominated the pop charts at times. Bobby Gentry's "Ode to Billy Joe" crossed over from country to pop.

For more about television, movies, and music of the following 12 months, see Appendix, Popular Culture: July 1967-June 1968.

# Daniel Boone Wagon Train, 1968

In 1968, the Daniel Boone Wagon Train continued in a pattern which had proven successful since 1964, when in its second year, North Wilkesboro was first made the starting spot. The "Pioneer Days" events had become a great weekend attraction to visitors and brought more potential shoppers into town. As they had before, "the Merchants Division of the Wilkes Chamber of Commerce will welcome the Wagon Train with entertainment, displays, music, and a special sales promotion here this weekend," reported the *Wilkes Journal-Patriot*. The merchants association paid for the entertainment at the two locations on Saturday night: one, a string band, the other, a combo. The merchants dressed up their window displays to entice passing shoppers to come in and to purchase one thing or another. Some stores displayed antique items and others offered goods which wagon trainers might need. The stores even engaged in a competition for window displays, and the winners were announced after the weekend. The sales people got into the act, too, dressing in pioneer garb—or at least what passed for such at the time and in the community.[1] All in all, it was a time-tested start to what all hoped would be another successful Daniel Boone Wagon Train. There was nothing new to try and no reason to. Just do it again, just like before.

### Campfire Girls, Canadian Friends, and a Good Cat Dog

But, some new things did happen, and that first time occurrence made

**Campfire Girls joined the wagon train from Cleveland, Ohio.**
from microfilm, courtesy of *Winston-Salem Journal*

them special and worth mentioning. A group of Campfire Girls from Cleveland, Ohio, were along on the trip for their first wagon train experience. Jack Hines, from Lincolnton, had been in the Wagon Train from the beginning and this year had 17 head of livestock pulling various wagons. He was hauling the Campfire Girls, it seemed, in several wagons.[2] Later in the event he would declare (tongue-in-cheek, he would admit), "I draw women like flies. If I start out with an empty wagon, I've got a load of women at the end." The first-time-wagon-training Campfire Girls apparently had more enthusiasm than energy, more spirit than stamina. Clambering aboard one of Smith's empty wagons had great appeal after a dozen or so miles of steady walking.

The Wagon Train also welcomed some international guests from Scarborough, Ontario, Canada. The Richard Pollards were goodwill ambassadors representing the Ontario Department of Tourism and the mayor of Scarborough. This included wife Carol and young daughters, Cathy and Heather. Ivey Moore had met the Pollards during a trout fishing and canoeing trip to Canada the year before. He had invited them to come join in the Wagon Train. Their "hands across the border" visit was sponsored by two local banks in Wilkes County.[3] [4] And the Wagon Train also welcomed its oldest wagon ever, one actu-

**The Pollard Family from Ontario, Canada, joined the wagon train as Goodwill Ambassadors.**
photo by John Hubbard, from newsprint courtesy of *Wilkes Journal-Patriot*

ally from Daniel Boone's era. It was really a family carriage with interior seats and it had a date of 1786 imprinted on it. It came along with Tommy Tucker of Asheboro.

Not surprisingly, the wagon train had its characters, too, but that was nothing new. One was Stanley Nicks, from Stone Mountain, and on this fifth Daniel Boone Wagon Train. He brought his handcrafted banjo with a drum head that he said was made of ground hog skin. "I had me a good cat dog," Nicks declared with a telltale gleam in his eye. "Ever time I'd turn him out he'd bring me a cat back, but some of the neighbors got attached to their cats, and I've started shooting ground hogs." He added how that was a tiring business. "It takes so long to get one, and then I've got to shoot it in the head or it ruins the skin."[5]

### Past and Future Sins

It was Arlene Edwards who solved the mystery. She was the latest reporter to be sent by the *Winston-Salem Journal* to cover the annual wagon train and she confided in her readers from the beginning that she was being punished. One suspects she was winking as she wrote her opening column for the 1968 edition of the expedition: "My bosses have decided that it's my turn to cover the Daniel Boone Wagon Train. … I'm not sure exactly what I'm being punished for, but I'm sure I'll suffer enough this week to make up for all past and future sins." Ms. Edwards was not an outdoorsy person, but she was game, and expecting to become gamey. "That's four days without plumbing or running water," she continued, "except, of course, for the icy mountain streams, and four nights without a bed, but plenty of bugs. … I've never slept out of doors before."[6]

With the schedule of events and the format of the wagon train being pretty much again what it had been for the prior five years, this reporter immersed herself into trying to find a good story to tell. She focused on her fellow wagon trainers and shared with readers mostly the odd situations she encountered and her own experiences as a reluctant participant. Her predecessor reporters had done some of that, too, of course. Indeed, the story of the Wagon Train had been told before at least five times, and perhaps there was not so much new to tell. The Daniel Boone Wagon Train was no longer a novelty. Nothing much had changed.

**Land of Freedom and Opportunity**

What had changed was the country. The mood of America was somber in the early summer of 1968. Escalation of the war in Vietnam, race riots, assassinations, campus unrest, and anti-war demonstrations—it had taken its toll on the sense of unity and community people were experiencing as Americans. Some folks were looking for a place to find a more stable, saner world. They looked back in time, as Americans often do, believing that things were better in the past, which of course, they had not been. They were only different, as those earlier times had their own challenges, threats, and conflicts; but, those earlier times also had their own rewards, victories, and happiness. If any of the participants shared their real reasons for coming on the wagon train, that sharing did not make it into the pages of the

*Winston-Salem Journal.*

The changing mood of the country could be read, however, in the editorials of the *Wilkes Journal-Patriot.* On June 24, the editor alluded to current events in remarks about the era celebrated by the Daniel Boone Wagon Train. No doubt, those sentiments expressed those of many in the community at the time, sentiments which were prevalent across the county in places not accustomed to such dramatic changes—threats as they perhaps saw them—to the fabric of American life. Dwight Nichols wrote:

> "[The Daniel Boone Wagon Train] serves to remind us that our country did not just happen. It developed because it was settled by people who had the fortitude and the courage to struggle against hardships to accomplish goals. The pioneers who settled this area and pushed westward in the formation of these 50 states had no Washington to go to for aid. They had no poor people's marches and nobody to give them handouts. Nobody was handing out surplus food or monetary aid. This country was formed by men and women who knew what they wanted and were willing to work and face all types of hardships to gain their objectives. Their principal purpose was to have a land of freedom and opportunity. Not an opportunity to get something for nothing; not an opportunity to be parasites on society; but to form a self-sustaining and free society. …
>
> "If we see the wagon train without reflecting on a meaning deeper than the opportunities it provides for an outing and recreation, we will have missed the mark."[7]

**Kit and Caboodle**

Reporter Edwards counted 103 wagons pulled by 208 "horses, mules, ponies, and four of the biggest steers you've ever seen." She numbered her fellow wagon trainers at 600.[8] "The whole kit and caboodle paraded through downtown North Wilkesboro late yesterday afternoon," she wrote, "and had their first bath of the trip while doing so. A light rain started falling about an hour before the parade left the park. It stopped right after the parade did. At least 1,000 people stood in the rain to watch the spectacle. Thirty-one Campfire Girls from Cleveland, Ohio, wearing granny dresses and bonnets they made, walked near the front of the parade."[9]

The rain had reduced the crowd of parade watchers to one of the smallest crowds ever, but when the rain stopped, people flooded into North Wilkesboro for the big square dance. "For a while it appeared that the there wasn't going to be a square dance," the *Journal-Patriot* reported. "Wayne Johnson's Brushy Mountain Boys hadn't shown. There was a reason for this. He and his 'boys' are on a North Wilkesboro Recreation Department softball team and had to complete the game before playing."[10]

"The old timers on the wagon train almost had me convinced that the trip was not going to be so bad," Edwards wrote. "Then I saw the Brame Drug Store ad in yesterday's *Journal-Patriot.* The Brame Brothers have a special on insect repellant, suntan lotion, sunglasses, toothpaste, aspirin, Alka-Seltzer and deodorant—half price."[11]

The Wagon Train got under way on Tuesday about 30 minutes late. "This one's so big it took us a long time to get lined up," declared Ivey Moore.[12] The Wagon Train's passage through neighboring Wilkesboro got some attention. "The construction crew building the new federal building in Wilkesboro perched on stacks of drainage pipe and metal siding until [the wagon train] passed. Summer school children stood in groups in sideditches to wave at the wagons. Barefooted toddlers with cowboy hats were in their front yards shooting [toy] pistols. At least six folks set up aluminum porch chairs on the courthouse lawn." Edwards added about the wagons arrival at Ferguson, "The sky was overcast most of the way, and a purple-black cloud rumbled and cracked as the wagon train rolled into camp."[13]

The Wagon Train arrived in Ferguson with the weather having cleared and crowd of 8,000-10,000 joined in for a big "hurrah." "By 10p.m. 1,000 chicken dinners had been served and countless hot dogs and hamburgers had been sold." The Brushy Mountain Boys provided the music for the crowd, "the largest we've seen at Ferguson." The dancing crowd was enthusiastic and it was treated to the authentic and energetic mountain dancing and clogging of a couple of folks, who "probably should have a prize for endurance." Another couple probably wanted less attention than they got for what they were doing. "One feller apparently got a little too friendly with a lady not his wife," the *Journal-Patriot* reported. "'Mama' arrived on the scene and 'papa' was last seen beating a hasty retreat saying 'I apologize, honey. I apologize.'"[14]

The second day's trip into Darby saw a reoccurrence of an old problem the organizers thought they had solved the year before. It seemed that when the wagons tried to pull into the campsite there, the horseback riders had once again pulled their trucks and trailers into the prime camping spots along Elk Creek as they had in 1966. The wagon trainers refused to pull into camp until the trucks were gone. Without the wagon train, there would not be much attraction for the visitors who were coming to buy the barbecue chicken and food the communities had planned to sell. It took awhile, but Chief Scout Ivey Moore and Wagon Train President John Dawson got the campsite cleared out. The wagon train pulled into camp.

Regardless of whatever strained relations existed between factions of the Wagon Train, the 8,000-10,000 visitors, who descended upon the camp, were eager for a party. That crowd "poured in and then almost evaporated when an unscheduled shower, lasting about an hour, put in an appearance," the *Journal-Patriot* reported. After the rain, about 3,000-4,000 remained and consumed about 1,250 chicken dinners. Revived, the crowd "took part in a gigantic square dance… . From about 9:30 pm until midnight, it was one dance after another and the participants were yelling for more music."[15] Reporter Edwards described it more succinctly, writing, "Last night there was a cooling rain, "Darbycued" chicken, hymn-singing, square dancing and much campfire sitting."[16]

That year's wagon train enjoyed the company of one celebrity, of sorts, "a real Indian," the *Journal-Patriot* declared. "Willard Blevins from Lenoir … is a half-blood Cherokee and qualifies for residency on the Qualla Boundary Reservation in Swain and Jackson Counties, but he likes Lenoir," the paper wrote.[17] Others knew better, they claimed. Blevins was a renowned character of Lenoir, reportedly seen walking around town often in one costume or another—Confederate soldier, Nazi, Indian, clown—whatever struck his fancy at the time. He had been doing this for years, even back into the 1950s. His wife followed him around, walking right behind him. Nobody really knew how he made a living or where he got his costumes, but he would come to the Wagon Train in Darby dressed as an Indian with one story or another made up. "Willard was one of the real characters of the day," said Edith Carter. [18]

**Executive Visit**

The next day "130 wagons and hundreds of horseback riders" made their way along "one of the prettiest parts of the trip, north high above crystal clear Elk Creek."[19] On the climb up from Darby to Triplett, the Wagon Train was greeted by a real celebrity, North Carolina's chief executive. Gov. Dan Moore—no evident relation to Ivey Moore—came riding down the road from Cook's Gap in a Cadillac. He was in the area to attend a Highway Commission meeting in Blowing Rock and to speak at the dedication of the E.B. Jeffress Park on the Blue Ridge Parkway near Deep Gap.[20] He took the opportunity to see the event which had been celebrating the state's birthday since 1963, though most of the participants had by then forgotten the origins of the Wagon Train experience. The two parties met about halfway on the nine-mile stretch of unpaved road. When the governor started talking about paving that stretch of road, Ivey Moore implored, "Don't pave it. Don't pave it. It's almost impossible to find an unpaved mountain road to make a wagon train on." The wagon trainers would have to wait to see if the governor got the message.[21] "This could mean good-bye to the wagon train," Ivey Moore, declared.[22]

**Gov. Dan Moore unveiled sign at E.B Jeffress Park with help of Mrs. James T. (Louise) Broyhill.**
from microfilm, courtesy of *Winston-Salem Journal*

The draft animals had about as much pavement as they could handle, but a paved road could be an economic boon for the folks in Darby; so, different factions had different interests at play. It was not surprising to find Ivey Moore back-pedaling as fast as he could on his remarks. "I opened my big fat mouth and put my moccasin in it," said Moore later. He acknowledged that he had written to the highway commissioner and to the governor imploring them to pave the "important secondary road" for the benefit of the people in that community.[23]

Someone suggested they find a horse for the governor to ride. But he was "shaved, showered, and cologned," the *Journal*'s Edwards noted, and so he had other ideas. He had his picture made with Mrs. Farris Buckels, the direct descendant of Israel Boone, who was back for her second Daniel Boone Wagon Train. Setting his sights on a story with an international angle, Gov. Moore also had his picture taken with the Dick Pollard family, the goodwill ambassadors from Canada.[24]

In addition to the potential loss of unpaved road, the Wagon Train was beset by a couple of real tragedies. One horse was kicked by another and then dashed off, plummeting over an embankment. The rider was injured and sent to the hospital in Boone. The horse, with a broken leg, had to be destroyed. Two others horses foundered while drinking too much water too quickly and died.[25] [26] But all these difficulties aside, on Friday, the Wagon Train "clanked and rattled its way into its final stop at the camp-

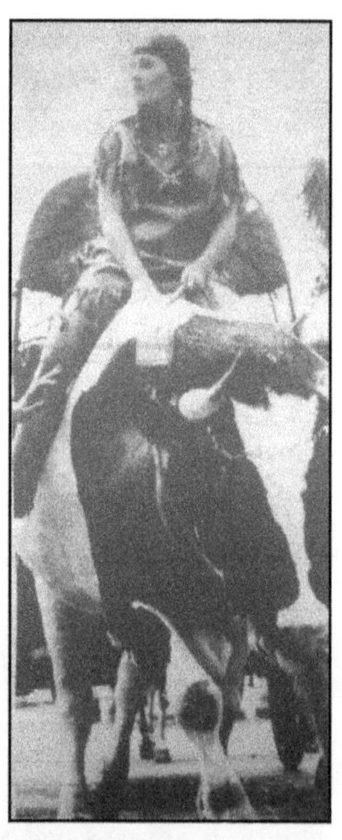

**Wagons by both A.J. White and Ernest Smith were pulled by large Holstein steers. Their massive size startled most who saw them.**
from microfilm, courtesy of *Watauga Democrat*

ground," Edwards wrote. They camped along US Hwy 321 in the southern part of the town. From there, some of the wagon trainers who had made the full trek would parade through Boone on Saturday morning. They would be joined by others coming for that event alone. In all, Ivey Moore reported 118 wagons and nearly 300 riders for the parade. The *Journal*'s readers were encouraged to look especially for Dave and Bill. They would be hard to miss. These two steers, pulling J. Ernest Smith's wagon, weighed together over 3,500 pounds. For show, they would be ridden by another set of twins, Margaret and Muriel Martin.[27]

The wagon train took about an hour to pass in review before an estimated 8,000 people who lined the streets in downtown Boone. The wagon train parade included 125 wagons and about 400 horseback riders, by another count. Many folks with wagons apparently joined in the final day's activities despite not having been on the Wagon Train during the week.[28] "Saturday's parade was livelier than any in the past, brought out larger crowds, and moved at a faster clip," declared the *Watauga Democrat.* But the fact was some of the wagons at the end of the long train got cut off from the parade. When people resumed their post-parade traffic patterns, some of those wagons turned down Depot Street to escape; others continued on the route amidst the cars and pedestrians who filled the streets of Boone.

The 1968 event closed with some concern for the health and future return of Ivey Moore. He had postponed some lung surgery scheduled for June so he could complete the Wagon Train, but on Monday, he was to report for surgery in Winston-Salem. Moore had been involved in the Daniel Boone Wagon Train from the very first year and had made many and long trips to promote the event. He had done so year after year without compensation except for his deerskin costume.[29] His involvement in the Daniel Boone Wagon Train would be sorely missed if he could not continue.

Accompanying the story of the 1968 Wagon Train's success in that Monday's *Journal-Patriot* was a story about another apparently successful (if clandestine) element of Wilkes County's economy. "A 500 gallon metal still with 24 fermenter boxes of 360 gallon capacity each," the article stated, "was raided and destroyed by Alcohol and Tobacco Tax agents from the Wilkesboro office early today in the Hamby's Mountain section west of Wilkesboro. … This was one of the largest liquor making outfits raided in Wilkes this year, agents said."[30]

And the world turned:

> The National Democratic Party convened in Chicago in August 1968 to nominate Hubert Humphrey for President as police took excessive action outside to halt anti-war protests. Over 20,000 Chicago police and Illinois National Guardsmen confronted 10,000 demonstrators, who chanted, "The whole world is watching!"
>
> A group called "New York Radical Women" protested the exploitation of women during the Miss America pageant in Atlantic City in early September. Two months later, Yale University announced that it would admit women.
>
> In mid-October, astronauts Wally Schirra, Donn Eisele, and Walter Cunningham aboard *Apollo 7*, tested the lunar docking module and broadcast live television images. During the 1968 Mexico Olympics, two black American athletes, Tommie Smith and John Carlos, gold and bronze winners respectively,

raised their arms with black-gloved hands in what was interpreted to be a Black Power salute during the playing of the *Star-Spangled Banner.*

On Halloween, President Johnson announced the cessation of bombardment of North Vietnam because of progress in the Paris peace talks.

Candidate Richard Nixon defeated Hubert Humphrey by 1% of the popular vote in one of the closest Presidential vote tallies ever. Third party candidate and Alabama's former governor George Wallace commanded 13%.

At Christmas, *Apollo 8* orbited the moon and returned safely making astronauts Frank Borman, James Lovell, and William Anders the first men to leave the earth's orbit, to see the whole earth from a distance and the dark side of the moon.

In 1969, Richard Nixon was inaugurated as the 37th president. Two months later, former-President and Supreme Allied Commander during WWII, Dwight Eisenhower, died of a heart attack at 78.

In early March, astronauts James McDivitt, David Scott, and Rusty Schweikart tested the lunar module and docking procedures in a low earth orbit aboard *Apollo 9.*

In April, Students for a Democratic Society (SDS) took over Harvard University's administration building. Similar disorder occurred at hundreds of campuses around the country.

In May, *Apollo 10* executed a successful rehearsal for a moon landing, including descent of the landing module to within nine miles of the lunar surface. Tom Stafford, Gene Cernan, and John Young were the astronauts.

In early June, President Nixon began to de-escalate the Vietnam War, announcing the return of 25,000 troops. During the previous year, 1968, US troops had died at a rate of 280 per week.

On June 22, singer and actress Judy Garland died in London at age 47 of an accidental overdose of medication.

On June 23, 1969, Warren Burger was sworn in as Chief Justice of the United States.

Meanwhile:
At Christmas, the world saw live on television a message of hope broadcast from *Apollo 8*, then circling the moon, as *Star Trek* was cancelled and the too-political *Smothers Brothers Comedy Hour* was replaced by *Hee Haw*. *Funny Girl*, Zeffirelli's *Romeo and Juliet*, and *Midnight Cowboy* drew movie audiences, but the musical *Oliver!* took the prize with 11 Academy Award nominations. The radio rocked with "Hey Jude" and "I Heard It Through the Grapevine" as Sly and the Family Stone sang "Everyday People." Jeannie C. Riley had a crossover hit with "Harper Valley PTA" and Merle Haggard sang "Mama Tried."

For more about television, movies, and music of the following 12 months, see Appendix, Popular Culture: July 1968-June 1969.

# Daniel Boone Wagon Train, 1969

The week before the 1969 Daniel Boone Wagon Train was to form had been a soggy one for Wilkes County. The campsite at Darby was flooded and some of the road along Elk Creek washed out. Acting optimistically, Wagon Train president John Dawson declared that everything would be ready. Repairs were under way as the wagons began to gather at Memorial Park.[1] Mayor Pro-Tem Rex Handy greeted the participants with a welcoming address at the park and the wagons and riders paraded through North Wilkesboro. Participants had joined in from New Jersey, Connecticut, Ohio, Florida, New York, South Carolina, and Iowa. Families without equipment made arrangements to book a ride with willing wagoners. Veteran wagon trainers Arnold Cooper, Robert Low, and Fred Cooper

**Some of the wagon train veterans offered spots on their wagons for paying passengers.**
from 1964 DBWT Souvenir Booklet

were three of those who had families in their care from Buffalo, New York; Palm Springs, Florida; and Muscatine, Iowa.[2]

### Bell Bottoms and Culottes

The weather was not the only changeable phenomenon. American society was in the throes of some dramatic revolutions during the late '60s, and some of those changes were being felt in the Daniel Boone Wagon Train of 1969. In the first year of the excursion and for many years afterward, the wagon trainers dressed the part of pioneers in period costume as they saw fit. Over the years, however, the purpose of what had become more-or-less a rolling party had been forgotten by some and so the dress code had become a little slack. In 1969, not all the women were wearing the long dresses. "Bell bottom pants, culottes, pant suits, and bare midriffs" were sported by some of the women making the trek with the Daniel Boone Wagon Train. The dress code had eased considerably, and the event continued to attract participants. Just before departure, the registrar reported 80 wagons and some 200 horseback riders.[3]

### Starshine

Another indicator of changing times was the immerging success of local singer, William Oliver Swofford. He was a graduate of Wilkes Central High School and a 1967 graduate of UNC-Chapel Hill. During the week before the 1969 wagon train, he was in North Wilkesboro visiting his mother and watching his hit single, "Good Morning, Starshine" reach #8 on the Billboard

**Wilkes County's own Bill Swofford, known as Oliver, had a hit song in 1969.**
from microfilm, courtesy of *Winston-Salem Journal*

Chart. Known to everyone else as Bill Swofford, he was also the solo, hit performer, Oliver, whose release of that song from the controversial, pop/rock musical *Hair* had catapulted him quickly to international fame and celebrity.[4] [5]

**A Loblolly**

The routine of the Wagon Train was so set by this point, that the *Winston-Salem Journal* reported its progress only cursorily. It noted that the wagon train arrived at Ferguson only a few minutes ahead of a thunderstorm, having passed by "within shouting distance" of the site of the Boone cabin at the mouth of Beaver Creek at the Yadkin River.[6] Tom Ferguson, 81, declared that the rain had turned the campground into "a loblolly for a while." But one spot of ground was bone dry, folks said. It was the plot where the wagon trainers and the visitors who came to see them had pounded the ground dry with their square dancing and other such prancing to music.[7]

The encampment at Darby was the occasion for another sizeable party, with thousands joining in the festivities of square dancing and eating "barbecued chicken hot off the grill." The number of visitors snarled "what must have been record traffic for Darby" all around, putting two Highway Patrol officers through their paces.[8]

**Chicken Thief**

The *Winston-Salem Journal*, despite its diminished coverage of the event compared to prior years, did share one new episode of adventure along the trail—the story of a chicken thief:

> DARBY—"The smell of 2,600 chicken halves barbequing over the charcoal here yesterday for the seventh annual Daniel Boone Wagon Train was just too much for one of Darby's younger residents. He waited until he thought nobody was

looking, grabbed one of the juiciest looking halves and started running. But somebody—Mrs. Beatrice Woods Whitson—had been looking. And she hiked up her flowered granny gown, held onto her sunbonnet and lit out after him. … The other Darby folks who were helping get the food ready for last night's mob, called out, 'Get him, Bea,' and applauded while she ran." She did not catch him, "But everyone agreed that the show she put on was worth far more that the $1.50 the chicken would have brought."[9]

**Chicken-thief chaser.**
from microfilm, courtesy of *Winston-Salem Journal*

**A Second Daniel Boone Wagon Train**

The only other news of sorts that year was the absence of Ivey Moore as chief scout. According to accounts given to the *Winston-Salem Journal*, he was reportedly ill, but that was just untrue. Moore was on his way to Canada to spend the summer above the Arctic Circle and to make trout surveys for the Canadian government. He stopped off in Pennsylvania at the request of the Kimmel family, who had been on the Wagon Train during the previous two years. While there, Moore did some research on the Boone family. This was of personal interest to him, but Moore was also the president of the Wilkes Genealogical Society. On June 19, he wrote a letter to the editor of the *Journal-Patriot* explaining his news about the George Boone family in Pennsylvania. This was Daniel's brother who came to Wilkes County after 1770 and then moved on to Kentucky in 1775 with Daniel and his family. During his visit, Moore had shown some of the films made of the Daniel Boone Wagon Train to folks in Somerset County, Pennsylvania, and they were all excited about starting a wagon train of their own depicting the departure of the Boone families from Pennsylvania in their migration to North Carolina. "In Pennsylvania, I feel," Moore wrote, "will be the beginning of the second Daniel Boone Wagon Train, in another great state and at the site of the other houses of the Boone Family."[10] (After Moore's meeting, Jean Kimmel organized the Appalachian Wagon Train Association. Its first wagon train was conducted in June 1970 in Somerset County from New Baltimore to Ligioner, a distance of about 50 miles. They had 20 wagons and 75 riders. The AWTA has conducted annual events continually since then and along different routes each year, completing its 43rd event in June 2012.[11] )

Moore was replaced in the duties of chief scout by Hubert Clodfelter of Kernersville.

**Horses or Hot Dogs**

It was a hot day on the road to Triplett and the wagon trainers were glad to reach the campground. Splashing in the creek and pitching horseshoes were nice and easy activities for such a hot day. [12] That evening, as usual, a big square dance was held. One young boy, declared, "Boy, I sure hope my horse's feet are not as sore as mine. If they are, we will never make the trip." A young mother said of her 2-year-old son, "I don't know which he's happier with, the horses or the hot dogs." It was a typical party at Triplett. "The crowds came early to the campsite," reported the *Winston-Salem Journal*, "and by nightfall one of the largest crowds during the train gathered to hear country music singing and to join in the square dancing."[13]

### A Carolina Calamity

But other news brought word of a great personal calamity to the family of North Carolinians. Mrs. Luther Hodges, former first lady of the state, had died in a house fire on Thursday evening in Chapel Hill. She was 70. The former governor who instigated the Carolina Charter Tercentenary celebration which gave birth to the Daniel Boone Wagon Train, was in the hospital afterward. He had suffered a broken foot and injured back jumping from the second floor of the house as fire swept the home. Still conscious when the firefighters arrived, he sent them into the house to retrieve his wife, but she had succumbed to smoke inhalation.[14]

### Every Bump

The wagon trainers gathered at a new campsite in Boone, at Optimist Park. There the Optimists and the Deep Gap Volunteer Fire Department served dinners on the grounds.[15] The weather was hot, reaching into the 90s. That had made for a challenging run from Triplett to Boone. One rider escaped serious injury when he rode too close to the edge of the road and his horse fell down the slope about

**The campsite at Optimist Park offered lots of room for the wagon train before the parade.**
from microfilm, photo by George Flowers, courtesy of *Winston-Salem Journal*

25 feet. But others faired some better. "This is our first experience on a train this size," said Mrs. John Sampter, of Buffalo, New York, "and we have enjoyed every bump the wagon has hit."[16]

From that Friday night campsite, the wagon trainers assembled on Saturday morning and paraded through the streets of Boone to complete their annual trek. They presented themselves in 77 wagons with about 250 riders, not all of whom had been on the four-day excursion. "It was the smoothest train ever," declared Wagon Master DeWitt Barnett. "Everybody enjoyed the entire trip."

And the world turned:

> On July 18, 1969, U.S. Senator Edward Kennedy, 37, drove off a narrow bridge across the salt marsh at Chappaquiddick, Massachusetts. The senator escaped. His 28-year-old passenger, Mary Jo Kopechne, a campaign aid to his assassinated brother, Robert, was trapped in the submerged car and drowned.

> On July 20, the *Eagle* landed and fulfilled President Kennedy's challenge to reach the moon by the end of the decade. U.S. astronauts Neil Armstrong and Buzz Aldrin stepped onto the lunar surface, leaving a plaque which read in part, "We came in peace for all mankind." Astronaut Michael Collins remained in the command capsule. They returned safely to Earth on July 24.

> On July 25, President Nixon announced his policy of "Vietnamization" of the war, expecting the South

Vietnamese to provide their own military defense.

From July 29 to August 5, *Mariner 6* and *Mariner 7* made close flybys of Mars returning data and pictures.

On August 9 and 10, Charles Manson and his "family" killed actress Sharon Tate and her friends at movie producer Roman Polanski's home and also Leno and Rosemary LaBianca in Los Angeles in the gruesome "Helter Skelter" murders.

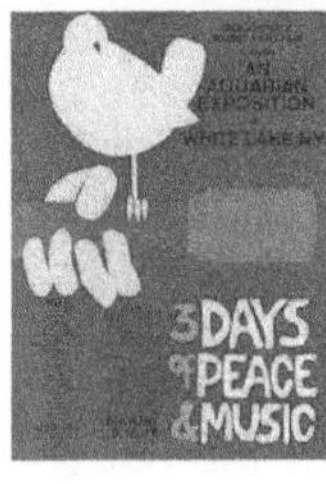


For three days in mid-August, 300,000 to 500,000 youth embraced rock music and the counter-culture at the Woodstock Festival in upstate New York. On August 17, Hurricane Camille, a Category 5, and possibly the most powerful hurricane to every make landfall, hit the Mississippi coast killing about 250 people and causing $1.5 billion in damage.

In September, the first automatic teller machine (ATM) was installed, in New York. In mid-October, hundreds of thousands demonstrated across the country against the Vietnam War.

In November, 250,000 to 500,000 demonstrators gathered in Washington, D.C., to protest the Vietnam War, becoming the nation's largest anti-war rally. Mid-month, *Apollo 12* with astronauts Pete Conrad, Alan Bean, and Richard Gordon returned to the moon as a reprise of the July lunar landing, and remained on the moon's surface for 31 hours.

Charged in September, Lt. William Calley went on trial in

November for premeditated murder in the massacre of 109 civilians in the village of My Lai in March 1968.

Seventy-eight militant American Indians seized control of the island of Alcatraz and its abandoned prison, claiming their right by treaty to lands abandoned by the federal government.

On December 1, the first draft lottery was held to establish by birth date the order in which draftees would be called.

Attempting to create a "Woodstock of the west," the Altamont Free Concert held in northern California and hosted by the Rolling Stones, ended in violence. It marked for some, "the end of the Sixties."

On February 17, 1970, it was later alleged, Jeffrey MacDonald killed his wife and children at Fort Bragg, NC, claiming that drugged hippies did it. In March, postal employees went on strike for two weeks.

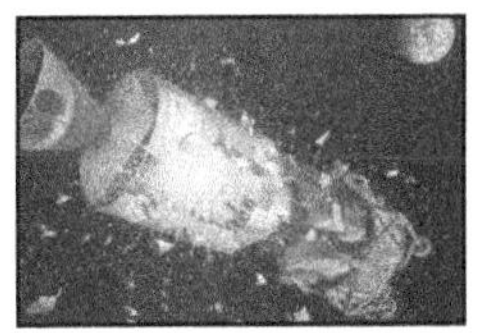

In mid-April, the world held its breath as astronauts aboard *Apollo 13*, Jim Lovell, Jack Swigert, and Fred Haise, dealt with a catastrophic malfunction that threatened their survival. They looped around the moon and returned safely, relying on the lunar landing craft for propulsion. (See movie, *Apollo 13*, [1995].)

On April 22, the first Earth Day was celebrated in the United States.

President Nixon sent 31,000 U.S. troops into Cambodia to attack pro-communist forces even as he also announced plans to reduce U.S. troop strength in Indochina by 150,000. Large anti-war protests were widespread.

On May 4, four student bystanders were killed at Kent State University as National Guardsmen fired at anti-war protesters. Ten days later, state police fired into a crowd of rock-and-bottle-throwing youths at Jackson State University in Mississippi, killing two and wounding 12. Four days later, unionized construction workers (called "Hard Hats" in the press) attacked about a thousand students and demonstrators marching in New York near Wall Street and Broad Street.

On May 11, Henry Morrow, a black man living in the segregated community in Oxford, NC, was beaten and shot by a white man and his son, witnesses said. Both suspects were later acquitted by an all-white jury. (See movie, *Blood Done Sign My Name*, 2010.)

In June, the voting age was lowered to 18 for federal elections, the U.S. Senate repealed the Gulf of Tonkin Resolution, and US troops withdrew from Cambodia.

Meanwhile:

On July 20, the world watched live on television as Neil Armstrong stepped onto the surface of the moon. That fall *The Brady Bunch* and *Sesame Street* began. At the movies, *Butch Cassidy and the Sundance Kid* and *M.A.S.H.* as well as the movie version of *Woodstock* were popular. On the radio, the Rolling Stones singing "Hony Tonk Women" and Peter, Paul and Mary singing "Leaving on a Jet Plane" spanned the wide range of popular tunes; but, "Let It Be" and "Bridge Over Troubled Water" dominated. On the country charts, "A Boy Named Sue" by Johnny Cash and Merle Haggard's "Okie from Muskogee" were memorable.

For more about television, movies, and music of the following 12 months, see Appendix, Popular Culture: July 1969-June 1970.

# Daniel Boone Wagon Train, 1970

A good party can be expensive to throw. The 1969 Daniel Boone Wagon Train had been the largest ever and prospects were good that the 1970 edition would be as big or bigger even without Ivey Moore's participation, except for one thing.

**This Stinks**

The problem was the town of North Wilkesboro had complaints about the foul odors and litter resulting from the wagon train, and they decided it was costing too much to clean up Memorial Park and the streets after each annual event. So, the Board of Commissioners, in a February 3rd vote, declined to host the Wagon Train in 1970.[1] That decision was not without its controversy, hurt feelings, and snide remarks.

After his organization's directors met, John Dawson, president of Daniel Boone Wagon Train, Inc., reminded North Wilkesboro of the positive publicity brought by the Wagon Train. It had received national TV coverage, national magazine coverage, and the event was covered by regional newspapers. It was even known across the Atlantic through broadcasts by Radio Free Europe. All this, Dawson suggested, worked to "offset some of the publicity about North Wilkesboro being the 'Moonshine Capital of the World.'" He then gave detailed statistics on the financial benefit which North Wilkesboro had enjoyed over seven years and would henceforth forfeit as he declared his openness to an invitation from any other town to assemble there. [2]

The editor of the *Wilkes Journal-Patriot* commented on the matter in an editorial, concluding that the town board had acted perhaps too rashly in a manner inconsistent with the facts.[3] But the damage had been done. North Wilkesboro's counterpart across the Yadkin River was indeed very pleased to extend the invitation. On June 21, the Daniel Boone Wagon Train would assemble in the town of Wilkesboro at Wilkesboro Park, on the ball fields and on open land adjacent to Cub Creek. The town worked feverishly to grade and gravel the roadway into the ball field, doing so right before the wagons arrived. On the eve of the gathering of wagons and horseback riders, the town, as first-time host, was sitting in what the *Journal-Patriot* knew well as, and called, "the quiet before the storm." [4]

But things would be different across the river from where the wagon train experience had bloomed during the 1960s. The Retail Merchants Association in Wilkesboro and the town itself did not offer to pay for

**Wilkesboro welcomed the wagon train to the park along Cub Creek.**
from microfilm, courtesy of *Wilkes Journal-Patriot*

entertainment, but they said the road adjacent to the courthouse could be roped off and used for a square dance, if someone wanted to have one, and they would open the park facilities. That was about it. And the citizenry and authorities of the community on the south side of the Yadkin River had to learn how to handle those gathering wagon trainers as temporary residents and not just as a parade passing through town. The wagon trainers were welcomed; but, one overly eager horseman, practicing for the parade, was ticketed for riding his horse on the sidewalk. Everyone was learning how to get along in a changed situation.[5]

The parade in Wilkesboro followed a new route from prior years, of course, and took about two hours for the 70-some wagons and over 100 horseback riders to make the route before the hundreds of spectators lining the streets and then to return to the park. The *Journal-Patriot* called it "the largest crowd gathered since the last hanging on the Tory Oak." (Patriot Colonel Benjamin Cleaveland, commander of the Wilkes County Militia, was notorious for hanging his Loyalist neighbors from the Tory Oak during the American Revolution.) The paper estimated more than 8,000 people came to the park to see the

**The wagon train rolls through Wilkesboro.**

from newsprint, courtesy of *Wilkes Journal-Patriot*

wagons. The square dance that night was called by Clayton Englebert, a well-known and experienced caller. The music was provided by Drake Walsh and his band, another well-known group. All in all, despite the change in venue, the Wagon Train seemed to be getting off to a good start. Wagon Master DeWitt Barnett said that the Wilkesboro camp was "well organized."[6] The Wilkesboro Park Supervisor, Jerry McGuire, even said that the wagon trainers were well behaved and left the park in "good shape."[7] [8]

**Silent Majority**

No doubt Dwight Nichols, editor of the *Journal-Patriot*, was aware of the changes to the Wagon Train, but it was the changes taking place across America that prompted his editorial comments which seemed to champion "the silent majority," a concept recently made popular by President Richard Nixon in comments televised in November 1969. Nichols wrote:

> "The dissidents, the demonstrators, the rioters, and the trouble makers in this country are getting far more attention than they deserve. They thrive on attention from news and communication media and therein lies the danger. This overemphasis and the practice of making a major production from each trouble-making incident give an erroneous impression. The media would have the public believe that the people are split down the middle or near middle, when there is no truth in that impression. The dissidents are a very small minority, and the hope of this country lies in the great majority who values our heritage and who fight and die, if necessary, to protect it. If the wagon trains fail to remind us of our past and inspire us to a better future, we will have missed the point."[9]

Editor Nichols might have taken exception to the article headline run in the *Winston-Salem Journal* on Wednesday explaining the problems which arose at the first campsite. "Dissent-Laden Train in Ferguson" it read. And, indeed, feelings were tender and the sense of camaraderie everyone wanted to prevail was once again in jeopardy. As the wagons reached the campgrounds at Ferguson, they discovered that trucks of some "outsiders" had taken many of the good spots, the ones the wagoners wanted. Wagon Master Barnett blamed the locals for letting the trucks in. The locals, including Tom Ferguson and Hill Carter, declared they had not been told to keep the trucks out. "We've got 30 acres of parking here," Carter said, "more than at any other stop. There's plenty of room for everybody."[10]

After the leaders spent a half-hour talking among themselves and considering even riding on to Darby, two of the wagoners had had enough. "I'm coming in," said Roy Jones, "the rest of them can do what they want to." "Count me in," agreed Roger Hamby. When the two teamsters turned their wagons into the fresh mowed field, that broke the stalemate and the camp took form after some time. The wagons rolled in. The crowds showed up, numbering "twelve to fifteen thousand" and ate chicken, hamburgers, and hotdogs.[11] They stayed around for the square dance which went on as planned. But bad feelings had developed. Some of the folks accused the wagon master and chief scout of playing favorites in the placing of wagons in the train. Ivey Moore, former chief scout, had gone off to Pennsylvania to start another wagon train, and some were not too happy with Hubert Clodfelter, Moore's replacement, even though it was his second year. Clodfelter was from Kernersville, about 60 miles east and some folks thought he and some others not from around there were trying to take over the Wagon Train. So, maybe the *Winston-Salem Journal* had got it about right. Maybe the wagon train was "dissent-laden"; or, maybe *Journal-Patriot* Editor Nichols was right and that was just the story the news media chose to share.[12]

Hurt feelings were not the only casualties, however. Two people escaped serious injury when their horse was "spooked" and "the wagon, occupants, and the horse went head over heels down a 30-foot embankment," reported the *Winston-Salem Journal*. "Roy Davis, 75, of Randolph County and Abigail Samuel, 13, of High Point were bruised but not seriously hurt." The horse was cut loose from the tangled harness and also escaped unhurt.[13]

**Fading Glory**

The second day's expedition, the trek along Elk Creek to Darby, ended successfully with the *Journal-Patriot* estimating 10,000 people coming to a "hurrah" there to eat "Darbycued" chicken and to square dance.[14] The next day's ride to Triplett was complicated some by rain, the *Winston-Salem Journal* reported. The weather "threatened a camp-out and square dance."[15] The *Journal*, which had embedded reporters in the annual wagon train for the first five or so years, was by 1970 giving the event scant attention. In addition to the story about the "dissent-laden train," the *Winston-Salem Journal* ran only one photograph and about six column-inches of copy in one additional article. Apparently the luster had come off this event as a newsworthy item for the Winton-Salem paper. It had for a few years been a storied experience worthy of covering in detail, but with the social turmoil in America that had intervened between 1963 and 1970, the Daniel Boone Wagon Train may have seemed perhaps too quaint and out of touch with current events to warrant reporting. Indeed, no mention of the annual event would enter the paper's pages at all the following year.

But closer to the mountains, where the draft animals which were pulling the wagons up the Blue Ridge Mountains could tell little difference between this excursion and the previous ones, the story and the event still held great appeal. As it had been for the past seven years, the Daniel Boone Wagon Train continued to be a spectacle and a rolling party. Despite the rain at Triplett, provisions were made for feeding a large crowd. "Twelve hundred pounds of country ham, six bushels of potato salad, 400 hundred pounds of cole slaw, and 300 hundred pounds of tomatoes," the *Watauga Democrat* reported, "are being prepared for the big feed at Triplett when the Daniel Boone Wagon Train camps there Thursday night."[16] When the entourage reached Boone, it would camp along State Farm Road across from Optimist Park, and the Deep Gap Volunteer Fire Department, famous for its fundraising dinners, would serve the food for the crowd. In Boone, they were expecting about 45 to 50 wagons and some 150 riders, down a bit from the earlier estimates of 75 wagons and 200 riders. One might have thought perhaps the rain discouraged a good number of the would-be pioneers. As it turned out, 90 wagons and 250 riders showed up at Boone for the parade.[17] [18] No one had dared declare the Wagon Train past its prime and its glory fading. If they had harbored such an opinion, the number of people turning out to participate and to watch could have certainly proved otherwise.

**A Real Good Hand**

Wagon Master DeWitt Barnett reminisced a little about the Daniel Boone Wagon Train completing its eighth expedition. He told the *Watauga Democrat* that he didn't "know how they ever made it the first year. Horses and mules were pulled out of the pasture, and hooked up to wagons that had been laid aside long since. Practically no one had new equipment or animals really in top shape for the long trip. Axles broke and other wagon pieces came apart, some of the animals could barely make it."

Barnett declared that those days were gone now. These days, people prepared their animals for the long, hard wagon train and readied their rigs, he said. He might have added that 200 years earlier, such preparation was actually a matter of survival for the migrating families, not merely an inconvenience as any such trouble would have been for the modern wagon trainers.

**Wagon Master Dewitt Barnett.**
from microfilm, courtesy of *Watauga Democrat*

Barnett praised his chief scout, Hubert Clodfelter, taking charge in his second year following Ivey Moore's six years of service. "He's a real good hand to keep them lined up. They don't string out like they used to. Sometimes you can look back and see them a mile off. Horseback riders are not all over the road like they used to be." Clodfelter had a scout helping him for every 10 wagons and was able to keep track of everyone.[19]

### Still a Boon

The festivities in Boone expanded some in 1970 to include some additional activities, mostly of interest in tapping into the pockets of the large crowds assembled. A flea market was scheduled for the day of the parade, and across the street and on the lawn of the Daniel Boone Hotel, the Boone Junior Woman's Club and the Juniorettes held a

Wagon Train Bazaar as a fundraiser for a cardiac unit in the hospital and for community parks. They sold handmade items and home-baked goods, reportedly in great quantities.[20]

The Wagon Train continued to attract the attention of elected officials, too. Congressman James T. Broyhill and Rufus Edmisten of Sen. Sam Ervin's office, both rode in the parade. Each spoke later at community events. Also participating in the parade was Carl Renfro of the Department of Conservation and Development, serving as a special representative of Gov. Bob Scott. [21]

Rachel Rivers Coffey described the parade for *Watauga Democrat* readers:

> "The parade through Boone escaped rain but had to endure threatening skies—as in some other years. The lead wagon, drawn by four horses belonged to R.C. Clodfelter & Sons, Route 3, Kernersville.
>
> "One of the entries was a huge prairie schooner, another wagon sported a cage with two [raccoons], there were horses aplenty, and one little girl was in the habit of rearing her peanut-colored pony for photographers. There were men with their hands full of reins, women in bonnets, children waving at spectators, a team of miniature mules, some pony-drawn wagons, and a one-eared horse.
>
> "And there was a man, up in years, who jogged alongside one of the wagons—how far, no one knows. He wore a woman's red felt hat, complete with grosgrain ribbon, and chatted occasionally with folks standing on the sidelines." [22]

And the world turned:

In August, 1970, the U.S. Post Office became an independent government corporation, expected to become self-sufficient. First class postage was 6 cents. Marin County Superior Court Judge Harold Haley was taken hostage and murdered in a failed attempt to free "the Soledad Brothers," members of the Black Panther Party, from police custody. Later indictments connected activist Angela Davis to the crime.

Many popular American music groups performed during the 1970 Isle of Wight Festival off the coast of England from August 26 to 31. With attendance estimated between 600,000 and 700,000 it was the largest-ever music festival, a step beyond Woodstock, but not profitable.

In September, over 340,000 members of United Auto Workers began a two-month strike, the largest in 20 years. In late September and early October, the world of rock and roll was shocked with the deaths of Jimi Hendrix and Janis Joplin just 16 days apart, both from alcohol and drug overdoses and each just 27 years old.

After the Communist delegates at the Paris peace talks rejected President Nixon's proposals, he announced withdrawal of 40,000 U.S. troops from Vietnam by year-end. A rocket-powered vehicle set the land speed record of 622 mph on the Bonneville Salt Flats in Utah.

On November 3, two future U.S. Presidents who would run against each other in 1980 each were elected as first-time gov-

Governor Reagan

ernors of their respective states: Jimmy Carter in Georgia and Ronald Reagan in California.

On November 14, an airplane carrying the football team and coaches of Marshall University crashed in West Virginia, killing all aboard. This was six weeks after most of the Wichita State University football team was lost in a plane crash in Colorado.

On November 21, under the distraction of seven hours of bombing of Hanoi, U.S. troops overran the Viet Cong prison camp Son Tay attempting to rescue prisoners of war. None were found there as they had been moved in anticipation of such a raid.

The U.S. population in 1970 was counted as 203 million. A strikingly diminished birthrate during the previous decade was attributed to later marriages, increased divorces, and smaller families. "The Pill" had been approved by FDA in 1960. (For comparison, the 2010 U.S. population was 309 million.)

The Environmental Protection Agency began operating on December 2. Two days before Christmas, the North Tower of the World Trade Center was topped, making it the tallest building in the world.

As of January 2, 1971, cigarettes could no longer be advertised on television or radio.

In February, the South Vietnam Army attacked Laos with heavy U.S. air support. The next day, *Apollo 14*, with astronauts Alan Shepard, Stuart Roosa, and Edgar Mitchell, returned after nine days, having spent 33 hours on the moon's surface from which Shepard hit two golf balls.

In March, a bomb exploded in the men's room at the U.S. Capitol. In the "Fight of the Century," undefeated boxing champions Joe Frazier and Muhammad Ali fought at Madison Square Garden to become the undisputed World Heavyweight Champion. Frazier won in a unanimous decision after 15 rounds. Found guilty of 22 murders at My Lai, Lt. William Calley was sentenced to life in prison. Charles Manson and three female followers, convicted of murder in January, were sentenced to death.

In April, the Supreme Court, reviewing *Swann v. Charlotte-Mecklenburg Board of Education*, upheld busing as a primary means of achieving integration of schools.

On April 22, John Kerry (later US Senator from Massachusetts and Secretary of State) testified before the Senate Foreign Relations Committee on behalf of Vietnam Veterans Against the War. He pointedly asked, "How do you ask a man to be the last man to die for a mistake?" Anti-war demonstrators, numbering in the hundreds of thousands, converged on Washington, D.C.; more joined in demonstrations in San Francisco. A Harris Poll revealed that 60% of Americans opposed the Vietnam War.

On May 1, Amtrak began providing intercity rail service.

In June 1971, the *New York Times* began publishing excerpts from the "Pentagon Papers" after their unauthorized release by Daniel Ellsberg, who wanted to expose what he regarded as unconstitutional behavior by a series of presidents in escalating the Vietnam War.

Meanwhile:
*Monday Night Football* premiered on television and PBS, Public Broadcasting Service, began operating. *The Odd Couple* and *All in the Family* premiered. In theaters, *The Owl and the Pussycat* entertained as did *Little Big Man*, but nothing drew like *Love Story*, with Ali McGraw. On the radio, Three Dog Night sang "Joy to the World" and Carole King sang "I Feel the Earth Move" as Edwin Star pounded out the anti-war anthem "War." On the Country charts, "For the Good Times" and "Sunday Mornin' Comin' Down" were big hits as was "Coal Miner's Daughter" and "Help Me Make It Through the Night."

For more about television, movies, and music of the following 12 months, see Appendix, Popular Culture: July 1970-June 1971.

# Daniel Boone Wagon Train, 1971

Time heals all wounds, and one year must have been long enough. Despite what bad feelings may have developed during parts of the 1970 Daniel Boone Wagon Train, the 1971 edition was greeted with eager enthusiasm. The overall routine was set for the week-long event, of course, and the wagons began to gather on the meadow belonging to B.S. Call adjacent to Wilkesboro Park as they had the year before for their second year of starting in Wilkesboro rather than North Wilkesboro. This year's event was beginning a little later in June so that it would arrive in time for the parade in Boone on Saturday, July 3, for the Independence Day celebrations.

**Some of the Nicest People**

The concessions at Wilkesboro Park were operated by the Rotary Club and the Wilkesboro Woman's Club as fundraisers for their community projects. They would have plenty of business including 16 Girl Scouts from Media, Pennsylvania, who with their four adult leaders were looking forward to their first wagon train experience. The girls had made their costumes and had been practicing their square dancing to prepare for the experience. They were riding in wagons provided by Fred Cooper, Arnold Cooper, and Robert Laws, all of Purlear.[1,2]

The Daniel Boone Wagon Train remained an attraction to many.

Indeed, John Dawson, president of the Daniel Boone Wagon Train, Inc., accompanied nearly 100 wagons during its parade through Wilkesboro and during the first day's journey to Ferguson. There and at the subsequent camps, the wagoners and visitors enjoyed the usual activities of music, barbecued chicken, country ham, and square dancing. Many wagoners returned from previous years. Others continued to join for the first time.[3] One wagon was joining from Vincennes, Indiana, and a retired shipyard worker from Jacksonville, Florida, was returning for his third experience. "I didn't have nothin' else to do …" he said. "These are some of the nicest people you'll ever meet." He rode along with wagoner Bud Moore. [4]

**John Dawson**
courtesy of
*Wilkes Journal-Patriot*

**Recalling an Era**

On the occasion of the ninth Daniel Boone Wagon Train, the *Journal-Patriot*'s editor echoed that positive sentiment and also challenged the organizers to put a little more emphasis on the historical interpretation. The editor may well have sensed that amidst all the changes of the last decade, a connection with the America of only a few generations before was rapidly slipping away. He wrote:

> "Wagon trains have become highly popular …. Thousands of people visit the wagon train's nightly encampments to see the wagons and horses, to eat food which is available in quantity and quality, and for the nightly entertainment which includes old time square dancing. But the underlying purpose of the Daniel Boone Wagon Train … is to give a demonstration in history of this area, recalling an era when pioneers were carving a nation from the wilderness. The trains also serve to educate children concerning the history of transportation, show-

**In the era of *Easy Rider*, motorcylces pass the slow-moving wagon train on the road to Ferguson.**
photo by John Wilkerson, from newsprint, courtesy of *Winston-Salem Journal*

ing again an era when freight was moved principally by wagons pulled by horses, mules, and oxen.

"When you visit a wagon train, tell and show the youngsters something about history lessons which are being demonstrated. Tell them about the difficulties pioneers faced in carrying the march of progress westward . . . . We would suggest to the Wagon Train officials that they emphasize pioneer dress and pioneer equipment for the wagon train personnel. In this way, history teaching will be enhanced and an atmosphere will prevail which will recall the pioneer life and habits of the Wilkes County residents of long ago."[5]

**Biggest Attraction**

The rains came on Friday as the Wagon Train was leaving from Triplett on the last leg of the excursion to Boone. About 70 wagons had arrived at Triplett, reported Wagon Master DeWitt Barnett, just a few short of the number leaving from Wilkesboro on Tuesday. But during that Friday rain, about half of the wagons had to pull out of the climb up to Cook's Gap. Some put their wagons and their livestock on flatbed trucks and made their way to the campsite in Boone, near Optimist Park. Others headed home. With a few more wagons joining in at Boone, the parade on Saturday enjoyed about 60 wagons in procession with about 150 horseback riders joining in.[6]

It was a good show for the record crowds that had descended on Boone for the Fourth of July weekend. "People, people, and more people flocked to such attractions as Tweetsie, *Horn in the West*, Grandfather Mountain, Wizard of Oz, and the Holiday Horse Show in Blowing Rock," reported the *Watauga Democrat.* "The wagon train turned out to be one of the biggest attractions to this section during the weekend."[7]

And the world turned:

On July 3, 1971, Jim Morrison, lead singer of *The Doors*, was found dead in Paris. Later that month, during the *Apollo 15* mission with astronauts David Scott, Alfred Worden, and James Irwin, a team spent three days on the lunar surface and used a lunar rover for the first time.

In August, President Nixon announced that the U.S. dollar would no longer be converted to gold at a fixed rate, thus unilaterally ending the Bretton Woods system, and making U.S .dollars a fiat currency. He also announced a 90-day freeze on wages, prices, and rents as one measure to address a sluggish economy and rising prices.

In September, the John F. Kennedy Center for the Performing Arts was inaugurated; and, one thousand New

York state troopers stormed Attica prison to stop a four-day riot. During the riot and rescue, 31 inmates were killed along with nine hostages. Cardinal Jozsef Mindszenty was allowed to leave Hungary, having taken refuge in the U.S. Embassy there since 1956.

On October 1, Walt Disney World opened in Orlando, Florida.

Supreme Court Justice Hugo Black, appointed by President Franklin Roosevelt in 1937, resigned from the court for health reasons.

Continuing his policy of "Vietnamization," in November, Nixon announced he would bring home another 45,000 U.S. troops from Vietnam by February 1, leaving a force of about 140,000.

Launched in May, *Mariner 9*, entered Martian orbit, the first spacecraft to do so; during its 12-month mission, it returned almost 8,000 images. Also in mid-November, Intel released the first commercially-available microprocessor. Later that month, "D.B. Cooper" parachuted from a jet airliner over the state of Washington with $2 million in ransom money. He was never seen again. In December, the Libertarian Party was established.

In January, 1972, President Nixon approved funding for the reusable space shuttle, costing $5.5 billion over six years. He brought home another 70,000 U.S. troops leaving troop strength in Vietnam at 69,000. The President also announced his budget, with a $25.5 billion deficit, the largest in U.S. peacetime history.

In February, President Nixon visited China in his "journey for peace," meeting with Mao Zedong. Nixon developed "normalized" relations with the Communist country. Attorney General John Mitchell resigned his post to become the chairman of the Committee to Re-elect the President. U.S. airlines began mandatory inspection of passengers and baggage.

The murder trial of black militant Angela Davis began in California for her association with the 1970 murder of Judge Harold Haley and others in the commandeering of a courtroom. After spending 18 months in jail, and becoming a cause célèbre, she was acquitted and freed.

In March, the U.S. Senate consented to the Equal Rights Amendment, so that it then went to the states for ratification. (Eventually it failed to be adopted.)

In mid-April, NASA launched *Apollo 16,* with astronauts John Young, Charles Duke, and Ken Mattingly. This followed the launching of *Pioneer 10* in March. It traveled 62 million miles to pass by Jupiter in fall 1973.

In May, after serving as FBI director for 48 years, J. Edgar Hoover died. Two weeks later, Gov. George C. Wallace was shot while campaigning for President.

He was paralyzed from the waist down. Three U.S. soldiers were killed in their barracks in Heidelberg, West Germany, by a bomb set by the Red Army Faction, an anti-imperialist urban guerilla group.

Also, in May, President Nixon traveled to Moscow, the first peacetime visit to the Soviet Union by a U.S. President. The leaders signed agreements on nuclear arsenals, trade, and a joint space mission.

In June, the Environmental Protection Division banned the pesticide DDT, a decade after Rachel Carson's *Silent Spring.*

On June 17, 1972, police in Washington, D.C., arrested five men while they were breaking into the Democratic National Headquarters in the Watergate complex. All five suspects worked for the Committee to Re-elect the President. An investigation began that would captivate national attention for more than a year.

A hurricane ravaged the East Coast for 10 days. The Supreme Court ruled that the death penalty could be "cruel and unusual punishment" and as practiced in some states might be unconstitutional under the Eighth Amendment. The California Supreme Court had already ruled similarly in February, and the death sentence of Charles Manson was commuted to life in prison.

Meanwhile, …

Television audiences welcomed *The Sonny and Cher Comedy Hour, Columbo*, and *Soul Train.* In the theaters, *The French Connection*, with Gene Hackman, and *Fiddler on the Roof* were big hits, but nothing beat Clint Eastwood in *Dirty Harry* for popularity until *The Godfather* arrived in the spring. The radio was filled with Rod Stewart singing "Maggie May" and Isaac Hayes with the "Theme from Shaft," as those were joined by Don McLean's "American Pie" and Sammy David, Jr.'s "Candy Man." Jerry Lee Lewis sang "Chantilly Lace" and Charley Pride sang "Kiss an Angel Good Mornin'."

For more about television, movies, and music of the following 12 months, see Appendix, Popular Culture: July 1971-June 1972.

# Daniel Boone Wagon Train, 1972

The 10th Daniel Boone Wagon Train received diminished acknowledgement by the regional media. Its unique means of celebrating the pioneer heritage of western North Carolina was no longer newsworthy, and frankly some of the communities were getting rather tired of it. The *Winston-Salem Journal* did not mention it at all; but, the *Wilkes Journal-Patriot* gave an account of the event which it had helped champion since the beginning. Still, North Wilkesboro had decided to place more emphasis on the Rotary Club Horse Show, an event that was drawing big crowds and putting Memorial Park to good use. The competitions involved 29 classes, with championships decided in categories such as Roadster Pony, Western Pleasure, Walking Horse, and Five Gaited, among others.[1] The horse show was a strong economic boon for North Wilkesboro after the Boone Wagon Train had ceased being thought of as such. People with show horses have trucks and trailers, and riding clothes, and are followed by a large entourage of well-heeled and well-behaved folks. It was correctly believed they have extra money they are willing to spend. A parade of old, wooden wagons drawn by mules and steers leaves a different impression about the economic viability of a community. And, some thought there was less need for a large police presence with the respectable audience attending a horse show than a horde of spirited revelers from out of town joining in a night-long frolic.

**Bicentennial Fever**

Another reason for the apparent decline in interest in the Wagon Train was that communities across the country had gotten "Bicentennial fever." Many were starting to plan how their communities would celebrate the country's 200$^{th}$ birthday anniversary then only four years away. The American Revolution Bicentennial Commission had already received plans from nearly 100 national organizations about their activities and suggestions. The commission chairman said that "parades and pageants, and fireworks" were fine, but he hoped communities would focus on programs "to add permanent values to America." Perhaps the Daniel Boone Wagon Train had come along too early; it would have seemed ripe for celebrating the Bicentennial. In any case, President Richard Nixon offered his public encouragements to "forge a new Spirit of '76," saying, "We want people all over this land to sense the greatness of this moment, to participate in it and help us all discover what that great spirit is."[2] As it happened, well before the Bicentennial would arrive, the American people would spend a good bit of time and energy trying to discover something else—something about this President.

**Story, NuWay, and Joppa**

The 1972 Wagon Train began under an aura of sadness, too, at least among the longtime residents of Wilkes County. Beloved public servant Thomas Edgar ("T.E.") Story had died on June 17 at the age of 84. He was an educator, an attorney, a state legislator, and devoted churchman. He was a public servant's public servant. And, he had championed the Daniel Boone Wagon Train in its early years. "T.E. Story's life was built on the principles of honesty, truth, integrity, rule by law, and loyalty to his God, his church, his community and every movement which he deemed worthwhile," said the *Journal-Patriot*.[3]

Story had graduated from the University of North Carolina at Chapel Hill in 1912, coincidentally, the year the Daughters of the American Revolution were planning their marking of Daniel Boone's Trail under the leadership of Mrs. Lindsay Patterson of Winston-Salem. (See *Trailing Daniel Boone*, 2012.) One of those bronze tablet markers was erected at the Wilkes County Courthouse square in 1913 and dedicated the following spring. The Daniel Boone Wagon Train had processed right by that marker each year on its way to Ferguson.

T.E. Story was a school principal in Wake County at the time of that 1913 marker placement in Wilkesboro, but by 1924 he had returned home to be the principal of Wilkesboro High School. He was in that position when another marker to Daniel Boone was erected in North Wilkesboro on June 27, 1928. The account of that marker's ceremony was recounted in the *Journal-Patriot* on June 29, 1972, in a column titled "In Wilkes County 44 Years Ago":

**A bronze tablet marking Daniel Boone's Trail was placed at the Wilkes Courthouse in 1913 by the DAR.**

*1972*

**"Boone Trail Marker Unveiled Here**

The unveiling of the Boone Trail marker at Forester's NuWay Service Station yesterday, afternoon was a beautiful and inspiring ceremony. Flags draped the railings of the balcony of the building and flags waved in the breeze on the numerous automobiles parked in every available space in the vicinity. A number of small boys and girls carried flags, altogether making an impressible [*sic*] scene.

"Rev. C.W. Robinson spoke the invocation. In opening the program, J.C. Reins presented attorney W.R. Baugess of Jefferson, who in turn introduced the principal speaker, Dr. B.B. Dougherty, president of the Appalachian State Normal [School]. Dr. Dougherty traced the history of Daniel Boone for whom the marker was being dedicated, and stressed Daniel Boone the citizen, rather than the hunter. Judge T.B. Finley, following the address, read an interesting paper written on Boone by John Hays Hammond. J. Hampton Rich, managing director of the Boone Trail Association, delivered a splendid address on the history of the work of marking the Boone Trail Highway across the continent.

"Misses Lina Forester, Florine Forester, Neil Gwynn, and Marjorie Deans pulled away the veil and revealed the Indian Arrow head on which were four tablets, two of Daniel Boone in hunting togs and two with a relief map of the route of the Boone Trail Highway. Miss Louise Vyne draped the marker with the Stars and Stripes as the larger number of people present bowed their heads."[4]

**The Boone Trail Highway marker was placed at NuWay Service Station (in background) in 1928 and later moved. The tablets show the commemorative route created by J. Hamption Rich to promote good roads, 1913-1938.**

As a modern expression of the community's pride in pioneer hero Daniel Boone, the *Journal-Patriot* published an article during the Daniel Boone Wagon Train about the nearby graves of Daniel Boone's parents. Apparently, Interstate 40 had just opened though Davie County in 1972, affording easier access to the Joppa Cemetery in Mocksville, where Daniel's parents, Squire and Sarah, were buried.[5]

### About the Regular Number

The Wagon Train gathered at Wilkesboro Park "under bright, sunny Wilkes County skies," the *Journal-Patriot* reported, and concession sales were good. The people were well-behaved, but a couple of horses got a little rowdy. One kicked in the windshield of one car and dented two others, doing about $600 in damage. The square dance ran into some trouble, too, starting about three hours late because the flatbed truck on which the band was to perform did not show up. The crowd dwindled a good bit because of the delay, but those who stayed around enjoyed Clayton Englebert calling the dance to the music of Jimmy Church and the Country Kings.[6]

The Wagon Train departed Wilkesboro with 58 wagons and "several hundred horseback riders" with another dozen apparently joining in at Ferguson.[7] Tom Ferguson reported on the encampment in Ferguson saying only that "about the regular number of wagons and horses" had passed through. He added, "The participants along with thousands of visitors were fed with Barbeque chicken, Hamburgers, and hot dogs."[8] The conflation of historic periods continued to plague the authenticity of the Daniel Boone Wagon Train; one wagon displayed the Confederate Stars and Bars across its canvas canopy. Or it might well have been a statement regarding current events involving racial desegregation. The caption to the photo in the *Journal-Patriot* only read "Unreconstructed Rebels."

The camps at Darby and Triplett were conducted with the same offering of barbecue chicken at Darby and country ham at Triplett. The number of wagons increased along the route with several joining at Darby and Triplett. A flood back home in East Bend and Kernersville had damaged the tobacco crops of some of the farmers and livelihood certainly took precedence over fun. But despite the preference for tradition in this reenactment excursion, changes had been made to the 1972 Wagon Train. Longtime Wagon Master DeWitt Barnett had retired from the role. Chief Scout Hubert Clodfelter stepped up to take on those responsibilities and Ray Pearson of Boomer became the chief scout.[9] Clodfelter, a stocky muscular man, raised percheron horses and worked for a trucking company.

### A Great Big Family

Reporter Mary Ellis Gibson for the *Watauga Democrat* asked Clodfelter about his new role when he arrived in Boone.

> "'You make some good friends doing this and a lot of good enemies,' the new wagon master of the Daniel Boone Wagon Train said with a good natured grin. … The wagon master confessed he has to be 'a little hardheaded' to keep the wagon train running smoothly. 'You get cussed a bit,' Clodfelter admitted.
>
> "The strictness of the wagon master and scouts has benefited the wagon train, Clodfelter said. 'It's got to where we sleep better than we used to,' he explained. 'There used to be a whole lot of drinking, but there's not much anymore. The rougher people go other places,' he continued, 'because there's so many other wagon trains they can ride in where

**Children enjoyed the wagon train, being outdoors and pretending to be frontier heroes.**
left photo by Lee Elliott, both courtesy of *Winston-Salem Journal*

they're freer to do what they want.' Clodfelter described his wagon train as a 'great big family—that's about what it amounts to.' When the wagon train makes camp, the people who drink and roughhouse usually camp on the outside, while the families camp in the middle of the area, Clodfelter said. 'The older people really enjoy the wagon train,' he said. 'And it's something for the children too. There're so many children who have never rode [*sic*] in a wagon in their life. … The Clodfelters make the wagon train their family vacation and many other families in the train do the same. 'The children do seem to love the train,' Clodfelter said. 'You can just turn them loose, and they play in the water when we camp and have a good time,' he added. Clodfelter estimated that at least 100 children were in the train this year."[10]

**Party Crashers**

Boone was having a special celebration when the Wagon Train arrived in 1972. It was the centennial anniversary of the town of Boone. The Daniel Boone Wagon Train was still the big draw for that Saturday and contributed to the festivities of the celebration. The parade had 77 wagons and 250 horseback riders.

In editorial comments on the success of the centennial festivities in the town of Boone, only one mention was made of the wagon train and it was not flattering. As Clodfelter had mentioned, some of the horseback riders were a rough crowd. The editor of the *Watauga Democrat* wrote in part: "Police and Sheriff patrols helped to keep the peace in the wagon train encampment. It is natural, we suppose, that a few of the riders in the train felt the need to kick up their heels a little after five days on the trail. The law enforcement patrols merely saw to it that the heels didn't kick too high."[11]

And the world turned:

In July 1972, Actress Jane Fonda toured North Vietnam and was photographed (tricked, she later declared) sitting on a North Vietnamese anti-aircraft gun and causing American outrage at "Hanoi Jane."

On July 8, President Nixon announced the U.S. would sell $750 billion in grain to the Soviet Union, hoping that trade would help ease tensions between the two superpowers.

At the National Democratic Convention in Miami, George McGovern, opposed to the Vietnam War and promising the immediate and complete withdrawal of U.S. troops, won the Democratic presidential nomination.

On July 25, U.S. health officials admitted that during the Tuskegee Study of Untreated Syphillis, Negro males were used as test subjects.

On August 10, a brilliant, daytime meteor skipped off the Earth's atmosphere. On August 12, 1972, the last U.S. ground forces withdrew from Vietnam, although by the end of November 27,000 troops remained.

On September 11, 1972, terrorists climbed over the walls of the athletes' compound at the Munich Olympics and killed eleven Israeli athletes.

In September, Bobby Fischer defeated Boris Spassky

to become the first American chess champion. In October, the Federal Bureau of Investigation hired its first female agents.

Congress addressed growing environmental concerns passing over a Presidential veto in October far-reaching amendments to the Clean Water Act.

The Nixon/Agnew ticket defeated the McGovern/Shriver ticket for President and Vice President of the United States, taking 60% of the popular vote and carrying all the states except Massachusetts. The landslide election also had the lowest voter turnout since 1948.

On November 14, the Dow Jones Industrial Average closed over 1,000 for the first time.

In mid-December, *Apollo 17*, the sixth moon landing, concluded America's lunar exploration with Gene Cernan being the last man to walk on the moon. He and fellow astronauts Ronald Evans and Harrison Schmitt returned to Earth on December 19.

The U.S. bombed North Vietnam during Christmas 1972 and received widespread criticism. The Swedish Prime Minister likened the U.S. bombing to Nazi massacres.

On January 14, 1973, Super Bowl VII ended with the Miami Dolphins completing the first perfect season in NFL history.

On January 22, the Supreme Court ruled in *Roe v Wade* the unconstitutionality of state laws prohibiting abortion up to the third trimester. Former President Lyndon Johnson died the same day at his ranch in Stonewall, Texas.

In Paris, on January 27, 1973, President Nixon's National Security Advisor Henry Kissinger signed the Paris Peace Accords with North Vietnam effectively ending the Vietnam War; the draft of civilians into military service was stopped. Nixon halted offensive actions in North Vietnam. The first American POWs were released on February 11.

In late February, 300 members of the militant American Indian Movement took over Wounded Knee, South Dakota, and staged a standoff which lasted 71 days.

On March 14, along with other POWs, Navy officer John McCain was released by North Vietnam after five-and-a-half years as a captive. On March 29, 1973, the last U.S. soldier left Vietnam.

On April 3, the first call was made in New York City from a handheld cellular phone. On April 17, Federal Express began operations for overnight delivery of packages.

In mid-May, NASA launched the unmanned *Skylab*. Two weeks later, they launched *Skylab 2*, with astronauts Pete Conrad, Paul Weitz, and Joseph Kerwin, to repair the orbiting space station which had been damaged in launch and to conduct experiments. They remained in space 28 days, doubling the prior U.S. record.

Despite such heroics above the Earth, the Watergate conspiracy took center stage in the public's focus during March, April, and May. Senate hearings on the matter began in May with Senator Sam Ervin of North Carolina presiding as chairman. *Washington Post* reporters Carl Bernstein and Bob Woodward continued to pursue the story as details of a cover-up came with the unraveling. They relied often on information provided by an anonymous source they referred to only as "Deep Throat." On June 25, former Presidential Counsel John Dean III testified that President Nixon was involved in the Watergate cover-up, but he had no proof to offer.

Meanwhile:
*Maude, The Waltons*, and *Kung Fu* were new programs that fall, and in the spring the televised daily Watergate hearings rotated among the three networks preempting regular programming every third day for each network. *Jeremiah Johnson, Sounder*, and *The Poseidon Adventure* drew people to the movie theaters, as did *Walking Tall*. On the radio, "Lean On Me" and "Alone Again (Naturally)" were big hits before "Carly Simon romped with "You're So Vain" and Roberta Flack topped with "Killing Me Softly with His Song." The Country charts welcomed "Eleven Roses" and "It's Not Love (But It's Not Bad)."

For more about television, movies, and music of the following 12 months, see Appendix, Popular Culture: July 1972-June 1973.

# Daniel Boone Wagon Train, 1973

Despite the problems reported at the Boone campsite during the 1972 Wagon Train, the 1973 version convened just the same. It began at a new gathering spot, however, one near but not in Wilkesboro. The wagons and riders assembled on Brown's Ford Road, west of town and near the dam for W. Kerr Scott Reservoir. They held the parade as before, through the streets of Wilkesboro, and then returned to the new gathering spot. Before the parade started, wagon train president John Dawson estimated they had between 50 and 75 wagons assembled, but he thought more would arrive before parade time.[1]

### Two Bests and a Better

Little additional information about the trek that year was recorded in some newspapers. A couple had lost interest in the Wagon Train altogether, it seemed. Again, the *Winston-Salem Journal* did not mention the wagon train at all. The *Wilkes Journal-Patriot* published the schedule in advance and the *Watauga Democrat* did as well. Those articles read as if they were written to fit any year and offered no specifics about what was planned for 1973. They suggested that the gathering at Darby was well attended, with crowds enjoying "Darbycue" chicken and later "Stuart Simmons' famous Triplett country ham." A square dance was held on the baseball field at Darby with Drake Walsh providing the music and Clayton Englebert calling.[2]

*1973*

The Thursday, June 28, edition of the *Wilkes Journal-Patriot*, however, did run a lengthy article based on first-hand interviews and observations by a reporter. The headline read "This Year's Boone Train Called One of the Best," but a closer reading revealed that claim was perhaps a bit of a stretch. Two youngsters had argued whether "the Boone Wagon Train was better than the Blue Ridge Wagon Train," the new Chief Scout, Sam Miller, said it was "the best group we've ever had as far as discipline," and the reporter claimed "participation in the dances has been about the best ever." So, perhaps the reporter felt that two "bests" and a "better" added up to enough to call this year's edition "one of the best." But the reporter had lost count as well referring repeatedly to the "12$^{th}$ annual" event, although it was clearly only the 11$^{th}$.

The only other account was printed in the *Watauga Democrat*, for which Jack Creech interviewed two wagon trainers while they were in camp at Boone. One was Sam English, and the interview was mostly about his life experiences and very little about the wagon train experience. But English did share, "There's people from everywhere out here. There's somebody from Indiana. … Last year we bought over $3,000 in ham in Triplett. That's the ham capitol [*sic*] of the world. It means a lot to those folks."[3]

**Trouble**

English then introduced the reporter to "a pretty girl," Pandora Hammond. She was a high school junior from Farmer, North Carolina, traveling in a wagon with her older sister, Candy. She was sleepy but not shy, reported Creech, who had awakened her from a well-deserved nap. "And as she spoke, her expression gained eagerness as if the words were waking her up." Her name might have seemed to suggest a familiarity with trouble, according to Greek mythology, but that did not appear to be the case, at least not trouble of her own making. In fact, she seemed to have done a pretty good job of avoiding what trouble was perhaps looking for her.

> "It's a lot like home, you know, out in the sticks. The only thing is you never get enough sleep with so much hoppin' and hollarin'. There's square dancing every night and I just love it. There was some drinking goin' on, but it was harmless. All they do is just stand around and scream a lot.
>
> "When I first started going on the train, a bunch of men would whistle and yell at me and it embarrassed me. Now I just go and talk to them, and I found out it pleases them just to talk. There are some real characters out there. It's fun just to watch 'em fall and trip over each other. You can't help but have a good time because they're havin' such a good time.
>
> "The best dancing is when there is a mob of people. I feel like a fool when I'm out there by myself. The only thing is you get so tired and everything gets so dirty. Some of the men put on bib overalls on Monday and didn't change clothes till Saturday. If they get tobacco stains on them, it stays on the whole week. … And you get so sorry while you're traveling. I don't even eat. I had to get up this morning at 5 a.m. and cook eggs for everybody. I just couldn't eat after that. Ugh! That ole' yellow yoke."[4]

Pandora was, perhaps, one of those young women coming of age during the Women's Liberation Movement of the early '70s. She might have been one who later would be incredulous that the Equal Rights Amendment, then out for ratification by the separate states, would be defeated. One doubts that failure would have stopped her from pursuing exactly what she wanted to do. She seemed to have spunk. And, in that regard, perhaps for some unlucky souls who might have stood in her way, Pandora may well have been "trouble."

Three photographs appeared with the Creech article. One picture was from the parade through Boone on King Street. The caption read, in part: "The wagon train contained 72 wagons and about 200 horseback riders, in this, its 11$^{th}$ year."

**Rules for Getting Along**

"One of the reasons we had to stop the Wagon Train," recalled Edith Ferguson Carter, "is because it got out of hand. It grew too big, too fast, and the rules were not kept. At first we just wanted to keep it as a nice, authentic-looking kind of camp with only covered wagons and horses and people dressed in costume. Then it got out of hand with more horseback riders wanting to come in with western clothes, carrying their guns, and so forth—and their whiskey. After awhile, I guess we thought they'd start showing up on motorcycles! It just got out of control. So, we decided here in our Ferguson community that we just couldn't handle it anymore.

"Darby is about eight miles from here; the wagon train would take all day to get there from Ferguson," Carter continued. "But when the rowdiness got really bad and we decided we just couldn't put up with the trouble, we told them they could not stop here anymore.—And it was trouble. The sheriff would be up here. It got really out of hand.—So, when they were coming up from Wilkesboro or from the reservoir, we didn't let them stop here and they had to go on up to Darby. That made for a really long first day. A year after we said we weren't going to deal with it anymore, Darby said they weren't either.

**Edith Ferguson Carter and friend on the porch of her "Daniel Boone Tavern," a log cabin she salvaged from Watauga County, now on display at Whippoorwill Village, the campsite of the Daniel Boone Wagon Train in 1963 and 1964.**

So, that's sort of when the Daniel Boone Wagon Train fell apart. It just crumbled. It wasn't the wagoners. And it wasn't all the horseback riders either, just enough of them. But that's all it took to spoil the party for everybody. A small group of people acting as if the rules for getting along did not apply to them, thinking they were special. That was it. But I guess we've seen that before, really all throughout human history."[5]

And the world turned:

> In July, 1973, North Carolina's Senator Sam Ervin, chairman, and the Senate Watergate Committee subpoenaed the White House audio tapes after learning that conversations there had been routinely recorded.
>
> *Skylab 3* was launched July 28, with astronauts Owen Garriott, Jack Lousma, and Alan Bean, to conduct scientific and medical experiments aboard the orbiting laboratory, *Skylab* (1973-1979).
>
> In August, the U.S. bombing of Cambodia ended.

In October, Vice-President Spiro Agnew resigned after pleading "no contest" to charges of tax evasion.

Egyptian and Syrian forces attacked Israeli-occupied lands in what came to be known as the Yom Kippur War (October 6-25, 1973). President Nixon pledged to resupply Israel in its fight against Arab states supplied by the U.S.S.R. The war ended with Israel recovering lands lost in the initial attack. These events led to the Camp David Accords in 1978, hosted by President Jimmy Carter, with the returning of Sinai to Egypt in exchange for the peaceful recognition of Israel by an Arab state.

The "Saturday Night Massacre" of October 20—the principled resignations of Attorney General Elliot Richardson and Deputy Attorney General William Ruckelshaus and the subsequent firing of Special Prosecutor Archibald Cox, an act on Presidential order the pair had refused to execute—led Congress to consider impeaching President Nixon.

In October, oil-producing Arab countries announced an embargo on exports to the U.S. in retaliation for U.S. support of Israel during the Yom Kippur War.

In mid-November, NASA launched *Skylab 4* with astronauts Gerald Carr, William Pogue, and Edward Gibson on a mission that would last 84 days. On the same day, Nixon signed the controversial Alaska Pipeline Bill to build an 800-mile pipeline across Alaska.

On December 6, House Minority Leader Gerald R. Ford was sworn in as Vice-President. Ten days later, the Buffalo Bill's O.J. Simpson became the first running back in NFL history to rush for 2,000 yards in a season.

With the Arab oil embargo, the Energy Crisis struck American drivers as gasoline was in short supply and prices rose sharply, going from 38 cents per gallon to 55 cents per gallon in six months. Cars lined up at pumps and followed rationing patterns until March 1974, when most OPEC (Organization of Petroleum Exporting Countries) members ended a five-month embargo against the United States, Europe, and Japan.

In February, heiress Patty Hearst was kidnapped by the Symbionese Liberation Army from her Berkley, California, apartment and held for ransom, at first the release of SLA members in custody and then changed to the donation of food to poor people in California.

On March 29, *Mariner 10*, launched in early November, became the first space probe to reach Mercury.

On April 3 & 4, an outbreak of 149 tornadoes hit 13 states and Canada killing 315 people and injuring over 5,000. On April 8, Atlanta Braves player Hank Aaron hit his 715th homerun to break Babe Ruth's career record.

Another outbreak—this one, of "streaking"—had overtaken the youth of America in the spring of 1974,

with hundreds of incidents, if not a thousand, reported on college campuses from late January to late May. Naked students running solo and in groups across college campuses in public places amused themselves and their peers in a spontaneous outburst of a silly diversion.[6] On a national stage, one person streaked the 46th Annual Academy Awards as David Niven was speaking.

During April, President Nixon agreed to pay back-taxes of over $400,000. He also announced the release of 1,200 pages of transcripts of the White House Tapes.

On May 9, the House Judiciary Committee opened impeachment hearings against the President. On May 16, former Attorney General Richard Kleindienst pled guilty to charges stemming from his Senate testimony.

On June 4, alcohol-fueled violence and intoxicated fans spilled from the stands onto the baseball field in Cleveland during the ill-advised "Ten Cent Beer Night" promotion.

In early June, President Nixon toured the Middle East for a week in an attempt to bring peace to the region. In late June, Nixon visited the Soviet Union a second time for summit talks with Leonid Brezhnev in Yalta. Agreements were signed but no breakthroughs occurred.

On June 30, in Atlanta, Alberta Williams King, mother of the assassinated Dr. Martin Luther King, Jr., was fatally shot during a church service.

Meanwhile:

*The Six Million Dollar Man* and *Happy Days* were new programs. *The Autobiography of Miss Jane Pittman* was a successful made-for-TV movie. At the theaters, *The Way We Were, The Exorcist*, and *Blazing Saddles* drew the audiences. On the radio, "Bad, Bad Leroy Brown" and "Time in a Bottle" were big hits for Jim Croce, as was "Sunshine On My Shoulders" for John Denver and "Bennie and the Jets" for Elton John. On the Country charts, Kris Christofferson sang "Why Me" and Dolly Parton topped with "Jolene."

For more about television, movies, and music of the following 12 months, see Appendix, Popular Culture: July 1973-August 1974.

# End of the Trail

In its 12th year, change once again came to the Daniel Boone Wagon Train. On June 3, 1974, the president of the Daniel Boone Wagon Train, Inc. made his announcement which ran on the front page of the *Wilkes Journal-Patriot.* The headline for the article read: "Boone Train Will Not Run." John Dawson explained that "because sites for the train are not available at Wilkesboro and Ferguson, the train will not run this year." The article continued, recounting the benefits of the event to the county and communities, although recently some had not appreciated its contributions as much as noted its faults. "Stops at Ferguson, Darby and Triplett brought more people into those communities than had ever been seen at one time," it said. "All the community organizations found the train a good money raiser for community projects. … Darbycued chicken became almost as famous as the Triplett country ham. There were 'hoedowns' on all the stops which lasted into the wee hours." John Dawson was clear to explain "the train hasn't stopped, that it's taking a year's rest."[1]

That year's rest was followed in 1975 with another announcement that the Daniel Boone Wagon Train would not run. Hoping to avoid the August rains that had plagued it previously, the organizers of the Blue Ridge Wagon Train moved its event to the last week of June, displacing the Daniel Boone Wagon Train on the calendar.[2] A year later, in 1976, the Blue Ridge Wagon Train ran again in the last week of June.

The Daniel Boone Wagon Train did not. It was finished, but not forgotten.[3] On July 1, 1976, the Wilkes County Board of Commissioners adopted a resolution dedicating the county's bicentennial celebrations to honor Ivey Moore. He was honored for a long list of civic service activities, among them serving as chief scout of the Daniel Boone Wagon Train from 1963 through 1968.

## A Different America

That rest in 1974 was probably what everyone most needed. The nation had changed considerably since the Daniel Boone Wagon Train had begun eleven years before. That change—social, scientific, and political—had come both in long, slow trajectories and in violent convulsions. America had been remade by the alchemy of the times through which it flowed. It was re-formed, transmuted into a new metal, perhaps, and different, indeed, having survived the crucible which was the Sixties. The America of 1963 had been pounded by the Vietnam War, ground down to its essential elements by the demands and demonstrations of the disenfranchised and disadvantaged. It had been subjected to the fire of assassinations and riots, and tested by the flames of cultural revolution and political corruption. The impurities of segregation and racial discord had begun to boil off, leaving behind the essentially American elixir of equality. Or at least the repeated utterance of that ideal reminded all of the nation's collective and continued shortcomings in its pursuit. And the country had been, as well, molded by its technological ambitions and achievements, giving rise to aspirations for a better future for all mankind. The United States was a different America in 1974, with new properties of uncertain quality and as yet untested reliability. It was hoped, of course, to be a stronger and more resilient America as it looked forward eagerly and immediately to celebrating in 1976 its bicentennial, its 200th birthday. America was, after all, a nation born of private dreams and desires, forged by individual determination and sacrifice, sustained by personal courage and diligence, and wrought thus, into its noble but imperfect form, during the life and times of Daniel Boone.

And the world turned:

On July 24, 1974, the Supreme Court ruled unanimously that President Nixon had to release all the White House tapes, not just ones of his choosing. By August 5, one of the newly released tapes had been determined to confirm the President's knowledge of the break-in at the Watergate offices well in advance of what he had acknowledged.

On August 7 in New York City, French high-wire artist Philippe Petit surreptitiously and illegally spanned the gap between the twin towers of the World Trade Center with a one-inch cable and successfully completed a most daring walk across that span, stopping in the middle to dance on the cable to taunt the policemen sent to remove him.[4] Unfortunately, the besieged President could not manage such fancy footwork and aerial artistry in his flaunting of constitutional authority, caught as he was in his own illegal and daring actions. The next day, on August 8, President Richard Milhouse Nixon announced his resignation from office effective at noon on August 9. Gerald R. Ford, Jr. was sworn in as the 38th President of the United States.

And the world turned.

courtesy of *Winston-Salem Journal*

# Epilogue

The Daniel Boone Wagon Train had a second life after taking a hiatus for nearly a decade. In 1982, another version of the annual event began and continued through at least 1986. Those in charge were keenly aware of the reasons the wagon train had stopped after 1973. "Excessive rowdiness," they said.[1] Indeed, the key to the success of the later version was strict adherence to specific rules: Horseback riders were assigned to specific wagons and had to ride behind that wagon for the duration of the event; no exceptions.[2]

The Boone Merchants Association sponsored the 1980's version of the Daniel Boone Wagon Train. Wagon Master Darrel Watson said the association wanted it started again but "it would have to be run right." The new version and the historic 1770s version were both centered around family, and that focus made the difference. One later family said they bought some horses for the 1983 wagon train after visiting it in 1982. "We wanted to see how the frontier people lived," said one. "We love to camp out, and it's a family trip." They chose to join in the wagon train, they said, because it was more exciting than going to the beach.[3]

Today, the lure of history continues. We Americans want to experience something from our collective past be it 50 years ago or 300. We seek a touchstone to test the authenticity of our modern lives. Innovations and conveniences are nice, of course, but without an appreciation of traditions fast held and the challenges endured and overcome by our ancestors, human nature can run toward feelings of entitlement and inordinate expectations. When we look back even 40 and 50 years ago, to the period 1963-1973, we see that achievements of merit and lasting value were accomplished at the expense of individual and collective effort and sacrifice. People invested their life energy and some gave their lives. Nothing came easily. Tragedies beyond control intervened on occasion, of course, but dedication, determination, discipline, and perseverance were the human qualities which moved America forward.

We are all pioneers in our own time. There is no script to follow, nothing preordained about how all of this is going to turn out. Civil rights demonstrators and anti-war protesters, NASA engineers and astronauts, statesmen of the people and for the people, poets and Olympic athletes, drafted soldiers and POWs, rocky-a-billy and hard rock musicians, Peace Corps volunteers and clandestine operatives, state troopers and national guardsmen, American Indian Movement protesters and feminists—all were venturing into the unknown landscape of their future, a wilderness of sorts for all.

Such is our calling today, to go forward, as they did, with hope and goodwill. So, when we look to the past, it may be that all we should really feel, perhaps, is profound gratitude for those who came before us: those who taught us, those who raised us, our parents and grandparents, our countless unknown ancestors, and their stalwart compatriots of their own respective eras, including, of course, for some the likes of Daniel Boone.

Take heart. Be strong. Wagons, Ho!

Bronze tableau of Daniel Boone in camp is along Rivers Street, campus of Appalachian State University, Boone, North Carolina. Sculpture by the late Sherry Edwards.

# Appendix

*Note: The information presented here was compiled from research of several Wikipedia sites. It is presented here for entertainment value to remind readers of "the times." The author has not independently confirmed the historical accuracy of this information about the popular culture; however, he lived through the era and has enjoyed having his own memories piqued by the mention of certain songs, TV shows, and movies. The author hopes you enjoy a similar experience.*

**Popular Culture: July 1963 - June 1964**

**On Television:**

In September, CBS, with news anchor Walter Cronkite, and then NBC expanded their evening newscasts to 30 minutes as Americans declared for the first time that they got more of their news from television than from newspapers. Programming was interrupted with the announcement of the assassination of President Kennedy; news reporting pre-empted programming for several days. Chet Huntley and David Brinkley went live on the air and remained there uninterrupted for hours reporting the developing story as it came in. On November 24, a live broadcast captured Jack Ruby shooting suspected assassin Lee Harvey Oswald. Instant Replay was used for the first time during the Army-Navy football game on Dec. 7.

*The Fugitive*, *Petticoat Junction*, and *The Patty Duke Show* premiered in September. *The Andy Griffith Show, The Flintstones, My Three Sons,* and *The Dick Van Dyke Show* continued in popularity.

The Beatles performed live on *The Ed Sullivan Show* three times in

February, 1964, breaking all ratings records. The Rolling Stones debuted on American TV on *The Hollywood Palace* on June 6.

**At the movies:**

*The Great Escape*, starring Steve McQueen, opened during the month of July. The second James Bond movie, *From Russia with Love*, premiered in October, following the opening of the year's eventual Academy Award-winning *Tom Jones*. The epic American comedy, *It's a Mad, Mad, Mad, Mad World*, opened in November. *The Pink Panther*, with Peter Sellers, entertained crowds beginning in March, 1964, and *Viva Las Vegas,* with Elvis Presley and Ann Margaret, did the same, opening in late May.

**On the radio:**

As the Daniel Boone Wagon Train made its way through the foothills of western North Carolina, the #1 pop song in America was a novelty song sung in Japanese, "Sukiyaki" by Kyu Sakamoto, enjoying the last of its three-week run in the top spot as the wagons rolled. "Easier Said Than Done," "Surf City," "My Boyfriend's Back," "Blue Velvet," and "Sugar Shack" finished out the calendar year among the #1 hits. The winter and spring airways of 1964 were filled with new sounds, especially songs from Great Britain. The Beatles commanded the #1 spot on the pop charts for 14 weeks with three songs: "I Want to Hold Your Hand," "She Loves You," and "Can't Buy Me Love." "Hello Dolly" and "Chapel of Love" were also immensely popular in May and June.

Johnny Cash singing "Ring of Fire" commanded the country charts during the summer and Buck Owens held the top spot for 16 weeks in the fall and winter with "Love's Gonna Live Here." The two repeated their dominant runs in the spring of 1964 with Cash's "Understand Your Man" and Owens's "My Heart Skips a Beat."

**Popular Culture: July 1964 – June 1965**

**On television:**

Using a geostationary communication satellite, the summer Olympics were broadcast live for the first time, from Tokyo. After the Rolling Stones performed on *The Ed Sullivan Show*, the host declared that he would never have them back. This followed by one week disgruntled—and unfunny—comedian Jackie Mason "flipping off" Ed Sullivan on the air.

The fall lineup of new programs saw the premiere of *Peyton Place, Shindig, Bewitched, The Addams Family, The Munsters, Flipper, Daniel Boone, Gomer Pyle, U.S.M.C, and Gilligan's Island.* The Christmas classic *Rudolf the Red-Nose Reindeer* premiered on December 6.

In March 1965, live images from the unmanned lunar probe, *Ranger 9*, are broadcast prior to its impact. The Beach Boys appeared on *Shindig* and the Rolling Stones returned to *The Ed Sullivan Show* after all.

**At the movies:**
The Beatles' first full-length movie, *A Hard Day's Night* opened in August to American audiences and great acclaim. Featuring North Carolina's own Ava Gardner with Richard Burton, *Night of the Iquana* opened in late summer. The fall was dominated by *My Fair Lady*, which won eight Academy Awards; *Goldfinger*, the third James Bond movie; and *Mary Poppins*, which earned an Academy Award for Julie Andrews. Nominated for seven academy awards, *Hush, Hush Sweet Charlotte* opened in December. The first half of 1965 welcomed the Academy's Best Picture of that year, *Sound of Music,* along with the ostensibly feline friendly *Cat Ballou*, and *What's New Pussycat?*

**On the radio:**
"Rag Doll" by the Four Seasons and "I Get Around" by the Beach Boys were big summer hits, followed by "House of the Rising Sun" by The Animals. Roy Orbison's "Pretty Woman" and "Baby Love" by the Supremes dominated the fall, but "Leader of the Pack" and Bobby Vinton's "Mr. Lonely" also reached the #1 spot. "I Feel Fine," another hit by the Beatles began 1965 along with "Downtown" by Petula Clark, "My Girl" by The Temptations, and "You've Lost That Lovin' Feeling" by the Righteous Brothers. "Eight Days a Week" and "Ticket to Ride" continued Beatlemania

which welcomed another British group, Herman's Hermits, with their big hit, "Mrs. Brown, You've Got a Lovely Daughter."

Roger Miller's "Dang Me" topped the country charts in the summer of 1964 as did "Gentleman Jim" Reeves' "I Guess I'm Crazy" after his untimely July 31 death in a plane crash. Connie Smith's debut single "Once a Day" topped the charts for eight weeks and Buck Owens did so for six more weeks with "I Don't Care (Just As Long As You Love Me)." He continued his run of hits in the spring with "I've Got a Tiger By the Trail" and "Before You Go." Roger Miller returned with another hit, "King of the Road."

**Popular Culture: July 1965 - June 1966**

**On television:**
In September, NBC began broadcasting *Today* in color. On Thanksgiving Day, CBS broadcast an NFL game in color for the first time. During the fall, new shows premiered including *The Big Valley, Lost in Space*, and *Green Acres. The Dean Martin Show, Hogan's Heroes, I Dream of Jeannie, Get Smart, and Wild, Wild West* also joined the mix of entertainment on the small screen. *Batman* debuted on ABC in January with twice weekly episodes. In February, the Rolling Stones returned again to *The Ed Sullivan Show*. On April 19, 1966, the *Academy Awards* were broadcast in color for the first time.

**At the movies:**
*The Great Race* with Jack Lemon, Tony Curtis, and Natalie Wood offered fun for summer viewing. *Von Ryan's Express* offered wartime action and *Shenandoah*, starring Jimmy Stewart, was praised for its strong antiwar theme. *Doctor Zchivago*, one of top 10 grossing U.S. movies of all time, and *Thunderball*, the fourth James Bond movie opened in December along with Disney's *That Darn Cat.* Released in February, Paul Newman starred with Lauren Becall in *Harper.* The British movie, *Alfie*, starring Michael Kane, opened in March.

**On the radio:**
Bob Dylan's song, "Mr. Tambourine Man," performed by The Byrds

reached # 1 in the summer of 1965. "I Can't Help Myself (Sugar Pie Honey Bunch)" by the Four Tops sat at #1 for four weeks as did The Rolling Stones' "(I Can't Get No) Satisfaction." Sonny and Cher dominated for three weeks with "I've Got You Babe" and The Beatles commanded the top spot for seven weeks with "Help!" and "Yesterday." "Hang on Sloopy" by the McCoys provided some break to the British dominance as did "Turn! Turn! Turn! (To Everything There Is a Season)" by The Byrds. The Beatles' "We Can Work It Out" swapped out with Simon and Garfunkel's "Sound of Silence" over the first five weeks of 1966 as the #1 hit. Nancy Sinatra captured attention with "These Boots Are Made for Walking," but Staff Sergeant Barry Sadler dominated the playlist during the spring with "Ballad of the Green Beret," staying in the top spot for five weeks. "(You're My) Soul and Inspiration" by the Righteous Brothers and "Monday, Monday" by The Mamas & The Papas were strong during the spring for three weeks each. The Rolling Stones welcomed the summer with "Paint It Black" at the top spot for two weeks.

"Is It Really Over?" by Jim Reeves (posthumously) reached #1 on the country charts for three weeks as did "Behind the Tears" by Sonny James. Johnnie Wright raised concerns about the war with "Hello Vietnam" for three weeks at the top spot and Eddie Arnold dominated December with "Make the World Go Away." The year 1966 welcomed Red Sovine back to a #1 tune for the first time in a decade with "Giddyup Go" riding high for six weeks. Buck Owens commanded seven weeks with "Waitin' in Your Welfare Line" and Eddie Arnold returned for six weeks with "I Want To Go With You." Again, Jim Reeves's music, although he was gone, enjoyed appreciation with four weeks in the top spot for "Distant Drums."

**Popular Culture: July 1966 - June 1967**

**On the television:**

*Dark Shadows*, the gothic American soap opera, debuted in late June and two weeks later *The Newlywed Game* debuted as well. In the fall, new programs included *Family Affair*, *That Girl*, and *The Monkees*, a program inspired by the movie *A Hard Day's Night. Mission: Impossible* and *Star Trek* started their runs as well. With mounting pressure from the NAACP, *The Amos & Andy Show* was pulled from the airways during 1966. In late June 1967, the first global TV broadcast "via satellite" was made to 30 countries with the offering of *Our World*, including performances by Mick Jagger, Marianne Faithful, Eric Clapton, Keith Moon, Graham Nash, and The Beatles.

**At the movies:**
The movies which dominated the screen over the following 12 months included the religious epic, *The Bible: In the Beginning*, and *Hawaii*, starring Julie Andrews, as well as *A Man for All Seasons*, and *Who's Afraid of Virginia Woolf*, starring Elizabeth Taylor and Richard Burton. The cold-war comedy, *The Russians Are Coming, The Russians Are Coming*, added some lightheartedness to the mix. In March, Julie Andrews returned with another grand performance in *Thoroughly Modern Millie*. In April, movie fans were treated to a spoof of the James Bond movies with the comedy *Casino Royale* and in a drama, Paul Newman in *Hombre*. The comedy, *Barefoot in the Park*, combined the talents of Robert Redford and Jane Fonda.

**On the radio:**
"Wild Thing" by the Troggs captivated the youth of America with its unexpected delivery just as "Summer in the City" by The Lovin' Spoonful got their collective motors running. But, love reigned as "You Can't Hurry Love" by The Supremes, "Cherish" by The Association, and "Reach Out I'll Be There" by The Four Tops each held the top spot for at least two weeks. The Monkees returned to the top with "Last Train to Clarksville" for one week and with "I'm a Believer" at the top spot for seven weeks. "Winchester Cathedral," Johnny River's "Poor Side of Town" and "You Keep Me Hanging On" by The Supremes joined with "Good Vibrations" by The Beach Boys to finish out 1966.

As 1967 rolled in, the songs of note were "Kind of a Drag" by The Buckinghams, "Ruby Tuesday" by The Rolling Stones and "Penny Lane" by The Beatles, each holding the #1 spot for a week. "Happy Together" by the Turtles endured for three weeks. But none out did "Old Blue Eyes" himself, Frank Sinatra, who joined with his daughter, Nancy Sinatra, to capture the top spot for four weeks with "Something Stupid." The Young Rascals did as well with "Groovin'," but their reign of four weeks was split in half for two weeks by Aretha Franklin offering up "Respect." The Supremes also continued their appearances on the charts with two popular songs, "Love Is Here and Now You're Gone" and "The Happening."

Buck Owens dominated the country charts in the second half of 1966 with "Think of Me" and "Open Up Your Heart" for a total of 10 weeks at #1. And few songs ever held the top spot longer than David Houston's "Almost Persuaded" at nine weeks. But, Jack Green was close with an eight–week stand at #1 for "There Goes My Everything." Eddy Arnold held it for half that with "Somebody Like Me." At Valentine's Day, Loretta Lynn held the top spot with "Don't Come Home A' Drinkin' (With Lovin' On Your Mind)." Buck Owens scored big with "Where Does the Good Times Go" and "Sam's Place."

## Popular Culture: July 1967 - June 1968

### On television:

The final episode of *The Fugitive* in August attracted the largest-ever television audience (viewed in over 25 million households), a record that lasted until 1980. Ed Sullivan banned The Doors from appearing again on his show after lead singer Jim Morrison did not alter lyrics Sullivan found too suggestive. The Who destroyed their instruments on stage during *The Smothers Brothers Comedy Hour*.

In the fall, *The Flying Nun* with Sally Field, *Spider-Man*, and *The High Chaparral* premiered along with *Ironside*, *Mannix*, and *The Carol Burnett Show*. In January, the sports world gained a new focus with the first prime-time broadcast of a men's collegiate basketball game (Houston vs. UCLA), an interest leading to what became known as "March Madness." The comedy program, Rowan and Martin's *Laugh-In*, debuted in January as did *Mister Rogers' Neighborhood* in February. On April 2, concern over social and racial taboos was piqued in program sponsors when white British singer Petula Clark touched on air the arm of dark-skinned, guest singer, Harry Belafonte (U.S.-born of Jamaican parents). In May, the British spy and science fiction series, *The Prisoner*, debuted in the US.

**At the movies:**
The theaters were filled in the summer with audiences watching the fifth James Bond movie, *You Only Live Twice, The Dirty Dozen*, and *To Sir With Love*, starring Sidney Poitier. He would star later that summer in *In the Heat of the Night* with Rod Steiger and in December would join with Kathryn Hepburn in *Guess Who's Coming to Dinner. Bonnie & Clyde, Valley of the Dolls*, Disney's animated *The Jungle Book* and *The Graduate* (the top-grossing movie of 1967) were released in the fall as were *Cool Hand Luke*, starring Paul Newman; *Wait Until Dark*, starring Audrey Hepburn; and Truman Capote's *In Cold Blood.* The musical *Camelot* was popular but did not gross as much at the box office as did *The Born Losers*, the first of the Billy Jack movies with a "half-Indian, Green Beret Viet Nam veteran" as hero.

The cinema year 1968 began with the creation of an epic (and eventual franchise) with *Planet of the Apes*, starring Charleton Heston. But nothing that year surpassed the draw of Stanley Kubrick's *2001: A Space Odyssey* which opened in April. During the spring, audiences laughed loud and long at *Yours, Mine, and Ours*, starring Lucille Ball and Henry Fonda. In June, viewers were shocked and surprised by the dramatically frightening and suspenseful *Rosemary's Baby*; and, John Wayne starred in *The Green Berets.*

**On the radio:**
The Association's "Windy" dominated the early summer for a month until it was overtaken for three weeks by The Doors' "Light My Fire," a six-minute song that first broke the standard convention for radio playtime. Bobby Gentry's country crossover hit "Ode to Billy Joe" captured the airwaves for four weeks as did "The Letter" by The Box Tops and "Daydream Believer" by The Monkees. But Lulu's "To Sir With Love" took charge of the fall for five weeks coincident with the movie's play in theaters.

As 1968 rolled in, the three-week run of "Hello, Goodbye" by The

Beatles continued. The orchestration of "Love Is Blue" offered by Paul Mauriat surprised listeners but apparently pleased them as it dominated the charts for five weeks. It was replaced by the posthumous release of Otis Redding's "(Sittin' by the) Dock of the Bay," which ran for four weeks at #1, and was itself followed by another five-week champion, the melancholy "Honey" by Bobby Goldboro. Archie Bell and the Drells reignited the party that was radio with "Tighten Up." Herb Alpert's "This Guy's In Love with You" carried four weeks before being replaced by the instrumental offered by South African trumpeter Hugh Masekela, "Grazing in the Grass."

Sonny James commanded the country music scene for nine weeks with "I'll Never Find Another You" and "It's the Little Things." Tammy Wynette had hits "I Don't Wanna Play House" and "My Elusive Dreams," joined on the second by David Houston. Houston had his own solo hit, "You Mean the World to Me." Henson Cargill released "Skip a Rope," which dominated the top spot for five weeks. Sonny James returned for three weeks with "A World of Our Own." Buck Owens, Loretta Lynn, Tammy Wynette, and Jack Green each returned with #1 hits in the spring before Merle Haggard released "The Legend of Bonnie and Clyde." Glenn Campbell dominated for three weeks with "I Wanna Live" and the pop hit "Honey" also played well on the country music scene commanding #1 for three weeks in the late spring.

## Popular Culture: July 1968 - June 1969

### On television:

In October, the first live broadcasts from an orbiting spacecraft showcased the flight of Apollo 7.

On November 17, NBC cut away from a professional football game with two minutes remaining to begin showing the movie *Heidi* (a remake, not the Shirley Temple version). The resulting outrage by sports fans led to the preeminence and sanctity of sports in the networks' schedules.

On November 22 during an episode of *Star Trek*, white actor William Shatner (Captain James T. Kirk) and black actress Nichelle Nichols (communications officer Lt. Uhura) shared TV's first interracial kiss.

On Christmas Eve, the crew of *Apollo 8* broadcast to Earth from its orbit around the moon, reading from the Book of Genesis.

In the fall, a new set of programs debuted, including *The Mod Squad, Land of the Giants, Hawaii-Five-O, Adam 12*, and the weekly CBS news show *60 Minutes*. On April 4, *The Smothers Brothers Comedy Hour,* which had embraced the counterculture and was popular with youth, was cancelled because of controversy with network censors about its antiwar position and political satire. It was replaced by *Hee Haw,* which premiered on June 5. *The Johnny Cash Show* followed with its premiere the same month. After only three seasons and because of low ratings, *Star Trek* was cancelled in
June, belying its enduring impact on popular culture. Leonard Nimoy then took the lead on *Mission: Impossible* for a while.

**At the movies:**

*Funny Girl*, starring Barbara Streisand (Best Actress, tied), Disney's *The Love Bug, The Odd Couple*, starring Jack Lemon and Walter Matthau, and *Bullitt*, starring Steve McQueen, entertained the movie-going public during the fall. *Lion in Winter* starring Peter O'Toole and Katharine Hepburn (Best Actress, tied) Italian director Franco Zeffirelli's *Romeo & Juliet* was a big hit with the teenaged audience. The original zombie movie, *Night of the Living Dead*, was released in October garnering domestic box office revenue over 100 times its production cost. *Oliver!* based on Charles Dickens' novel, *Oliver Twist*, won Best Picture and other Oscars among its 11 nominations.

In the new year, theaters welcomed *True Grit*, which earned John Wayne, as Rooster Cogburn, his only Academy Award, and *Midnight Cowboy*, which launched the career of Jon Voight and strengthened the appeal of Dustin Hoffman. It won the Academy's Best Picture award, the first "X-rated" film to do so. The French-language film, *Z*, about political intrigues in Greece did surprisingly well with

American audiences. *Goodbye, Columbus* introduced Ali McGraw, and *Winning*, starring Paul Newman and Joan Crawford, showcased the sport of Formula 1 racing.

**On the radio:**

During the summer, The Doors pounded out "Hello, I Love You," but The Rascals captured the mood of the nation with "People Got To Be Free," at the top spot for five weeks. "Harper Valley PTA" was a crossover country hit by Jeannie C. Riley, holding the #1 spot on the pop charts for one week until The Beatles dominated for nine weeks with "Hey, Jude." Showcasing her vocal dominance in the group and changing the name accordingly, Diana Ross & the Supremes charted "Love Child" to the #1 spot before Marvin Gaye replaced it for seven weeks with what became a classic, "I Heard It Through the Grapevine" bridging December into January.

"Crimson and Clover," "Everyday People" by Sly & the Family Stone, and "Dizzy" by Tommy Roe took the top spots for 10 weeks into mid-April. "Aquarius/Let the Sunshine In" by the 5$^{th}$ Dimension commanded the #1 spot for six weeks as the musical *Hair* and the counterculture rose in popularity. The Beatles (with Billy Preston) again dominated the late spring with "Get Back" for five weeks. But the #2 spot hosted some great music, too. Blood, Sweat, and Tears had two #2 songs that spring with "You've Made Me So Very Happy" in March and again in May with the Grammy Award-winning "Spinning Wheel."

On the country music charts, the summer of 1968 began with Tammy Wynette singing "D-I-V-O-R-C-E" for three weeks. Johnny Cash dominated for four weeks with "Folsom Prison Blues" and Merle Haggard did the same in September with "Mama Tried." "Harper Valley PTA" reigned for three weeks on the country charts as did Tammy Wynette's "Stand By Your Man." Glen Campbell scored a crossover hit with "Wichita Lineman" in December. John Cash captured the top spot for six weeks in the winter with "Daddy Sang Bass" as Jack Greene and Jerry Lee Lewis followed with hits. Sonny James commanded the airwaves in June with "Running Bear."

## Popular Culture: July 1969 - June 1970

**On television:**
On July 20 at 10:56 p.m. EDT, 720 million people around the world watched live images from the moon of U.S. astronauts Neil Armstrong and and then Buzz Aldrin stepping onto the lunar surface.

In the fall, new shows premiered, including *The Brady Bunch; Marcus Welby, M.D; Sesame Street*; *Room 222; Love, American Style;* and *The Courtship of Eddie's Father.*

**At the movies:**
*Easy Rider*, starring Peter Fonda and Dennis Hooper, with Jack Nicholson, was "a touchstone for a generation," critics declared. *Butch Cassidy and the Sundance Kid*, starring Paul Newman and Robert Redford, was a massive box office hit and garnered four academy awards. It dominated the big screen that fall although several other movies did well, including the musical *Hello, Dolly*; the titillating and suggestive *Bob and Carol and Ted and Alice*; *Paint Your Wagon*, starring Lee Marvin and Clint Eastwood; and *On Her Majesty's Secret Service*, a sixth James Bond movie with a new lead actor, one-time Bond, George Lazenby.

The year 1970 began with the February release of *M.A.S.H.*, a comedy set during the Korean War and surprisingly successful given the national angst over the long and continuing Vietnam War. *Airport*, based on Arthur Haley's novel, was a critical success and a moneymaker. *Patton* returned the public's attention to war and its leaders. It received the Academy's Best Picture and for George C. Scott, Best Actor, an award he refused to accept. *Woodstock*, a documentary about the three-day music festival in upstate New York the previous August, profited from the public's interest in the counterculture phenomenon. In June, theaters offered the satirical war film *Catch 22*, a dark comedy.

**On the radio:**
"The Love Theme from Romeo & Juliet" started the summer music fest, but was soon supplanted by the provocative "In the Year 2525," which dominated for five weeks. The Rolling Stone's "Honky Tonk Women" and "Sugar, Sugar" by The Archies each topped the charts for four weeks. Blood, Sweat, and Tears had another #2 hit with "When I Die" in August. "I Can't Get Next to You" by the Temptations and "Suspicious Minds" by Elvis Presley combined for three weeks as did The 5th Dimension with "Wedding Bell Blues." "Come Together/Something" by The Beatles, "Leaving on a Jet Plane" by Peter, Paul, and Mary; and Someday We'll Be Together" by Diana Ross & the Supremes each captured the top spot for a week. Steam with "Na Na Hey Hey Kiss Him Goodbye" dominated for two.

The hit song "Raindrops Keep Fallin' on My Head" by B.J. Thomas from the Butch-Sundance movie dominate for four weeks. "Bridge Over Troubled Water" by Simon & Garfunkel was the #1 song for five weeks and was the #1 song for 1970. The Beatles returned for two weeks with "Let It Be" and two more with "The Long and Winding Road." The Jackson 5 had hits with "I Want You Back" and "The Love You Save." Ray Stevens hit the top for two weeks with "Everything Is Beautiful," and The Guess Who dominated for three weeks with "American Woman."

The big country hits during the second half of 1969 included "Statue of a Fool" by Jack Greene, "Johnny B. Goode" by Buck Owens, and Johnny Cash's "A Boy Named Sue" at #1 for five weeks. Sonny James topped the charts for three weeks with "Since I Met You Baby" and Conway Twitty had two hits with "To See My Angel Cry" and "I Love You More Today." Merle Haggard held #1 for four weeks in November and December with "Okie from Muskogee." The new year was greeted with "Baby, Baby (I Know You're a Lady)" by David Houston for four weeks at #1 as was "It's Just a Matter of Time" by Sonny James, who returned in May with the hit "My Love." Merle Haggard led the charts for three weeks in the spring with "The Fightin' Side of Me."

**Popular Culture: July 1970 - June 1971**

**On television:**
On September 21, *NFL Monday Night Football* premiered. In October, PBS, Public Broadcasting Service, began operating. Other series premieres that fall included *The Mary Tyler Moore Show, The Flip Wilson Show, The Odd Couple*, starring Tony Randall and Jack Klugman, and *The Partridge Family.*
Cigarette advertising on television was banned after January 1, 1971. *All in the Family* premiered in January with a warning of potentially offensive material. PBS premiered *Masterpiece Theatre* in January and *The Lawrence Welk Show*, on ABC since 1955, was cancelled as a network program in March after 16 years.

**At the movies:**
Released in September, *Tora! Tora! Tora!* dramatized the Japanese surprise attack on Pearl Harbor. *Ryan's Daughter*, a love story set in Ireland in 1916 was released in November as was *The Owl and the Pussycat,* a comedy starring Barbra Streisand and George Segal. *Love Story*, starring Ryan O'Neal and the achingly attractive Ali McGraw, appeared in December, dominating the box office into the spring. Also released in December was *Little Big Man*, starring Dustin Hoffman, followed in the new year by *Summer of '42*, virtually the only notable film that opened that spring.

**On the radio:**
The summer tunes of 1970 included some songs that did not make it to #1 but which remained iconic of the era, including Chicago's "25 or 6 to 4," which reached #4 in the charts in the summer of 1970. The chart toppers included Three Dog Night's "Mama Told Me (Not To Come)" and for four weeks, "Close to You," by the brother-sister duo, The Carpenters. Edwin Starr's anti-war anthem, "War" dominated for three weeks before Diana Ross captured the top tune for another three weeks with "Ain't No Mountain High Enough." "Cracklin' Rosie" by Neil Diamond and "The Tears of a Clown" by Smokey Robinson & The Miracles got good play, but The Jackson Five dominated for five weeks with "I'll Be There" and

the Partridge Family for three weeks with "I Think I Love You." At the top spot, George Harrison captured four weeks with "My Sweet Lord" before Tony Orlando & Dawn and The Osmonds dominated eight weeks with "Knock Three Times" and "One Bad Apple," respectively. A posthumous release of a recording by Janis Joplin, who died October 4, dominated for two weeks—"Me and Bobby McGee." Three Dog Night returned to #1 with "Joy to the World" for six weeks; it was 1971's top song. Carole King took the top spot for five weeks with two tracks from her album, *Tapestry*: "It's Too Late" and "I Feel the Earth Move."

On the country charts, the summer of 1970 included Tammy Wynette's "He Loves Me All the Way" and Charley Pride singing "Wonder Could I Live There Anymore." Sonny James commanded the top spot for four weeks with "Don't Keep Me Hangin' On." Hanks Williams Jr. appeared at the top spot for the first time and for two weeks with "All for the Love of Sunshine." Ray Price sang "For the Good Times" and Johnny Cash sang "Sunday Mornin' Comin' Down." Sonny James sang "Endlessly," a three-week chart topper supplanted by Loretta Lynn's "Coal Miner's Daughter." The new year belonged to Lynn Anderson for five weeks with "Rose Garden" at the top. Johnny Cash sang "Flesh and Blood" and Dolly Parton, "Joshua," her first Billboard chart #1 hit. She was followed by Sammi Smith singing, "Help Me Make It Through the Night" and Charley Pride singing "I'd Rather Love You," each song for three weeks at the top. Conway Twitty and Loretta Lynn teamed up for the hit "After the Fire Is Gone."

**Popular Culture: July 1971 - June 1972**

**On television:**

The fall lineup of programming included the premieres of several programs, including *The Sonny & Cher Comedy Hour, Columbo, McMillian & Wife*, and *The New Dick Van Dyke Show. Soul Train* began its 35-year run as a showcase for R&B, soul, and hip hop artists; and, PBS debuted *The Electric Company* to help develop reading skills.

**At the movies:**
*Carnal Knowledge*, starring Jack Nicholson, Art Garfunkel, Candice Bergen, and Ann Margaret, pressed the sensibilities of American society. The movie received nominations and awards from critics; but, in some communities, copies of the film were seized and theater proprietors were convicted of distributing obscene materials. During the fall, theaters welcomed a string of new releases including *The French Connection*, starring Gene Hackman (Oscar, Best Actor) and *The Last Picture Show*, starring Cybill Shepherd in an early role. *Fiddler On the Roof*, released in November dominated the box office that year, but December welcomed *Diamonds Are Forever*, the sixth James Bond movie, and made with the return of Sean Connery. *A Clockwork Orange* shocked audiences with its violence, and the satire of *The Hospital* taught consumers of healthcare to be more skeptical of the medical-business complex. *Dirty Harry*, starring Clint Eastwood, delighted American audiences with a new "cowboy cop" hero.

The year 1972 soon saw the release of a film adaptation of the Broadway musical *Cabaret* starring Liza Minnelli (Oscar, Best Actress). *The Godfather* dominated the box office, but *What's Up, Doc?* starring Barbra Streisand and Ryan O'Neal was popular. As a sign of the times, explicit sexuality was featured in two particular films in the spring, *Felix the Cat*, an animated X-rated movie, and *Deep Throat*, whose title thus entered the lexicon of popular culture.

**On the radio:**
The early summer was filled with the driving beat of Paul Revere and the Raiders pounding out "Indian Reservation." That contrasted with James Taylor singing "You've Got a Friend." The Bee Gees, of later disco fame, dominated the chart for four weeks with "How Can You Mend a Broken Heart." Paul and Linda McCartney sang "Uncle Albert/Admiral Halsey." Donny Osmond had a hit for three weeks with "Go Away Little Girl," but Rod Stewart captured the spot for five weeks with "Maggie May" and "Reason to Believe." Cher, singing solo, released "Gypsies, Tramps, and Thieves." Isaac Hayes' "Theme from Shaft" and "Family Affair" by Sly and the Family stone kept the top spot wrapped up for five weeks through

Christmas.

Melanie held the top spot for three weeks into 1972 with "Brand New Key" before Don McLean dominated for a month with "American Pie." Al Green and Neil Young captured the #1 spot for a week each with "Let's Stay Together" and "Heart of Gold," respectively. Nilsson dominated for four weeks with "Without You." America held the top spot for three weeks with "A Horse with No Name" before Robert Flack dominated the chart for six weeks with "The First Time Ever I Saw Your Face." The Chi-Lites sang "Oh Girl" a top spot song for one week as was "I'll Take You There" by the Staple Singers. Sammy Davis, Jr. rolled to the top for three weeks with "Candy Man."

Charley Pride's "I'm Just Me" topped the country charts for four weeks followed by five weeks of Tammy Wynette singing "Good Lovin'(Makes It Right)" and "Easy Loving" by Freddie Hart. Tom T. Hall followed with "The Year Clayton Delaney Died." Charley Pride finished the year with a chart topper for five weeks, "Kiss an Angel Good Mornin'."

Merle Haggard had a three week hit with "Carolyn" and Loretta Lynn sang "One's on the Way." But, Freddie Hart's hit, "My Hang Up Is You," dominated the chart's top spot for six weeks, only to be replaced by Jerry Lee Lewis singing "Chantilly Lace." Merle Haggard sang "Grandma Harp" and Conway Twitty sang "(Lost Her Love) On Our Last Date." Donna Fargo commanded the #1 spot for three weeks with "The Happiest Girl in the Whole U.S.A.," the year's top song. Sonny James sang "That's Why I Love You Like I Do."

In March, California Gov. Ronald Reagan pardoned Merle Haggard for a conviction in a 1957 robbery. In June, the Opryland USA theme park opened in Nashville, Tennessee.

**Popular Culture: July 1972 - June 1973**

**On television:**
A presidential campaign was under way during the summer and fall,

but a public eager to escape from politics had a number of choices among the new shows introduced in the fall. They included *Maude, The Waltons*, and *The Bob Newhart Show* as well as *The (New) Price Is Right*. Other shows including *M.A.S.H., Kung Fu*, and *The Streets of San Francisco* debuted, too. *Great Performances* began its decades-long and continuing run on PBS.

In January, Elvis Presley's concert *Aloha From Hawaii-Via Satellite* was beamed to 40 countries and an audience of 1 billion. Because the historic event coincided with Super Bowl VII, it was not seen in the U.S. until April.

*School House Rock* and *Barnaby Jones* premiered in January. *Police Story* and *The Young and the Restless* debuted in March. From May 17 to August 7, the Watergate Hearings pre-empted daytime television programming with each of the three networks taking a day in rotation.

**At the movies:**

The unusual perils of an outdoor adventure were suggested in the drama *Deliverance*, starring Burt Reynolds and Jon Voight. Woody Allen teased the public's inquisitive nature with the comedy *Everything You Always Wanted To Now About Sex (But Were Afraid to Ask). Sounder*, starring Cicely Tyson, and *Lady Sings the Blues*, the biographical drama of the life of singer Billie Hollday played by Diana Ross, opened in the fall. At year's end, *The Poseidon Adventure, The Getaway*, and *Jeremiah Johnson*, starring Robert Redford made their appearances. The controversial and X-rated *Last Tango in Paris,* starring Marlin Brando, was released in December as well.

In February, *Walking Tall* starring Joe Don Baker as Sheriff Buford Pusser was a surprise hit. In May, *Paper Moon*, starred father-daughter pair, Ryan and Tatum O'Neal. In late June, the eighth James Bond movie, *Live and Let Die,* and starring Roger Moore, opened in theaters.

**On the radio:**

Neil Diamond had a hit with "Song Sung Blue" and Bill Withers dominated for three weeks with "Lean On Me." Gilbert O'Sullivan topped the charts with "Alone Again (Naturally)" for six weeks, though that run was interrupted for a week by "Brandy (You're a Fine Girl)" by Looking Glass. Mac Davis sang "Baby, Don't Get Hooked on Me" at #1 for three weeks and Michael Jackson with "Ben" and Three Dog Night with "Black and White" each held the top spot. Chuck Berry sang "My Ding-a-Ling" and Johnny Nash took honors for a month with "I Can See Clearly Now." "Papa Was a Rollin' Stone" by The Temptations and Billy Paul singing "Me and Mrs. Jones" reached the top spot by year end.

Carly Simon rode a wave of approval for "You're So Vain" for three weeks as did "Crocodile Rock" by Elton John. Stevie Wonder sang "Superstition" at #1 between those two. Roberta Flack returned to the top with "Killing Me Softly With His Song" for five weeks, with "Love Train" by The O'Jays stealing it for a week. The spring was alive with "The Night the Lights Went Out in Georgia" by Vicky Lawrence and Dawn Featuring Tony Orlando had a huge hit with "Tie a Yellow Ribbon Round the Ole Oak Tree" for four weeks. That was followed by another Stevie Wonder hit, "You Are the Sunshine of My Life." The Edgar Winter Group took the top spot with "Frankenstein," followed by "My Love" by Paul McCartney and Wings for four weeks and "Give Me Love (Give Me Peace on Earth)" by George Harrison for a week.

On the country charts, Hank Williams, Jr. sang "Eleven Roses," and Charley Pride sang "It's Gonna Take a Little Bit Longer." Mel Tillis claimed the top spot for two weeks with "I Ain't Never" and Donna Fargo did the same for three weeks with "Funny Face." "It's Not Love (But It's Not Bad)" by Merle Haggard and Tammy Wynette with "My Man (Understands)" were chart toppers.

That October, Loretta Lynn became the first woman to win the CMA's Entertainer of the Year Award.

Charlie Rich hit the #1 spot for the first time with "Behind Closed Doors" and Jeanne Pruett commanded the top spot for three weeks with "Satin Sheets." Other songs during the winter and spring were "(Old Dogs, Children And) Watermelon Wine" by Tom T. Hall and

"I Wonder If They Ever Think of Me" by Merle Haggard.

**Popular Culture: July 1973 – August 1974**

**On television:**
The game show *Match Game* premiered in July and in November *A Charlie Brown Thanksgiving* aired for the first time. The new fall shows of note included *Kojak* with Telly Savalas and *The Six Million Dollar Man* starring Lee Majors.

*Happy Days* debuted on January 15 and ran for 10 years, spawning eight spin-offs. In January, Cicely Tyson starred in the Emmy-winning production of *The Autobiography of Miss Jane Pittman.* In March, audiences watched the made-for-TV film, *The Execution of Private Slovik.*

On August 9, networks carried the live resignation of President Richard Nixon.

**At the movies:**
The late summer screen hits included *Enter the Dragon* starring Brue Lee, who had died shortly before its release. The film version of the Broadway hit *Jesus Christ Superstar* hit theaters in August as did *American Graffiti.* During the fall, *The Way We Were* starring Barbra Streisand and Robert Redford dominated the box office. Disney released the animated *Robin Hood* with celebrity voice talent in November. December saw the release of several movies: *Serpico, Papillon, The Exorcist*, *Magnum Force*, and *The Sting*, starring Robert Redford and Paul Newman.

*Blazing Saddles*, a western comedy, was the surprise hit movie of the spring of 1974. *The Great Gatsby* was released in March, followed in June by *Chinatown*, starring Jack Nicholson. A compilation movie, *That's Entertainment,* was released to celebrate the 50th anniversary of MGM; it featured Frank Sinatra, Bing Crosby, Fred Astaire, and Gene Kelly. *Death Wish* starring Charles Bronson was released in July 1974.

**On the radio:**
The summer of 1973 began with Billy Preston singing "Will It Go Round in Circles" and Jim Croce singing "Bad, Bad Leroy Brown." Maureen McGovern captured the top spot for two weeks with "The Morning After" followed by Diana Ross's "Touch Me in the Morning." Stories captured the #1 spot for two weeks with "Brother Louie" and Marvin Gaye captured two weeks with "Let's Get It On" separated by one week dominated by Helen Reddy singing "Delta Dawn." Grand Funk (Railroad) pumped out "We're an American Band" and The Rolling Stones sang "Angie." Cher captured the top spot for two weeks with "Half Breed." Gladys Knight and the Pips topped the charts for two weeks with "Midnight Train to Georgia" and Eddie Kendricks did the same with "Keep On Truckin' (Part 1)." Ringo Starr sang "Photograph" and The Carpenters delivered with "Top of the World" for two weeks. Charlie Rich was at the top spot for two weeks with "The Most Beautiful Girl." The old year finished and the new year began with Jim Croce singing "Time in a Bottle," at the top for two weeks. (Croce had died in a plane crash in September.)

The Steve Miller Band sang "The Joker," Al Wilson sang "Show and Tell," and Ringo Starr sang "You're Sixteen." Barbra Streisand topped the charts for three weeks with "The Way We Were" interrupted for a week by "Love's Theme" by Love Unlimited Orchestra. Terry Jacks topped the chart for three weeks with "Seasons in the Sun." March and April saw a string of one-week chart toppers: "Dark Lady" by Cher, "Sunshine on My Shoulders" by John Denver, "Hooked on a Feeling" by Blue Swede, and "Bennie and the Jets" by Elton John. "The Sound of Philadelphia" (the theme for *Soul Train*) by Mother Father Sister Brother charted at the top for two weeks. Grand Funk (Railroad) returned to the top for two weeks with "The Loco-Motion" until Ray Stevens captured the mood of the country with "The Streak," at the top for three weeks. Paul McCartney and Wings sang "Band on the Run" and Bo Donaldson and The Heywoods topped the chart for two weeks with "Billy Don't Be a Hero." Gordon Lightfoot sang "Sundown."

Into the summer of 1974, Hues Corporation sang "Rock the Boat" and George McCrae sang "Rock Your Baby." For the two weeks leading into August, John Denver dominated with "Annie's Song."

On the country charts, Kris Kristofferson sang "Why Me." Loretta Lynn topped the chart for two weeks with "Love Is a Fountain" and Merle Haggard did the same with "Everybody's Had the Blues." Conway Twitty dominated for three weeks with "You've Never Been This Far Before," the #1 song of the year. Johnny Rodriguez returned to the top for two weeks with "Ridin' My Thumb to Mexico." George Jones and Tammy Wynette doubled up on "We're Gonna Hold On." Marie Osmond took the top spot for two weeks with "Paper Roses" and Charlie Rich captured #1 for three weeks with "The Most Beautiful Girl." Charley Pride had a hit with "Amazing Love" followed by a four-week run at #1 by Merle Haggard with "If We Make It Through December." In 1974, Tom T. Hall sang "I Love," at the top for two weeks and Dolly Parton hit #1 with "Jolene."

On March 16, 1974, The Grand Ole Opry moved from the Ryman Auditorium after 41 years. President Richard Nixon attended the last Opry show at the Ryman.

Conway Twitty performed "There's a Honky Tonk Angel (Who'll Take Me Back In)." Tanya Tucker sang "Would You Lay with Me (In a Field of Stone)" and Charlie Rich topped the chart for three weeks with "A Very Special Love Song." Dolly Parton sang "I Will Always Love You."

Whether prophetic of the coming resignation of President Nixon or not, into the summer of 1974 Donna Fargo performed "You Can't Be a Beacon If Your Light Don't Shine." That was followed during the first full week of August 1974 by Billy "Crash" Craddock singing "Rub It In."

And the world turned.

# Acknowledgements

I could not possibly have compiled this book without the help of many others. I did not live in North Carolina during the time of the Daniel Boone Wagon Train, but I met and listened to a few people who recalled that event clearly and were interested in helping me bring that story back into the public's awareness. I am grateful to those individuals and to others who helped me track down photographs or who directed me toward other possible sources of information. Each has helped to enrich the story by his or her efforts and I thank all for their kindness and assistance to me and for their enabling this story to be told much better than it could have been otherwise. Any failings or shortcomings, however, and all errors are mine and mine alone.

I wish to thank (in alphabetic order):
Edith Ferguson Carter for her keen memory of events and for her collection of newspaper clippings diligently kept for five decades; recognizing her family's willingness to host the event in 1963 and 1964 and champion it afterward; and for her father, Tom Ferguson, and his thorough columns and artistic writing about the Upper Yadkin River

Chris Crooks, son of Leroy Crooks, for stories about filming the Daniel Boone Wagon Train and photos from Nagagamasisis Lake.

Brian Fannon, doctoral candidate and dedicated reenactor, for sharing his knowledge and insights about the original trails through and the history of Watauga County, North Carolina;

Marcus Green for permission to reprint images from the *Winston-Salem Journal.*

Terry and Suzanne Hamilton for their enthusiasm for the project, recollections of the event, and comments on a few early chapters;

Jule Hubbard for permission to reprint images from the *Wilkes Journal-Patriot* and for locating two high-quality images;

Betty Greene Koontz for sharing her newspaper clippings, DBWT ribbons, and recollections of Clyde Greene, her father, and his involvement as the originator of the wagon train in 1963;

Dr. H.G. Jones for his willingness to read the manuscript and to write a foreword for a book that reached back into his early career as a historian for the State of North Carolina and to his undergraduate alma mater, Appalachian State Teachers College;

Tom Mayer for permission to reprint images from *Watauga Democrat*;

Dudley Moore for his willingness to share recollections of his father, Ivey Moore, and as well as family photos and memorabilia and his own accounts of his boyhood in North Wilkesboro;

Molly Grogan Rawls, Forsyth County Public Library Photography Collection, for her interest in this project and for searching her archives to provide images for use;

Harry C. Steele, a neighbor and a native of North Wilkesboro, who knew the story and helped me locate Dudley Moore to interview; and,

Janet Wooten, eagle-eyed proof reader and champion of proper usage.

I wish to thank the archivists at the Division of Archives and History in Raleigh and at the Outer Banks History Center for their help in locating records for the Carolina Charter Tercentenary Commission. I wish to thank the library staff for access to and assistance with newspaper and other archives at the Carolina Room, Forsyth County Public Library; Wilkes County Public Library; Watauga County Public Library; Caldwell County Public Library, and, the Pardue Library, Wilkes Community College.

I want to thank all the newspaper reporters and photographers of that day who made the professional effort to capture in words and pictures the images that help us all appreciate today the experience of being on the Daniel Boone Wagon Train. I have credited the reporters for their writing and when the information was available, I have credited the photographers for their work as well.

I also wish to thank the people who went on the Daniel Boone Wagon Train—some for many years and some also from far away—as a way of honoring the legacy of America's pioneer hero, Daniel Boone, here in North Carolina. It is through their individual and collective efforts to honor history that they created history of their own. It is to all the participants of the Daniel Boone Wagon Train from 1963 to 1973 that this book is truly dedicated.

Congratulations with sincere appreciation to you all.

## Reaching Across Time

White House Photo, National Archives

President Richard Nixon and Elvis Presley
meet in the White House
December 21, 1970.

# Notes

**Chapter 1 - Wagons, Ho!**

[1] Having debuted in September 1957, Wagon Train was the #1 TV series in 1961-62 season. (http://en.wikipedia.org/wiki/Wagon_Train)

[2] Wagon Train (1957-1965). TV series starring Ward Bond, who died midseries in 1960. http://www.imdb.com/title/tt0050073/

**Chapter 2 - DBWT, 1963**

[1] Interview with Edith Ferguson Carter at Whippoorwill Academy, Ferguson, NC, July 14, 2011.

[2] Thompson, Roy, "New Pioneers on Old Trail" (Winston-Salem, NC: Winston-Salem Journal, June 26, 1963), p. 7

[3] Jesse Poindexter, "Wagon Train Still Going—While Officers Direct Traffic" (Winston-Salem, NC: Winston-Salem Journal, July 2, 1964)

[4] Oxen and steers are basically the same; both are castrated males. Steers are raised for meat. Oxen are raised as draught animals. Some cows have been used as draught animals, too.

[5] Some will argue origins from the Dutch word "heiweg" from the 10th century, meaning a path through the moors. The sense of staying on the high ground would still apply.

[6] The Boone family may have taken the route followed by the wagon-trainers in 1963, but that route would have been too steep for Boone's horses. That climb up Sampson's Mountain to Cook's Gap was the route Boone probably took when he was on foot. When he was mounted, he most likely took another path through Watauga County, one that later became known as the Buffalo Trail. It was the oldest wagon route through Watauga County passing from Deep Gap to Rich Gap and on the way passing by Meat Camp, the site where Boone and other long hunters reportedly hung the meat they had shot. However, Brian Fannon, historian, reenactor, and doctoral candidate, offers another possibility as the source of that name, Meat Camp. On one early map he found the name Neat Camp. He admits it could be a mapmaker's error, but the term "neat" is an old English word for cow. (Neat's Foot oil is made by boiling cow hooves to remove the organic oil which then floats to the surface for skimming.) The name Neat Camp would simply refer to a cow camp, a place for the herders who tended to the cattle pastured on the Blue Ridge. Benjamin Howard, for whom Howard' Knob is named, was a well-known cattleman in the area when Boone was hunting. It was Howard's enslaved man, Burrell, who told Daniel Boone about the route through the Blue Ridge Mountains to the Holston Valley by way of today's Mountain City, TN, and Damascus, VA. Although the original name could have been Neat Camp and not Meat Camp, the latter name has stuck in the public's consciousness and as well to the maps that have been created.

[7] Much of the emphasis that comes today on historical accuracy in reenactment came after the 1976 Bicentennial when many people realized they had been relying on Hollywood to define the dress and manner of entire era's of American history. An even greater emphasis on research and authenticity has come about since the formation in 1999 of the National Rendezvous and Living History Foundation, Inc., www.nrlhf.org.

[8] Roy Thompson, "Oxen Ready for Slow Trip" (Winston-Salem, NC: Winston-Salem Journal, June 27, 1963)

[9] Larry Penley, "Final Wagon Train Plans Made; To Camp at Darby," (Boone, NC: Watauga

Democrat, June 27, 1963), p. 1
[10] Roy Thompson, "Old Dan'l Had Problems, But Not Like This…" (Winston-Salem, NC: Winston-Salem Journal, June 28, 1963)
[11] "Boone Wagon Train Completes 3-Day Trip," (Wilkesboro, NC: Journal-Patriot, July 1, 1963)
[12] Ibid.
[13] Roy Thompson, "Old Dan'l Had Problems, But Not Like This…" (Winston-Salem, NC: Winston-Salem Journal, June 28, 1963)
[14] "Boone Wagon Train Completes 3-Day Trip," (Wilkesboro, NC: Journal-Patriot, July 1, 1963)
[15] Roy Thompson, "Old Dan'l Had Problems, But Not Like This…" (Winston-Salem, NC: Winston-Salem Journal, June 28, 1963)
[16] Edith Carter interview
[17] "Wagon Train Begins Blue Ridge Journey," (North Wilkesboro, NC: Journal-Patriot, June 27, 1963)
[18] T.W. Ferguson, "News from Ferguson," (North Wilkesboro, NC: Journal-Patriot, July 4, 1963)
[19] Boone Wagon Train Completes 3-Day Trip," (Wilkesboro, NC: Journal-Patriot, July 1, 1963)
[20] Nancy Alexander, "Ancestor of Wagon Train Scout Left Priceless Weapons," (Boone, NC: Watauga Democrat, July 11, 1963)
[21] "Final Wagon Train Plans Made; To Camp at Darby," (Boone, NC: Watauga Democrat, June 27, 1963)
[22] Boone Wagon Train Completes 3-Day Trip," (Wilkesboro, NC: Journal-Patriot, July 1, 1963)
[23] Boone Wagon Train Completes 3-Day Trip," (Wilkesboro, NC: Journal-Patriot, July 1, 1963)
[24] Boone Wagon Train Completes 3-Day Trip," (Wilkesboro, NC: Journal-Patriot, July 1, 1963)
[25] Edith Carter interview
[26] T.W. Ferguson, "News from Ferguson," (North Wilkesboro, NC: Journal-Patriot, July 4, 1963)
[27] Thompson, Roy, "Boone-Bound Wagon Train on Last Weary Leg" (Winston-Salem, NC: Winston-Salem Journal, June 29, 1963)
[28] T.W. Ferguson, "News from Ferguson," (North Wilkesboro, NC: Journal-Patriot, July 4, 1963)
[29] "Daniel Boone Crosses the Blue Ridge Official Program," (Boone, NC: Watauga Democrat, June 27, 1963), p. 1
[30] Final Wagon Train Plans Made; To Camp at Darby," (Boone, NC: Watauga Democrat, June 27, 1963)
[31] Roy Thompson, "Wagon Train Welcomed to Boone" (Winston-Salem, NC: Winston-Salem Journal, June 30, 1963)
[32] Ibid.
[33] Dale Gaddy, "Parade Covered Wagons Draws Throngs to City," (Boone, NC: Watauga Democrat, July 4, 1963)
[34] "Secretary Hodges Sponsored Celebration As Governor," (Boone, NC: Watauga Democrat, July 4, 1963)
[35] "Secretary Hodges Sponsored Celebration As Governor," (Boone, NC: Watauga Democrat, July 4, 1963)
[36] "New York Taxi Drivers on Goodwill Tour to Boone Saturday," (Boone, NC: Watauga Democrat, June 27, 1963)
[37] "Daniel Boone Gardens To Be Dedicated During Observance," (Boone, NC: Watauga Democrat, June 27, 1963)
[38] "Daniel Boone Gardens To Be Dedicated During Observance," (Boone, NC: Watauga Democrat, June 27, 1963)
[39] R.C. Rivers, Jr., editor, "It Was A Big Day," (Boone, NC: Watauga Democrat, July 4, 1963)
[40] Carolina Charter Tercentenary Commission, "Commemorative Events – Watauga County," (Raleigh, NC: Tercentenary News, July 1963), p. 5

**Chapter 3 - Carolina Charter Tercentenary**
[1] McLennan, S. (2012, January 18). Jamestown 350th Anniversary, 1957. Retrieved October 15, 2012, from *Encyclopedia Virginia*: http://www.EncyclopediaVirginia.org/Jamestown_350th_Anniversary_1957
[2] John Filson, *The Adventures of Colonel Daniel Boon*, 1784
[3] Francis E. Winslow, "Report of the Carolina Charter Tercentenary Commission," (Raleigh, NC: State Dept. of Archives and History, Dec. 31, 1963)
[4] "'Curly' Wilcox Is Untiring Man Behind Wagon Train Promotion," (Boone, NC: *Watauga Democrat*, June 27, 1963)
[5] 1963 Wagon Train Committee:
General Chairman – Herman W. Wilcox
Finance Chairman – Alfred T. Adams
Invitation of Guests – Dr. D.J. Whitener
Parade – Robert Brietenstein
Publicity – Larry Penley
Decoration – Jack Williams
Traffic – W.R. Winkler
Transportation – Glenn Andrews
ASTC 60th Anniversary – Herman R. Eggers
Dedication Daniel Boone Botanical Gardens – Mrs. H.W. Stallings
Entertainment – James Marsh, Grady Farthing
Wagon Train – Clyde R. Greene
Music – Wade E. Brown
Reservations – Miss Laura Foster, Mrs. Rachel Klutz, Mrs. Georgia Matheson
Special Events – Jack Groce
Golf Tournament – Joe Maples
Picnic and Banquets – Stanley A. Harris
*Watauga Democrat* 75th Anniversary – R.C. Rivers, Jr.
Costumes – Mrs. Boyce Brooks
[6] "Ivey Moore Chief Scout Wagon Train," (North Wilkesboro, NC: *Wilkes Journal-Patriot*, undated clipping, 1963)
[7] "Boone Wagon Train Forming for Three-Day Trek," (Carolina Charter Tercentenary Commission, *Tercentenary News*, May 1963)
[8] Larry Penley, "Press Release of Parade Committee," April 8, 1963, (Carolina Charter Tercentenary Commission, 1960-1963, Committee on Commemorative Events, N.C. State Archives)

**Chapter 4 - DBWT, 1964**
[1] Daniel J. Whitener, "Daniel Boone Wagon Train Crosses the Blue Ridge," The Daniel Boone Wagon Train souvenir program, (Boone, NC: unknown publisher, 1964), p. 1
[2] "North Carolina Youngsters Write Essays To Enhance Boone Legend," (Boone, NC: Watauga Democrat, July 2, 1964)
[3] "Library Memorial Is Planned In Memory of Dr. Whitener," (Boone, NC: Watauga Democrat, July 2, 1964)
[4] Ibid.
[5] "They Had A Whiskey Wagon in the Original Wagon Train." (Boone, NC: Watauga Democrat, July 2, 1964)
[6] Editorial, "Wagon Train—Glimpse into Past," North Wilkesboro, NC: Wilkes Patriot-Journal, June 25, 1964), p.4
[7] "Authentic Music Will Be Heard," (North Wilkesboro, NC: Wilkes Journal-Patriot, June 25, 1964)
[8] Ibid., p.4

[9] "2,000 Chickens Will Be Barbecued Here," (North Wilkesboro, NC: Wilkes Journal-Patriot, June 25, 1964)
[10] "Wagon Train Assembles Here for Trip to Boone," (North Wilkesboro, NC: Wilkes Journal-Patriot, June 29, 1964), p.4
[11] "Pioneer Days Event May Draw Record Crowd," (North Wilkesboro, NC: Wilkes Journal-Patriot, June 25, 1964), p.4
[12] Jesse Poindexter, "Wagon Train Stages Parade, Starts Rolling Westward Today," (Winston-Salem, NC: Winston-Salem Journal, June 30, 1964)
[13] "Wagon Train Assembles Here for Trip to Boone," (North Wilkesboro, NC: Wilkes Journal-Patriot, June 29, 1964), p.1
[14] _____, "Wagon Train Is Assembling To Follow Daniel Boone Trail" (Winston-Salem, NC: Winston-Salem Journal, June 28, 1964)
[15] "Thousands Attend Big Square Dance Here," (North Wilkesboro, NC: Wilkes Journal-Patriot, July 2, 1964), Sec. 3, p.1
[16] Jesse Poindexter, "Wagon Train Stages Parade, Starts Rolling Westward Today," (Winston-Salem, NC: Winston-Salem Journal, June 30, 1964)
[17] Jesse Poindexter, "Wagon Train Stages Parade, Starts Rolling Westward Today," (Winston-Salem, NC: Winston-Salem Journal, June 30, 1964)
[18] Jesse Poindexter, "Wagon Train Still Going—While Officers Direct Traffic" (Winston-Salem, NC: Winston-Salem Journal, July 2, 1964)
[19] See A Guide to the Overmountain Victory National Historic Trail, (Winston-Salem, NC: Daniel Boone Footsteps, 2011), p. 27
[20] Jesse Poindexter, "Westward Ho, Despite Cast" (Winston-Salem, NC: Winston-Salem Journal, July 1, 1964)
[21] "Mile-long Wagon Train Rolls into Watauga Area," (North Wilkesboro, NC: Wilkes Journal-Patriot, July 2, 1964)
[22] "Thousands Visit Wagon Train at Ferguson Site," (North Wilkesboro, NC: Wilkes Journal-Patriot, July 2, 1964), Sec. 2, p.1
[23] Ibid.
[24] Jesse Poindexter, "Wagon Train 'Pioneers' Welcome Visitors" (Winston-Salem, NC: Winston-Salem Journal, July 3, 1964)
[25] "Thousands Throng To Camp Site at Darby," (North Wilkesboro, NC: Wilkes Journal-Patriot, July 2, 1964), p.8
[26] Ibid.
[27] Ibid.
[28] Jesse Poindexter, "Wagon Train 'Pioneers' Welcome Visitors" (Winston-Salem, NC: Winston-Salem Journal, July 3, 1964)
[29] Jesse Poindexter, "Wagons Reach Trail's End" (Winston-Salem, NC: Winston-Salem Journal, July 4, 1964)
[30] Jesse Poindexter, "Wagon Train Highlights Rainy Celebration in Boone" (Winston-Salem, NC: Winston-Salem Journal, July 5, 1964)
[31] Jesse Poindexter, "Wagons Reach Trail's End" (Winston-Salem, NC: Winston-Salem Journal, July 4, 1964)
[32] "New Marker Marks Original Trail of Boone Thru Watauga," (Boone, NC: Watauga Democrat, June 25, 1964)
[33] "Wagon Train Leaders Choose Valley Near Horn for Camp," (Boone, NC: Watauga Democrat, July 2, 1964)
[34] "Costume Contest Set for Thursday, Friday," (Boone, NC: Watauga Democrat, July 2, 1964)
[35] Jesse Poindexter, "Wagon Train Highlights Rainy Celebration in Boone" (Winston-Salem, NC: Winston-Salem Journal, July 5, 1964)
[36] "Hot Time in Old Town Seen For Wagon Train," (Boone, NC: Watauga Democrat, July 2, 1964)
[37] Rachel Rivers, "Parade—the Crowning Point," (Boone, NC: Watauga Democrat, July 9, 1964)

[38] Jesse Poindexter, "Wagon Train Highlights Rainy Celebration in Boone" (Winston-Salem, NC: Winston-Salem Journal, July 5, 1964)
[39] Livingston Taylor, "House Calls 'Boone' Show 'Insult to Intelligence,'" (Louisville, KY: Courier Journal, March 3, 1966), p. A1
[40] http://en.wikipedia.org/wiki/Daniel_Boone_(TV_series)

**Chapter 5 - Chief Scout Ivey Moore**
[1] Dudley Moore, interview by author, High Point, NC, Oct. 18, 2011
[2] Ivey Moore, taped interview, Wilkes Community College Library, 1974; transcribed by author, Nov. 30, 2011
[3] "Three Known Dead in Wilkes; Property Loss $5,000,000; Number Homeless and Jobless," (North Wilkesboro, NC: *Wilkes Journal-Patriot*, Aug. 15, 1940)
[4] "Three Known Dead in Wilkes; Property Loss $5,000,000; Number Homeless and Jobless," (North Wilkesboro, NC: *Wilkes Journal-Patriot*, Aug. 15, 1940)
[5] Interview with Harry Steele, a young resident of North Wilkesboro at the time of the flood, 2011.
[6] Ivey Moore, taped interview, Wilkes Community College Library, 1974; transcribed by author, Nov. 30, 2011
[7] Ivey Moore, taped interview, Wilkes Community College Library, 1974; transcribed by author, Nov. 30, 2011
[8] Ivey Moore, taped interview, Wilkes Community College Library, 1974; transcribed by author, Nov. 30, 2011
[9] Ivey Moore, taped interview, Wilkes Community College Library, 1974; transcribed by author, Nov. 30, 2011
[10] Dudley Moore, interview by author, High Point, NC, Oct. 18, 2011
[11] "Bicentennial Kickoff Will Be on April 10, Moore and Party of Eight Set To Walk Boone Trail," (*Wilkes Journal-Patriot*, April 3, 1975)
[12] Jeanne Moore (daughter), handwritten biography of Ivey Moore, (provided by Dudley Moore), 1984
[13] Jeanne Moore (daughter), handwritten biography of Ivey Moore, (provided by Dudley Moore), 1984
[14] Jeanne Moore (daughter), handwritten biography of Ivey Moore, (provided by Dudley Moore), 1984
[15] Dudley Moore, interview by author, High Point, NC, Oct. 18, 2011

**Chapter 6 - DBWT, 1965**
[1] Editorial,"Daniel Boone Wagon Train," (North Wilkesboro, NC: Journal Patriot, June 28, 1965). p. 4
[2] "Dula's Grave On Route of Unique Wagon Train," (Boone, NC: Watauga Democrat, July 15, 1965)
[3] In error, the reporter continually wrote "Hiawassee Lodge."
[4] "Wagon Train Ready to Roll," (North Wilkesboro, NC: Journal Patriot, June 28, 1965), p.1; reporter names "Hiawassee Lodge." The local OA lodge is actually "Wahissa."
[5] "Boone Train Heads Out On Daniel's Trail," (North Wilkesboro, NC: Journal Patriot, July 1, 1965), Sec. 2, p. 1
[6] "Boone Train Heads Out On Daniel's Trail," (North Wilkesboro, NC: Journal Patriot, July 1, 1965), Sec. 2, p. 1
[7] Joe Goodman later became the managing editor of the Winston-Salem Journal.
[8] Joe Goodman, "Days Are Long, Night Short On Wagon Train Caravan" (Winston-Salem, NC: Winston-Salem Journal, June 30, 1965)
9 The author is an Eagle Scout, 1965, Chickasaw Council, Memphis, TN, and was inducted into the Order of the Arrow.
[10] Goodman, WSJ, June 30, '65

[11] Joe Goodman, "Taste of Bygone Days" (Winston-Salem, NC: Winston-Salem Journal, June 29, 1965)
[12] Goodman, WSJ, June 29, '65
[13] T.W. Ferguson, "News of Ferguson," (North Wilkesboro, NC: Journal-Patriot, July 1, 1965), p. 5
[14] Joe Goodman, "Stream Ends Wagon Train's Woes" (Winston-Salem, NC: Winston-Salem Journal, July 1, 1965)
[15] Goodman, WSJ, July 1, '65
[16] Ibid.
[17] Ibid.
[18] Goodman reported crowds of 3,000 to 4,000. The Journal-Patriot reported 12,000 at Ferguson and 10,000 at Darby. "Thousands Flock to Wagon Train at Overnight Camp," (North Wilkesboro, NC: Journal-Patriot, July 1, 1965)
[19] Joe Goodman, "Campsite is Scene of Hoedown" Winston-Salem, NC: Winston-Salem Journal, July 2, 1965)
[20] "Thousands Flock to Wagon Train at Overnight Camp," (North Wilkesboro, NC: Journal-Patriot, July 1, 1965)
[21] Goodman, WSJ, July 2, '65
[22] Joe Goodman, "Hot Dogs Signal Civilization as Wagon Trek Hits Boone" Winston-Salem, NC: Winston-Salem Journal, July 3, 1965)
[23] Goodman, WSJ, July 2, '65
[24] Joe Goodman, "Hot Dogs Signal Civilization as Wagon Trek Hits Boone" (Winston-Salem, NC: Winston-Salem Journal, July 3, 1965)
[25] Ibid.
[26] "Wagon Train Parade To Stretch Mile Down King Street Saturday," (Boone, NC: Watauga Democrat, July 1, 1965)
[27] "Miller Family and 19 Children Will Head Wagon Train Parade," (Boone, NC: Watauga Democrat, July 1, 1965)
[28] "Wagon Train Parade To Stretch Mile Down King Street Saturday," (Boone, NC: Watauga Democrat, July 1, 1965)
[29] Joe Goodman, "Hot Dogs Signal Civilization as Wagon Trek Hits Boone" (Winston-Salem, NC: Winston-Salem Journal, July 3, 1965)
[30] "Miller Family and 19 Children Will Head Wagon Train Parade," (Boone, NC: Watauga Democrat, July 1, 1965)
[31] "Dula's Grave On Route of Unique Wagon Train," (Boone, NC: Watauga Democrat, July 15, 1965)
[32] "I Raised My Hand To Volunteer, Students Protest in 1960s Chapel Hill," Part 2: Speaker Ban Controversy, UNC University Library, <http://www.lib.unc.edu/mss/exhibits/protests/ban.html>, (accessed Dec. 23, 2012)

**Chapter 7 - DBWT, 1966**

[1] "Chief Wagon Train Scout Is Enthusiastic about '66 Trip," (Boone, NC: *Watauga Democrat*, May 19, 1966)
[2] Herman Wilcox, "Screen Star Parker Father of Year; Will Visit "Horn," (Boone, NC: *Watauga Democrat*, June 2, 1966); One unconfirmed account suggests that Wilcox actually "hijacked" Parker for his appearances at *Horn in the West* as Parker had actually contracted to appear at Tweetsie Railroad.
[3] "Record Number Attractions Lure Visitors to High Country," (Boone, NC: *Watauga Democrat*, June 16, 1966)
[4] Farnum Gray, "Wagon Train Hits the Trail" (Winston-Salem, NC: *Winston-Salem Journal*, June 28, 1966)
*Wilkes Journal-Patriot* reported Moore's count as 69 wagons and 202 riders and his estimate as 100 wagons and 300 horseback riders. June 27, 1966.

[5] Farnum Gray, "It's Boone or Bust: Wagon Train Hits the Trail," (Winston-Salem, NC: *Winston-Salem Journal*, June 28, 1966)
[6] "Thousands View Train in Down Town Parade," (North Wilkesboro, NC: *Wilkes Journal-Patriot*, June 30, 1966); It is doubtful that the train was moving at 4 mph if folks were walking in a parade. The reporter may have noted the time incorrectly or over-estimated the length of the wagon train.
[7] Farnum Gray, "Wagon Train Hits the Trail" (Winston-Salem, NC: *Winston-Salem Journal*, June 28, 1966)
[8] Farnum Gray, "Wagon Train Hits the Trail" (Winston-Salem, NC: *Winston-Salem Journal*, June 28, 1966)
[9] "Thousands View Train in Down Town Parade," (North Wilkesboro, NC: *Wilkes Journal-Patriot*, June 30, 1966)
[10] Editorial, "The Wagon Train and History," (North Wilkesboro, NC: *Wilkes Journal-Patriot*, June 27, 1966)
[11] Farnum Gray, "Wagon Train Hits the Trail" (Winston-Salem, NC: *Winston-Salem Journal*, June 28, 1966)
[12] Farnum Gray, "Old-time Style of Train Favored," (Winston-Salem, NC: *Winston-Salem Journal*, June 29, 1966)
[13] Farnum Gray, "Old Time Style of Train Favored" (Winston-Salem, NC: *Winston-Salem Journal*, June 29, 1966)
[14] Farnum Gray, "Old Time Style of Train Favored" (Winston-Salem, NC: *Winston-Salem Journal*, June 29, 1966)
[15] Farnum Gray, "Old Time Style of Train Favored" (Winston-Salem, NC: *Winston-Salem Journal*, June 29, 1966)
[16] http://en.wikipedia.org/wiki/Hootenanny_(US_TV_Show)
[17] Farnum Gray, "Old Time Style of Train Favored" (Winston-Salem, NC: *Winston-Salem Journal*, June 29, 1966)
[18] Farnum Gray, "Old Time Style of Train Favored" (Winston-Salem, NC: *Winston-Salem Journal*, June 29, 1966)
[19] Farnum Gray, "Old Time Style of Train Favored" (Winston-Salem, NC: *Winston-Salem Journal*, June 29, 1966)
[20] Farnum Gray estimated 10,000. The next day he reported a highway patrol estimate of 18,000 visitors.
[21] "Wagon Train Show Has One Night Stand," (North Wilkesboro, NC: *Wilkes Journal-Patriot*, June 30, 1966)
[22] Farnum Gray, "Four Wagons Leave Train" (Winston-Salem, NC: *Winston-Salem Journal*, June 30, 1966)
[23] "Wagon Train Show Has One Night Stand," (North Wilkesboro, NC: *Wilkes Journal-Patriot*, June 30, 1966)
[24] Farnum Gray, "Four Wagons Leave Train" (Winston-Salem, NC: *Winston-Salem Journal*, June 30, 1966)
[25] "Wagon Train Show Has One Night Stand," (North Wilkesboro, NC: *Wilkes Journal-Patriot*, June 30, 1966)
[26] Farnum Gray, "Covered Wagons Are Given Better Choice of Campsites" (Winston-Salem, NC: *Winston-Salem Journal*, July 1, 1966)
[27] Farnum Gray, "Four Wagons Leave Train" (Winston-Salem, NC: *Winston-Salem Journal*, June 30, 1966)
[28] Ibid.
[29] "Wagons Headed for Triplett: Boone Train in Watauga," (North Wilkesboro, NC: *Wilkes Journal-Patriot*, June 30, 1966)
[30] Farnum Gray, "Covered Wagons Are Given Better Choice of Campsites" (Winston-Salem, NC: *Winston-Salem Journal*, July 1, 1966)
[31] Farnum Gray, "Covered Wagons Are Given Better Choice of Campsites" (Winston-Salem, NC: *Winston-Salem Journal*, July 1, 1966)

[32] Farnum Gray, "Train's Scout Says 'Last Year'" (Winston-Salem, NC: *Winston-Salem Journal*, July 2, 1966)
[33] Rachel Rivers, "Bright, Gay Wagon Train Rattling Along DB's Trail," (Boone, NC: *Watauga Democrat*, June30, 1966)
[34] "Wagon Train Days Focus Attention on Boone Stores," (Boone, NC: *Watauga Democrat*, June 30, 1966)
[35] Rachel Rivers, "Wagons, Teams, Riders Form Mile-Long Parade," (Boone, NC: *Watauga Democrat*, July 7, 1966)
[36] Rachel Rivers, "Bright, Gay Wagon Train Rattling Along DB's Trail," (Boone, NC: *Watauga Democrat*, June30, 1966)
[37] Rachel Rivers, "Wagons, Teams, Riders Form Mile-Long Parade," (Boone, NC: *Watauga Democrat*, July 7, 1966)

**Chapter 8 - DBWT, 1967**

[1] "Scout Just Couldn't Quit," (Winston-Salem, NC: *Winston-Salem Journal*, June 29, 1967)
[2] Martin Howard, "Wagon Train Rolls Out Today," (Winston-Salem, NC: *Winston-Salem Journal*, June 27, 1967)
[3] "Boone Descendants Are Honored Today,"(North Wilkesboro, NC: *Wilkes Journal-Patriot*, June 26, 1967)
[4] "Wagon Train Greeted," (North Wilkesboro, NC: *Wilkes Journal-Patriot*, June 29, 1967) Sec 3, p 1
[5] "Wagon Train Greeted," (North Wilkesboro, NC: *Wilkes Journal-Patriot*, June 29, 1967) Sec 3, p 1
[6] Martin Howard, "Wagon Train Rolls Out Today," (Winston-Salem, NC: *Winston-Salem Journal*, June 27, 1967), p.10
[7] Martin Howard, "Wagon Train Rolls Out Today," (Winston-Salem, NC: *Winston-Salem Journal*, June 27, 1967), p.10
[8] Jeanette Reid, "Wagon Train Is Like County Fair and Old-Time Reunion," (Winston-Salem, NC: *Winston-Salem Journal*, June 30, 1967)
[9] "Boone Descendants Are Honored Today,"(North Wilkesboro, NC: *Wilkes Journal-Patriot*, June 26, 1967)
[10] "Boone Descendants Coming for Train," (North Wilkesboro, NC: *Wilkes Journal-Patriot*, June 22, 1967)
[11] "Boone Descendants Are Honored Today,"(North Wilkesboro, NC: *Wilkes Journal-Patriot*, June 26, 1967)
[12] Rachel Rivers, "Descendant of Boone Is Having Fun on Journey," (Boone, NC: *Watauga Democrat*, June 29, 1967)
[13] Janette Reid, "Wagon Train Makes Good Time First Day," (Winston-Salem, NC: *Winston-Salem Journal*, June 28, 1967) p.24
[14] Jeanette Reid, "Wagon Train Is Like County Fair and Old-Time Reunion," (Winston-Salem, NC: *Winston-Salem Journal*, June 30, 1967)
[15] "Boone Descendants Are Honored Today,"(North Wilkesboro, NC: *Wilkes Journal-Patriot*, June 26, 1967)
[16] Rachel Rivers, "Descendant of Boone Is Having Fun on Journey," (Boone, NC: *Watauga Democrat*, June 29, 1967)
[17] Martin Howard, "Wagon Train Rolls Out Today," (Winston-Salem, NC: *Winston-Salem Journal*, June 27, 1967), p.10
[18] "Wagon Train To Parade Over 100 Wagons Monday," (North Wilkesboro, NC: *Wilkes Journal-Patriot*, June 22, 1967)
[19] "New Train Rule To Stop Trouble," North Wilkesboro, NC: *Wilkes Journal-Patriot*, June 29, 1967), Sec 3, p 1
[20] "New Train Rule To Stop Trouble," North Wilkesboro, NC: *Wilkes Journal-Patriot*, June 29, 1967), Sec 3, p 1

[21] "Wagon Train Greeted," (North Wilkesboro, NC: *Wilkes Journal-Patriot*, June 29, 1967) Sec 3, p 1
[22] "Movies of Wagon Train '66 Will Be Shown in Wilkes," (North Wilkesboro, NC: *Wilkes Journal-Patriot*, June 22, 1967)
[23] "Voice of America To Tell Horn Story Around World," (Boone, NC: *Watauga Democrat*, June 22, 1967)
[24] Martin Howard, "Wagon Train Rolls Out Today," (Winston-Salem, NC: *Winston-Salem Journal*, June 27, 1967), p.10
[25] Janette Reid, "Wagon Train Makes Good Time First Day," (Winston-Salem, NC: *Winston-Salem Journal*, June 28, 1967) p.24
[26] "Huge Square Dance Is Held at Ferguson," (North Wilkesboro, NC: *Wilkes Journal-Patriot*, June 29, 1967)
[27] Janette Reid, "Varied Reasons for Going on Train," (Winston-Salem, NC: *Winston-Salem Journal*, June 29, 1967)
[28] Janette Reid, "Varied Reasons for Going on Train," (Winston-Salem, NC: *Winston-Salem Journal*, June 29, 1967)
[29] Jeanette Reid, "Wagon Train Is Like County Fair and Old-Time Reunion," (Winston-Salem, NC: *Winston-Salem Journal*, June 30, 1967)
[30] "Wagon Train To Parade Over 100 Wagons Monday," (North Wilkesboro, NC: *Wilkes Journal-Patriot*, June 22, 1967)
[31] "Wagon Train on Blue Ridge," (North Wilkesboro, NC: *Wilkes Journal-Patriot*, June 29, 1967)
[32] "Best Train Reaches End of the Trail," (Winston-Salem, NC: *Winston-Salem Journal*, July 1, 1967)
[33] "Wagon Train Parade To Climax Long Trip." (Boone, NC: *Watauga Democrat*, June 29, 1967)
[34] Editorial, "The Wagon Train," (Boone, NC: *Watauga Democrat*, July 6, 1967)
[35] "It's Now Appalachian State University," (Boone, NC: *Watauga Democrat*, July 6, 1967)
[36] "I Raised My Hand To Volunteer, Students Protest in 1960s Chapel Hill," Part 2: Speaker Ban Controversy, UNC University Library, <*http://www.lib.unc.edu/mss/exhibits/protests/ban.html*>, (accessed Dec. 23, 2012)

**Chapter 9 - DBWT, 1968**

[1] "Saturday Is Pioneer Day Here," (North Wilkesboro, NC: *Wilkes Journal-Patriot*, June 20, 1968)
[2] "Thousands See Wagon Train Parade Here Today—100 Wagons in Annual Event," (North Wilkesboro, NC: *Wilkes Journal-Patriot*, June 24, 1968)
[3] "Banks Sponsor Canadian Family on Wagon Train," (North Wilkesboro, NC: *Wilkes Journal-Patriot*, June 24, 1968)
[4] Rachel Rivers, "Last Week's Wagon Train Was Grandest of Them All." (Boone, NC: *Watauga Democrat*, July 4, 1968)
[5] "Thousands See Wagon Train Parade Here Today—100 Wagons in Annual Event," (North Wilkesboro, NC: *Wilkes Journal-Patriot*, June 24, 1968)
[6] Arlene Edwards, "Wagon No. 13 Bounces Toward Boone," (Winston-Salem, NC: *Winston-Salem Journal*, June 25, 1968)
[7] Editorial, "Daniel Boone Wagon Train," (North Wilkesboro, NC: *Wilkes Journal-Patriot*, June 24, 1968)
[8] Arlene Edwards, "Wagon No. 13 Bounces Toward Boone," (Winston-Salem, NC: *Winston-Salem Journal*, June 25, 1968)
[9] Arlene Edwards, "Wagon No. 13 Bounces Toward Boone," (Winston-Salem, NC: *Winston-Salem Journal*, June 25, 1968)
[10] "Crowd Views Train in Light Rain Here," (North Wilkesboro, NC: *Wilkes Journal-Patriot*, June 27, 1968, Sec. 3)
[11] Arlene Edwards, "Wagon No. 13 Bounces Toward Boone," (Winston-Salem, NC: *Winston-Salem Journal*, June 25, 1968)

[12] "Crowd Views Train in Light Rain Here," (North Wilkesboro, NC: *Wilkes Journal-Patriot*, June 27, 1968, Sec. 3)
[13] Arlene Edwards, "Wagon Train Goes 15 miles—Troubles and All," (Winston-Salem, NC: *Winston-Salem Journal*, June 26, 1968)
[14] "Big Celebration at Ferguson," (North Wilkesboro, NC: *Wilkes Journal-Patriot*, June 27, 1968, Sec. 4)
[15] "Wagon Train Winds Way Out of Wilkes, (North Wilkesboro, NC: *Wilkes Journal-Patriot*, June 27, 1968, Sec. 1)
[16] Arlene Edwards, "Sore Ride With Two in the Saddle," (Winston-Salem, NC: *Winston-Salem Journal*, June 27, 1968)
[17] "Wagon Train Winds Way Out of Wilkes, (North Wilkesboro, NC: *Wilkes Journal-Patriot*, June 27, 1968, Sec. 1)
[18] Interview with Edith Carter, July 14, 2011
[19] "Wagon Train Winds Way Out of Wilkes, (North Wilkesboro, NC: *Wilkes Journal-Patriot*, June 27, 1968, Sec. 1)
[20] "Boone Wagon Train Is Termed Huge Success," (North Wilkesboro, NC: *Wilkes Journal-Patriot*, July 1, 1968)
[21] Arlene Edwards, "A Natty Gov. Moore Pays Visit to Dusty Wagon Train," (Winston-Salem, NC: *Winston-Salem Journal*, June 28, 1968)
[22] Rachel Rivers, "Last Week's Wagon Train Was Grandest of Them All." (Boone, NC: *Watauga Democrat*, July 4, 1968)
[23] "Boone Wagon Train Is Termed Huge Success," (North Wilkesboro, NC: *Wilkes Journal-Patriot*, July 1, 1968)
[24] Arlene Edwards, "A Natty Gov. Moore Pays Visit to Dusty Wagon Train," (Winston-Salem, NC: *Winston-Salem Journal*, June 28, 1968)
[25] Rachel Rivers, "Last Week's Wagon Train Was Grandest of Them All." (Boone, NC: *Watauga Democrat*, July 4, 1968)
[26] "Boone Wagon Train Is Termed Huge Success," (North Wilkesboro, NC: *Wilkes Journal-Patriot*, July 1, 1968)
[27] Arlene Edwards, "Train to Mark Journey's End With Parade in Boone Today," (Winston-Salem, NC: *Winston-Salem Journal*, June 29, 1968)
[28] "Wagon Train Ends Trip With Parade," (Winston-Salem, NC: *Winston-Salem Journal*, June 30, 1968)
[29] Rachel Rivers, "Last Week's Wagon Train Was Grandest of Them All." (Boone, NC: *Watauga Democrat*, July 4, 1968)
[30] "Huge Still 'Cut' Early This Morning," (North Wilkesboro, NC: *Wilkes Journal-Patriot*, July 1, 1968)

**Chapter 10 - DBWT, 1969**

[1] "Daniel Boone Wagon Train Forms This Weekend," (North Wilkesboro, NC: *Wilkes Journal-Patriot*, June 19, 1969)
[2] "Ninety Wagon Registered for Daniel Boone Wagon Train," (North Wilkesboro, NC: *Wilkes Journal-Patriot*, June 23, 1969)
[3] Jeanette Reid, "Wagon Train Styles Change," (Winston-Salem, NC: *Winston-Salem Journal*, June 24, 1969)
[4] "'Good Morning Starshine' Is Wilkes Man's Success," (Winston-Salem, NC: *Winston-Salem Journal*, June 25, 1969)
[5] "Good Morning Starshine" reached #3 in July, selling 1 million copies. In August his second hit. "Jean" reached #2. Oliver's brother was John Swofford, a quarterback at UNC-CH, then athletics director and later commissioner for the Atlantic Coast Conference. Oliver retired from music and went into real estate in Louisiana where he also was the business manager for a pharmaceutical company. He died of cancer at age 54 in February 2000. In 2010, he was inducted into the NC Music Hall of Fame. See *Wikipedia*.

[6] "Wagons Roll Ahead of Thunderstorm," (Winston-Salem, NC: *Winston-Salem Journal*, June 25, 1969)
[7] "He's Off and Running … Pilfered Chicken in Hand," (Winston-Salem, NC: *Winston-Salem Journal*, June 26, 1969)
[8] "Thousands View Wagon Train at Darby Camp," (North Wilkesboro, NC: *Wilkes Journal-Patriot*, June 26, 1969)
[9] "He's Off and Running … Pilfered Chicken in Hand," (Winston-Salem, NC: *Winston-Salem Journal*, June 26, 1969)
[10] "Moore Finds More Boone History," (North Wilkesboro, NC: *Wilkes Journal-Patriot*, June 19, 1969)
[11] "Appalachian Wagon Train" home page, < *http://muleshoepa.com/AWT/AWT.HTM*>, accessed Nov. 12, 2012
[12] "Wagon Train has New Chief Scout," (Winston-Salem, NC: *Winston-Salem Journal*, June 27, 1969)
[13] Lee Elliott, "Wagon Train Ends Its Trek to Boone," (Winston-Salem, NC: *Winston-Salem Journal*, June 28, 1969)
[14] "Mrs. Hodges Loses Life," (Winston-Salem, NC: *Winston-Salem Journal*, June 28, 1969)
[15] "Wagon Train Is Called Best in Its Seven Years." (Boone, NC: Watauga Democrat, July 3, 1969)
[16] Lee Elliott, "Wagon Train Ends Its Trek to Boone," (Winston-Salem, NC: *Winston-Salem Journal*, June 28, 1969)

**Chapter 11 - DBWT, 1970**
[1] "2 Wagon Train Heads Blast Action of Board, (North Wilkesboro, NC: *Wilkes Journal-Patriot*, Feb. 19, 1970)
[2] "2 Wagon Train Heads Blast Action of Board, (North Wilkesboro, NC: *Wilkes Journal-Patriot*, Feb. 19, 1970)
[3] Editorial, "Wagon Train Situation," (North Wilkesboro, NC: *Wilkes Journal-Patriot*, Feb. 23, 1970)
[4] "Wagon Train Will Assemble Sunday," (North Wilkesboro, NC: *Wilkes Journal-Patriot*, June 18, 1970)
[5] "Wagon Train Will Assemble Sunday," (North Wilkesboro, NC: *Wilkes Journal-Patriot*, June 18, 1970)
[6] Wagon Train Rolling Toward Triplett Encampment," (North Wilkesboro, NC: *Wilkes Journal-Patriot*, June 25, 1970)
[7] "Wagon Train Ready To Roll," (North Wilkesboro, NC: *Wilkes Journal-Patriot*, June 22, 1970)
[8] Wagon Train Rolling Toward Triplett Encampment," (North Wilkesboro, NC: *Wilkes Journal-Patriot*, June 25, 1970)
[9] Editorial, "Reminders of Heritage," (North Wilkesboro, NC: *Wilkes Journal-Patriot*, June 25, 1970)
[10] "Dissent-Laden Train in Ferguson," (Winston-Salem, NC: *Winston-Salem Journal*, June 24, 1970)
[11] T.W. Ferguson, "Ferguson News," North Wilkesboro, NC: *Wilkes Journal-Patriot*, June 25, 1970)
[12] "Dissent-Laden Train in Ferguson," (Winston-Salem, NC: *Winston-Salem Journal*, June 24, 1970)
[13] "Dissent-Laden Train in Ferguson," (Winston-Salem, NC: *Winston-Salem Journal*, June 24, 1970)
[14] Wagon Train Rolling Toward Triplett Encampment," (North Wilkesboro, NC: *Wilkes Journal-Patriot*, June 25, 1970)
[15] "Wagon Train Rolls On Last Leg of Trip," (Winston-Salem, NC: *Winston-Salem Journal*, June 26, 1970)
[16] "Wagon Train ___ To Have 75 Vehicles," (Boone, NC: *Watauga Democrat*, June 25, 1970)
[17] "Wagon Train ___ To Have 75 Vehicles," (Boone, NC: *Watauga Democrat*, June 25, 1970)

[18] Rachel Rivers Coffey, "Wagon Train Has Over 90 Vehicles," (Boone, NC: *Watauga Democrat*, July 2, 1970)
[19] Rachel Rivers Coffey, "Wagon Train Has Over 90 Vehicles," (Boone, NC: *Watauga Democrat*, July 2, 1970)
[20] "Wagon Train ___ To Have 75 Vehicles," (Boone, NC: *Watauga Democrat*, June 25, 1970)
[21] "Wagon Train ___ To Have 75 Vehicles," (Boone, NC: *Watauga Democrat*, June 25, 1970)
[22] Rachel Rivers Coffey, "Wagon Train Has Over 90 Vehicles," (Boone, NC: *Watauga Democrat*, July 2, 1970)

**Chapter 12 - DBWT, 1971**
[1] "Boone Wagon Train Will Assemble June 26 and 27," (North Wilkesboro, NC: *Wilkes Journal-Patriot*, June 21, 1971)
[2] "Wagons Gather for Boone Trip," (North Wilkesboro, NC: *Wilkes Journal-Patriot*, June 28, 1971)
[3] "Wagons Are Rolling on Narrow, Historic Trail," (Boone, NC: *Watauga Democrat*, July 1, 1971)
[4] "Wagons Gather for Boone Trip," (North Wilkesboro, NC: *Wilkes Journal-Patriot*, June 28, 1971)
[5] Editorial, "Wagon Trains and History," (North Wilkesboro, NC: *Wilkes Journal-Patriot*, June 24, 1971)
[6] "Throngs Flock to Area for Holiday," (Boone, NC: *Watauga Democrat*, July 8, 1971)
[7] "Throngs Flock to Area for Holiday," (Boone, NC: *Watauga Democrat*, July 8, 1971)

**Chapter 13 - DBWT, 1972**
[1] "Huge Crowds Attend Rotary Horse Show," (North Wilkesboro, NC: *Wilkes Journal-Patriot*, July 3, 1972)
[2] "Bicentennial Boosted Throughout the Nation," (North Wilkesboro, NC: *Wilkes Journal-Patriot*, June 29, 1972)
[3] Editorial, "T.E. Story, Public Servant," (North Wilkesboro, NC: *Wilkes Journal-Patriot*, June 22, 1972)
[4] "In Wilkes County 44 Years Ago," (North Wilkesboro, NC: *Wilkes Journal-Patriot*, June 29, 1972)
[5] "Boone's Parents Buried in Davie," (North Wilkesboro, NC: *Wilkes Journal-Patriot*, June 29, 1972)
[6] "Daniel Boone Train On Way to Triplett," (North Wilkesboro, NC: *Wilkes Journal-Patriot*, June 29, 1972)
[7] "Daniel Boone Train On Way to Triplett," (North Wilkesboro, NC: *Wilkes Journal-Patriot*, June 29, 1972)
[8] T.W. Ferguson, "Ferguson News," (North Wilkesboro, NC: *Wilkes Journal-Patriot*, June 29, 1972)
[9] "Wagon Train Expected To Arrive Here Friday," (Boone, NC: *Watauga Democrat*, June 29, 1972)
[10] Mary Ellis Gibson, "A Little Bit Hard Headed and He Gets Cussed a Bit," (Boone, NC: *Watauga Democrat*, July 3, 1972)
[11] Editorial, "About the Celebration," (Boone, NC: *Watauga Democrat*, July 3, 1972)

**Chapter 14 - DBWT, 1973**
[1] "Wagon Train Ready to Roll," (North Wilkesboro, NC: *Wilkes Journal-Patriot*, June 25, 1973)
[2] "Wagon Train Is On Way to Triplett," (North Wilkesboro, NC: *Wilkes Journal-Patriot*, June 28, 1973)
[3] "An Old Man and a Young Girl Dance Their Way to Boone On Wagon Train," (Boone, NC: Watauga Democrat, July 2, 1973)
[4] Ibid.
[5] Edith Carter, in-person interview by author, July 14, 2011.

[6] Kirkpatrick, Bill, "'It Beats Rocks and Tear Gas': Streaking and Cultural Politics in the Post-Vietnam Era." Journal of Popular Culture 43:5 (October 2010), 1023-1047

**Chapter 15 - End of the Trail**

[1] "Boone Train Will Not Run," (North Wilkesboro, NC: *Wilkes Journal-Patriot*, June 3, 1973)
[2] "Blue Ridge Wagon Train Assembles This Weekend," (North Wilkesboro, NC: *Wilkes Journal-Patriot*, June 26, 1975)
[3] Another round of Daniel Boone Wagon Train events began around 1983 and continued for three or four years. That history is beyond the scope of this book.
[4] "Biography: Tightrope Between the Towers," (PBS: American Experience) <http://www.pbs.org/wgbh/americanexperience/features/biography/newyork-tightrope/> (Accessed Dec. 31, 2012)

**Epilogue**

[1] Valeria DuSold, "Wagon Train Combines History with Family Togetherness," (North Wilkesboro: Wilkes Journal-Patriot, June 30, 1983)
[2] John Hubbard, "Daniel Boone Wagon Train," (North Wilkesboro: Wilkes Journal-Patriot, July 3, 1986)
[3] Valeria DuSold, "Wagon Train Combines History with Family Togetherness," (North Wilkesboro: Wilkes Journal-Patriot, June 30, 1983)

# Bibliography


## Articles

Kirkpatrick, Bill. "'It Beats Rocks and Tear Gas': Streaking and Cultural Politics in the Post-Vietnam Era." *Journal of Popular Culture*, 43:5 (October 2010), 1023-1047

Taylor, Livingston, "House Calls 'Boone' Show 'Insult to Intelligence,'" (Louisville, KY: *Courier Journal*, March 3, 1966)

## Periodicals

*Lenoir News-Topic*, Lenoir, NC, 1963-1968
*Tercentenary News*, Carolina Charter Tercentenary Commission, Raleigh, NC, 1963
*Watauga Democrat*, Boone, NC, 1968-1976, 1983, 1986
*Wilkes Journal-Patriot*, North Wilkesboro, NC, 1963-1976
*Winston-Salem Journal*, Winston-Salem, NC, 1940, 1963-1976

## Collections

"The Daniel Boone Wagon Train Scrapbook," Edith Ferguson Carter
Forsyth County Public Library Photography Collection, Winston-Salem, NC
Taped interview of Ivey Moore, 1974, Pardue Library, Wilkes Community College, Wilkesboro, NC

## Interviews

Edith Ferguson Carter, Ferguson, NC, July 14, 2011
Dudley Moore, High Point, NC, October 28, 2011
Betty Greene Koontz, Boone, NC, February 11, 2013

## Reports

_______, "Daniel Boone Wagon Train" Souvenir Booklet, Daniel Boone Wagon Train, Inc., (Boone, NC: Rivers Printing Co., 1964)
Winslow, Francis E., "Report of the Carolina Charter Tercentenary Commission," (Raleigh, NC: State Dept. of Archives and History, Dec. 31, 1963)

## Online

Appalachian Wagon Train, <http://muleshoepa.com/AWT/AWT.HTM>

*"Biography: Tightrope between the Towers," American Experience, PBS*, <http://www.pbs.org/wgbh/americanexperience/features/biography/newyork-tightrope/>

Daniel Boone (TV Series), *http://en.wikipedia.org/wiki/Daniel_Boone_(TV_series)*

"I Raise My Hand to Volunteer, Student Protest in 1960s Chapel Hill, Part 2: Speaker Ban Controversy," Manuscripts Department, UNC University Library, *http://www.lib.unc.edu/mss/exhibits/protests/ban.html*

McLennan, Sarah. "Jamestown 350th Anniversary, 1957." Encyclopedia Virginia. Ed. Brendan Wolfe. 18 Feb. 2013. Virginia Foundation for the Humanities. 18 Jan. 2012 <http://www.EncyclopediaVirginia.org/Jamestown_350th_Anniversary_1957>

Wagon Train, *<http://en.wikipedia.org/wiki/Wagon_Train>*

Wagon Train, Internet Movie Database, *<http://www.imdb.com/title/tt0050073/>*

# Index

(This index is for the body of the text and does not include references to the chronology of national events following each chapter nor to the Appendix listing the music, movies, and television programs.)

www.ingramcontent.com/pod-product-compliance
Lightning Source LLC
Chambersburg PA
CBHW030715110426
42739CB00030B/417
* 9 7 8 0 9 7 6 9 1 4 9 7 6 *